Y0-AIG-058

Thompson

Command

CASUALTY INVESTIGATION CHECKLISTS

by

PAT MAGARICK

Second Edition, 1977

**Clark Boardman Company, Ltd.
New York, New York**

Copyright © 1977 by Clark Boardman Company, Ltd.

Fourth Printing, May 1980

Library of Congress Cataloging in Publication Data

Magarick, Patrick.
  Casualty investigation checklists.

  Includes index.
  1. Insurance, Casualty—United States—Adjustment of claims.   I. Title.
KF1215.M3 1977   346′.73′086   77-24444
ISBN 0-87632-154-6

PREFACE

This book is intended to be used as a practical working guide for the investigator of negligence claims and attorneys who practice negligence and compensation law. Because it was fashioned as a usable tool, it has been shorn of all extraneous matter and is made up of investigation checklists only.

A tool can only be as good as the workman using it. It cannot work for you without your assistance. This applies particularly to the checklists which you will find in this book and which can be used as important aids in the investigation of claims. These checklists are meant to augment your own thoughts and imagination, but cannot replace them.

This book will cover most of the usual situations confronting the average claims man or negligence attorney and should give you enough of a head-start on any investigation so that you should have little trouble developing your material from the leads given.

The important thing to remember is that the book should be used as a tool—not as a crutch. Properly used, it will make your investigations better and more comprehensive. It should also avoid unnecessary call-backs and time consuming re-investigations. No list can be so complete as to cover every possible contingency. The field is entirely too vast. Contrariwise, very few cases will call for the complete and detailed investigations outlined in this book. It is obvious, therefore, that you will have to use judgment in applying whatever may be pertinent in the checklists to the accident under investigation.

This revised edition of the original 1955 publication contains much new material covering the fields of Accident and Health, Fidelity, Suit and Trial Preparation, new areas of Products Liability, Professional Liability, and Personal Liability, factors involved in taking Signed Statements and Reserve Evaluation.

I can readily recall the feeling of confusion and almost hopelessness that I felt many years ago when I was a neophyte, with no book to turn to for help. These checklists were written with that in mind.

P.M.

PUBLISHER'S NOTE

Mr. Magarick is the author of *Successful Handling of Casualty Claims,* which has remained the accepted text for many insurance company and independent adjuster schools, as well as some colleges and universities that give claim courses. It has recently been revised to about twice its original size and contains much new material that brings it up to date.

He is also the author of *Excess Liability,* a legal text that deals with the responsibility of an insurance company for liability in excess of its policy limits under certain circumstances and includes a treatment of punitive damages in both first- and third-party cases.

Using the checklists in *Successful Handling of Casualty Claims* as a nucleus, Mr. Magarick has expanded and enlarged them and added much new material. The format has been arranged for easy reference and the entire book has been designed for practical use as a working tool for the investigator or attorney.

The author is exceptionally well-qualified in his field, having spent almost fifty years in the claim and legal professions. Retired from his most recent position as Vice President in charge of world-wide claim operations of the American International Underwriters Corporation, he was also, prior to that, Vice President of the Trans America claim operation.

Mr. Magarick has worked as investigator, supervisor, branch manager and home office examiner for a number of insurance companies. Presently, he is working as a consultant and expert in his field, continues to write a monthly column for the "Insurance Adjuster" magazine and has various writing projects that he hopes to have the time to complete.

Mr. Magarick received the degree of J.D. from the Dickinson School of Law and an LL.B. degree from the Brooklyn Law School. He is a member of the New York and Federal Bars.

TABLE OF CONTENTS

CHAPTER I

Automobile Liability and Property Investigation

	PAGE
A. Coverage Information	1
How and when obtained	1
Possible violations	2
Regular drivers	2
Purpose of automobile	2
Commercial Radius Endorsement	3
B. Identification of the Insured's Vehicle	3
Personal identification	3
Condition of vehicle	4
Vehicle not listed in policy	5
Replacement vehicle	5
Additional automobile	5
C. Insured's Investigation	6
Background and introductory matter	6
Permissive use of vehicle	8
Distractions	10
Fatigue	11
Alcoholic or drug consumption	11
Guest statutes	12
Official reports	14
Factual details	14
Injuries	18
Property damage	19
Witnesses obtained from insured	20
D. Claimant's Investigation	21
Background and introductory matter	21
Distractions	25

		PAGE
	Passengers	25
	Pedestrians	26
	Official reports	27
	Economic status	27
	Insurance carriers	27
	Factual details	27
	Bus or trolley passengers	29
	Medical information	30
	Property damage	32
	Witnesses	33
E.	Medical Information	34
	Detailed information from claimant	34
	Doctor's report	34
	Hospital records	36
	Physical examination	36
	Additional interviews	38
	Possible malpractice	38
F.	Physical Facts	38
	Description of scene of accident	39
	Weather conditions	40
	Traffic controls	40
	Lighting	41
	Condition of vehicles	41
	Witness' possible vantage points	42
	Diagrams	42
	Photographs and snapshots	42
	Other prepared evidence	43
	Hearings and hearing reports	43
G.	Witnesses' Investigation	44
	Identification and background	44
	Location of and reason for witness' presence	45
	Factual details	45
	Injuries	46
	Property damage	47
	Neighborhood canvass	47

TABLE OF CONTENTS ix

	PAGE
H. Special Damages	49
Lost time and earnings	49
Automobile property damage	50
Other property damage	52
Medical expenses	52
Fatal claims	53
Expected future monetary losses	53
Pain and suffering	53
Loss of services or support	53
Cosmetic disfigurement	53

CHAPTER II

Additional Automobile Investigations

A. Automobile Medical Payments Investigation	55
Coverage information	55
Factual details	56
Medical information	56
Expenses	56
B. Automobile Non-Ownership Coverage Investigation	57
Ownership and control	57
Statement from owner and operator	57
Statement from insured	58
Corroborate allegations	58
Determine primary insurance	59
Contacting claimant	59
C. Automobile Physical Damages Investigation	59
Identification of vehicle and determination of coverage	59
Investigation of total losses	61
Investigation of theft losses	61
Investigation of fire losses	62
In the event of suspected arson	63

TABLE OF CONTENTS

PAGE

- D. Investigation of Claims Involving I.C.C. or
    P.S.C. Certificates 63
    Legal requirements 63
    Registration and ownership 64
    Leased trucks 64
    Control of the driver 64
- E. Investigation of Coverage Problems
    in Automobile Claims 66
    Review of the application 66
    Date of accident 66
    Delayed notice 67
    Ownership of vehicle 69
    Regular driver 69
    Purposes of use of vehicle 70
    Uninsured vehicles 70
    Commercial Radius Endorsement 71
- F. Investigation of Uninsured
    Motorist's Claims 71

CHAPTER III

General or Public Liability Investigation

- A. Description and Identification of Premises 73
- B. Ownership and Control 74
- C. Coverage 75
    Edible product 76
    Completed operations 76
- D. Insured's Investigation 77
    Notice 77
    Physical facts 78
    Repairs 81
    Injuries 82
    Witnesses 83
- E. Claimant's Investigation 83
    Background information and introductory matter ... 83

		PAGE
	Marital status and dependency	84
	Employment history	84
	Educational background	84
	Pensions, insurance or welfare help	85
	Physical condition	85
	Possible distractions	86
	Accident records	87
	Clothing	87
	Nature and purpose of trip	87
	Previous knowledge of condition	88
	Factual details	88
	Blind accidents	89
	Medical information	90
	Witnesses	92
F.	Medical Investigation	93
	Doctor's report	93
	Hospital records	95
	Physical examination	95
	Additional interviews	97
G.	Physical Facts	97
	Diagrams	97
	Photographs or snapshots	98
	Other prepared evidence	98
	Hearings and reports	98
H.	Witnesses' Investigation	99
	Identification and background	99
	Reason for witness' presence	100
	Factual details	100
	Injuries	101
	Description of property damage	101
	Neighborhood canvass	101
I.	Special Damages	101
	Lost time and earnings	101
	Property damage	102
	Medical expenses	103

	PAGE
Fatal claims	103
Expected future monetary loss	103
Pain and suffering	104
Loss of services or support	104
Cosmetic disfigurement	104

CHAPTER IV

Some Specific Public Liability Investigations

A.	Amusement Parks and Fairs	105
B.	Animals	107
	Dogs	109
	Saddle horses	110
C.	Attractive Nuisance	113
D.	Blasting	114
E.	Blind Accidents	115
F.	Boiler Explosions	117
G.	Carbon Monoxide	119
H.	Ceiling Cases—Falling Plaster	122
I.	Construction Cases	124
J.	Crop Dusting	127
K.	Doors	130
	Transparent	130
	Swinging	131
	Revolving	131
L.	Elevators	131
M.	Entrances and Lobbies	136
N.	Escalators	137
O.	Falling Objects	138
P.	Floor Accidents	140
Q.	Liquor Liability Law	142
R.	Machinery Claims	143
S.	Playgrounds	144
T.	Pollution Claims	146
U.	Porcelain Handles	148

		PAGE
V.	Road Construction	149
W.	Sidewalk Claims	151
X.	Sporting Events	154
Y.	Stairways	156
Z.	Swimming Pools	158
AA.	Tenancy Claims	160
AB.	Theatres and Auditoriums	162

CHAPTER V

Investigation of Products Liability Claims

A.	Coverage	165
B.	Description and Identification	165
C.	Insured's Investigation	166
D.	Claimant's Investigation	169
	Background information	169
	Marital status and dependency	170
	Employment history	170
	Factual details	171
	Medical information	172
	Witnesses through claimant	174
E.	Medical Investigation	174
F.	Special Damages	174
	Lost time and earnings	174
	Medical expenses	175
	Fatal claims	175

CHAPTER VI

Some Specific Products Liability Investigations

A.	Automobiles	177
	Brake failure	178
B.	Bottling Claims	179
	Bottle fragments	179

xiv   TABLE OF CONTENTS

PAGE

    Mouse claims 180
C. Crop Dusting or Spraying 180
D. Drugs or Cosmetics 182
E. Electrical Appliances 185
F. Food Contamination or Foreign Substance 186
G. Inflammables 189
H. Motorcycles and Snowmobiles 190
I. Percussion Caps 191
J. Power Mowers 192
K. Pressure Spray Containers 195
L. Trichinosis 196

CHAPTER VII

Investigation of Claims Under Professional Liability Policies

A. Coverage 200
B. Insured's Investigation 201
    Background 201
    Factual details 202
C. Claimant's Investigation 204
    Background and introductory matter 204
    Marital status and dependency 205
    Employment history 205
    Educational background 205
    Factual details 206
D. Medical Investigation 206
    Doctor's reports 206
    Hospital records 207
E. Witnesses' Investigation 208
F. Special Damages 208
    Lost time and earnings 208
    Medical expenses 209
    Fatal claims 209
    Future monetary losses 209

Pain and suffering	209
Loss of services or support	210
Cosmetic disfigurement	210

CHAPTER VIII

Some Specific Professional Liability Investigations

A.	Accountant's Liability	211
B.	Agent's Errors and Omissions	212
C.	Architects and Engineers	214
D.	Druggist's Liability	216
E.	Hospital Malpractice	218
F.	Lawyers	220
G.	Nurses	222
H.	Surgeons	224
I.	Teachers	226

CHAPTER IX

Workmen's Compensation Investigation

A.	Coverage	229
	Jurisdiction or extraterritoriality	229
	Occupational disease	230
	Dual or multiple employment	230
	Voluntary compensation	231
	General	231
B.	Factual Information	232
C.	Insured's Investigation	235
	Background information	235
	Details of incident	236
	Type of employment	237
	Salary details	239
	Forms	240
D.	Claimant's Investigation	240

		PAGE
	Background information	240
	Dependency	241
	General information	243
	Medical information	243
E.	Medical Investigation	244
	Doctor's reports	245
	Hospital records	247
	Physical examination	247
F.	Physical Facts	249
G.	Occupational Diseases	249
H.	Determination of Employee Status	251
I.	Employee versus Independent Contractor	252

CHAPTER X

Crime Insurance Investigation

BURGLARY AND ROBBERY		255
A.	Residence Investigation	255
	Insured's information	255
B.	Loss From Premises	256
C.	Loss From a Depository	257
D.	Nature of the Loss	258
E.	Damage to Property or Premises	259
F.	Suspects	260
G.	Settlement Negotiations	260
MERCANTILE INVESTIGATIONS		261
A.	Commercial Losses—General	261
	Insured's information	261
	Nature of loss	262
	Suspects	264
B.	Safe Burglary Claims	264
C.	Messenger Losses	264
D.	Robbery Claims	265
E.	Subrogation, Salvage or Contribution	265

	PAGE
F. Confidential Report to Underwriters	266
FIDELITY CLAIMS	266
A. General Guidelines	267
B. Investigation	268

CHAPTER XI

Accident and Health, Personal Injury and Plate Glass Investigations

ACCIDENT AND HEALTH CLAIMS	273
A. Coverage	273
B. Misrepresentations in the Application	274
C. Reasonable Bills	274
D. Over-Insurance	274
E. Dismemberment, Loss of Sight or Total Disability	274
F. Physical Examination	275
G. Death Claims	275
H. Suicide or Voluntary Injury	275
I. Forms	277
J. Independent of Other Causes	278
K. Medical Substantiation	278
PERSONAL INJURY CLAIMS	278
A. Defamation, Libel and Slander	279
B. False Arrest or Imprisonment	279
PLATE GLASS LOSSES	281

CHAPTER XII

Some Special Aspects of Liability Investigations

A. Investigation of Accidents Involving Children	283
B. Investigation of Fatal Accidents	284
C. Investigation of Claims Involving Fraud	285
Background	285

	PAGE
Medical information	286
Special damages	286
D. Suit Reviews	287
Attorney's review	287
Claim manager's or supervisor's review	288
Checklist for trial preparation	288
Final review of file	290
E. Locating the Missing Witness	294

CHAPTER XIII

Factors Involved in Taking Signed Statements

A.	Rules	297
B.	Construction of a Signed Statement	301

CHAPTER XIV

Casualty Reserves and Evaluation and Reports to Underwriters

RESERVES	305
A. Serious Injury Liability Claims	305
B. Fatal Liability Claims	307
C. Workmen's Compensation Cases	308
REPORT TO UNDERWRITERS	310

INDEX 313

CHAPTER I

Automobile Liability and Property Investigations

A. **Coverage Information**

The first step in the investigation of a claim or suit is to determine whether the reported incident was properly covered under the policy of insurance issued to the insured. It is accordingly necessary to:

1. Determine that the incident occurred within the policy period. An accident that allegedly occurred within a day or two of the inception date of the policy is one that should be checked carefully in order to make sure that the policy had actually been purchased before the accident occurred. In cases of doubt, the following information should be obtained from the insured in the form of a signed statement:
    a. The exact date and time when the policy was ordered.
    b. Determine the manner in which it was ordered, whether by telephone, mail or in person.
    c. Get the exact name of the person from whom the policy was ordered.
    d. Determine the conversations and surrounding circumstances of the order.
2. Obtain a signed statement from the person with whom the original order was placed, covering the information as in 1.
3. Check the date stamp of the binder in the agent's office.
4. Check any other written notations or memoranda that the agent may be able to produce.
5. Check the company's records if necessary, to deter-

mine the exact date and time when notice was received by the company concerning any binder or policy.
6. Check the date of the accident carefully through police records, witnesses, claimant's version or other means that might make the date conclusive.
7. Determine possible violations of policy declarations:
    a. Find out who owns the vehicle involved in the accident:
        (1) Is it an individual, partnership or corporation?
        (2) Is it an estate, trusteeship, municipality or other entity?
        (3) Is the owner someone other than the named insured? If he is, obtain full details.
    b. Determine who regularly drives the vehicle named in the policy.
        (1) Is the vehicle driven by members of the insured's family or household?
        (2) Is it driven by employees of the insured?
        (3) Obtain the exact ages of all regular drivers.
    c. Determine the purposes for which the automobile is used:
        (1) Business or pleasure.
        (2) Other purposes.
        (3) Average number of miles per year the car is driven.
    d. Determine where the automobile is principally garaged.
    e. Determine whether there are any other automobiles in the same household:
        (1) How many?

> (2) Who owns them?
> (3) Find out if the insured owns or regularly drives any other automobiles.
> (4) Find out if they are insured and, if so, by what company.
>
> f. If a Commercial Radius Endorsement is involved:
>
> > (1) Determine whether the truck is ever driven outside the permitted limits.
> > (2) If so, find out how often. Give locations and times as nearly as possible.
>
> 8. Determine whether there is any excess insurance and, if so, the name of the company and the policy limits. Find out if the insured has reported the accident to the excess carrier.

B. **Identification of the Insured's Vehicle**

One purpose of making a personal identification of the insured's vehicle is to determine whether the automobile involved in the accident is the one that is intended to be covered under the policy.

Since the advent of the Standard Family Automobile Liability policy, the Personal Auto policy and new provisions in other policies giving automatic coverage, under certain circumstances, for additional automobiles, personal identification of the vehicle is today of much less importance than it used to be.

Nevertheless, there are still occasions when it is necessary to make sure that the vehicle in the accident was the same one covered by the policy.

It is also good practice to personally inspect the insured's car where the location of the damage, or lack of it, could give an indication of the manner in which the accident happened. The following checklists could be helpful in those instances where personal identification of the insured's vehicle may be warranted.

1. Examine the owner's license or registration certificate, and, where possible, compare it with the policy information:
   a. Check the make, year, color and model of the vehicle.
   b. Check the motor and serial numbers.
   c. Determine the registration numbers.
2. Examine the vehicle personally for any evidence of contact resulting from the accident in order to be certain that the vehicle allegedly involved in the accident is the one that was actually involved.
3. Check the make, year, color, model and license numbers from personal observation if there is any doubt or uncertainty concerning the identification.
4. Check the condition of the vehicle, including specific items which may have contributed to, or been involved in, the accident such as:
   a. Headlights and taillights.
   b. Windshields and windows, for visibility.
   c. Windshield wipers and windows for operation.
   d. Brakes.
   e. Tires (worn tread, puncture, blowout).
   f. Steering wheel and gear.
   g. Speedometer (may have been frozen to indicate speed at the time of impact).
   h. Directional signal indicators for operation.
5. Report to the underwriting department any defects that might affect the safety of the vehicle or the desirability of the risk.
6. Examine any damage carefully to determine:
   a. Exact point of impact.
   b. Force of impact and estimated speed by the extent of the damage.

AUTOMOBILE LIABILITY & PROPERTY INVESTIGATIONS

    c. Determine which car was struck.
    d. Determine the type of accident (sideswipe, rear-end, right angle, etc.).

7. Check the odometer mileage figures and compare them with the age of the vehicle to determine the average number of miles driven per year. If excessive for classification, report to the underwriters.
8. If the vehicle involved in the accident is not the one listed on the policy, determine:

    a. Where the vehicle listed in the policy is located and why.
    b. Determine who owns the vehicle.
    c. Find out if there is any primary insurance on the car. If so, determine the carrier.
    d. Find out if it is a temporary substitute vehicle.
    e. Determine the purpose for which the car was used.
    f. If it was a hired vehicle, determine:

        (1) Who hired it.
        (2) How often it was hired, by whom, and from whom.
        (3) Check all allegations.

    g. If the vehicle involved in the accident is a replacement, obtain:

        (1) Date of sale of the old vehicle.
        (2) Date of purchase of the new vehicle.
        (3) Signed statement, where necessary, from the insured concerning notice of change, or the lack of it, to the agent or company.
        (4) Corroborating evidence of any kind, such as bills of sale, registration certificates, copies of letters, etc.

    h. If the vehicle involved in the accident is an additional automobile, obtain:

        (1) Date of purchase.

(2) Corroborating evidence by examining the bill of sale or registration certificate.
(3) Signed statement, where necessary, concerning notice to the agent or company, of the purchase of the new vehicle.
(4) Information concerning possibility of any other insurance on the vehicle in question.
(5) Description of all vehicles owned by the insured and insurance information thereon.

C. **Insured's Investigation**

This section is devoted to the information which must be obtained from the insured and his driver, if someone other than himself. Wherever possible and where warranted, a signed statement should be obtained from the insured and the driver. Matters dealing with coverage that necessitate the mention of insurance should be confined to a separate statement.

The suggested investigation covers all matters on which comment should be made in the report, some of which obviously cannot be included in a signed statement.

1. *Driver's background and introductory matter:*
    a. Name and address. If present address is temporary, obtain driver's permanent address or the permanent address of a close relative through whom the driver can always be reached.
    b. Age and general appearance, for example:
        (1) Mental disabilities such as incoherence, slowwittedness, irrationality, etc.
        (2) Temperamental defects such as overaggressiveness or pugnaciousness, "trigger temper," etc.

(3) Physical defects such as blindness in one eye, poor eyesight, poor hearing or deafness, crippling that might affect driving ability, heart trouble, epilepsy, etc.

(4) Physical appearance that might affect jury opinion such as dirtiness, shifty-eyed, etc.

c. Marital status, including children, if any.
d. Occupational status, as it may affect ability to appear as a witness.
e. Name and address of employer, nature of job or position, and length of employment.
f. Report on insured's apparent economic status and financial responsibility where warranted.
g. Driving experience.
h. Driving record, including dates, locations and details of previous major accidents:

(1) Is driver licensed? Does he have a driver's license, chauffer's license, truck driver's license or learner's permit?

(2) How long has driver had license or permit?

(3) If driver has learner's permit, was he or she accompanied by a properly licensed driver? Obtain name, address and statement from such accompanying driver.

(4) Is driver required to wear glasses? If so, was he or she wearing them?

(5) Does the license or permit show any recorded traffic violations? If so, obtain details.

(6) Was the driver ever convicted of any other traffic violations? If so, obtain details.

(7) Was driver's license ever revoked or suspended? If so, obtain details.

2. *Permissive use of vehicle:*

If the driver was someone other than the named insured, determine if he or she was driving with the permission of the named insured as follows:

   a. Find out if the named insured gave express permission to the driver.
   b. If not, find out if he or she had ever given permission previously to drive:
      (1) Determine if the previous situations were similar to the one under investigation.
      (2) Find out how many times such previous permission had been granted and under what circumstances.
      (3) Determine if the named insured voiced any objections on this or any previous occasions.
      (4) Find out if the car was taken in spite of any voiced objections and, if so, get details.
   c. Learn if the driver was a close relative of the named insured.
   d. Learn if the driver was a member of named insured's household.
   e. Find out if the driver was unable to legally drive the vehicle for any reason, such as not having a driver's license or being under the legal age for drivers.
   f. If so, determine if the named insured was aware of this disability.
   g. Determine if any limitation was placed on the use of the vehicle such as:
      (1) Time within which the vehicle was to be returned.
      (2) Purpose for which the vehicle was to be used.

AUTOMOBILE LIABILITY & PROPERTY INVESTIGATIONS 9

- (3) Place to which vehicle was to be driven or not driven.
- (4) Route which was to be taken.
- (5) Speed or manner in which the vehicle was to be driven.
- (6) Passengers to be taken or not to be taken.

h. Find out if there were any material deviations from any limited permission to drive:

- (1) Obtain list of the exact places visited and the order in which they were visited.
- (2) Determine the exact routes taken.
- (3) Determine the time consumed while the vehicle was in the driver's possesion.
- (4) Determine the reason for any deviation of the permission granted:
    - (a) Find out if it was a matter of necessity.
    - (b) Find out if it was for the driver's own convenience or pleasure.
    - (c) Find out if it was done for the ostensible benefit of the named insured.

i. Determine if the driver permitted someone else to drive the vehicle. If so, obtain a signed statement from the second permittee, as well as from the named insured and the first permittee, incorporating the following information:

- (1) Find out if the named insured gave express permission for the second permittee to drive.
- (2) Find out if the insured was in the vehicle at the time.
- (3) If not, find out if he or she knew that the second permittee would drive.

(4) Find out if the named insured knew that the first permittee had permitted the second permittee to drive on previous occasions.
   (5) Find out if the named insured expressly forbade the driving by the second permittee.
   (6) Find out if the named insured ever previously forbade the driving by the second permittee.
   (7) Learn if it was customary, because of the nature of the employment, or for any other reason, for the second permittee to drive.
   (8) Learn if the second permittee was allowed to drive because of necessity or because of an emergency such as:
      (a) Sudden illness or accident to the first permittee.
      (b) Intoxication of the first permittee.
      (c) Any other emergency.
   (9) Find out if it was in the business interests of the named insured for the second permittee to drive.

3. *Driving distractions:*
   a. Find out if the driver was familiar with the area in which he was driving.
   b. Find out if the driver was talking to someone in the vehicle or otherwise distracted.
   c. Find out if the driver was watching someone or something outside.
   d. Learn if the driver was daydreaming.
   e. Determine if there was a dangling object in front of the driver's view inside the windshield.
   f. Find out if the radio was in operation or whether he was operating a C.B. radio.

AUTOMOBILE LIABILITY & PROPERTY INVESTIGATIONS 11

- g. Determine if the driver was smoking, and, if so, whether the smoke or ashes distracted the driver.
- h. Find out if the driver was worried or under emotional strain.
- i. Determine if the driver was in a hurry for any reason.

4. *Driver fatigue:*
   - a. Learn how long the driver had been driving continuously before the accident.
   - b. Find out where the trip had originated.
   - c. Learn the starting time.
   - d. Determine the distance traveled.
   - e. Determine what route was taken.
   - f. Find out the destination.
   - g. Find out how much rest the driver got immediately preceding the trip.

5. *Alcoholic or drug consumption:*
   - a. Determine the nature of the drinks or drugs.
   - b. Find out how much was taken and where.
   - c. Determine when the drinking started and at what intervals drinks were taken. Same if drugs were involved.
   - d. Find out if the driver felt any effects of the drinking or drugs.
   - e. Determine if the driver was intoxicated or drugged or accused of it. If so, find out by whom and under what circumstances.
   - f. Find out if there was any charge of intoxication or drug use brought against the driver and get details.
   - g. Determine if any test was made to determine intoxication or drug use and, if so, obtain the result.
   - h. Determine if the driver had taken any pills or

other drugs and get all details as to time and amount.

6. *Injury to passengers in the insured's vehicle (guest statutes)*

Not all states have guest statutes, and some of those that did enact such statutes have since declared them unconstitutional. There are, however, enough jurisdictions that follow the guest statute law to warrant inclusion of this checklist:

  a. Determine the exact nature of the trip:
     (1) Find out who suggested it.
     (2) Determine the purpose of the trip and whether it was for pleasure or business.
     (3) Find out if it was a joint enterprise for the benefit of both.
     (4) Determine if the driver received any material benefit from the trip.
     (5) Find out if the trip was for purely social reasons.

  b. Determine the exact route, including the starting point and the exact destination. Check if necessary.

  c. Find out if the passenger made any contribution toward the expense of the trip.
     (1) Determine if any arrangement was made for contribution before the trip was started.
     (2) Find out who paid for the gasoline and oil.
     (3) Find out if the passenger paid for road or bridge tolls, meals, or other items of expense.
     (4) Determine if the trip was on a share-the-ride plan.

(5) Find out if the passenger made a cash payment or gave other material consideration of any kind for the ride.
d. Obtain the names and addresses of all occupants and possible witnesses to the financial or other arrangements of the trip and obtain corroboration of information given by the parties in interest.
e. Determine if the passenger or driver was intoxicated or under the influence of drugs. Find out if the passenger knew that the driver drank or took drugs regularly.
f. If the driver was going fast or driving recklessly, determine if the passenger objected. If so, find out in what manner.
g. Determine if the driver was tired or sleepy, and if the passenger was aware of this.
h. Find out how well the passenger knew the driver.
   (1) Determine if they were related.
   (2) Find out if they were co-employees.
   (3) Learn if they were friends of long standing.
   (4) Determine if the passenger knew that the driver usually drove fast and recklessly.
   (5) Find out if the passenger knew of any possible driving defects of a mental or physical nature that might affect the driver's driving ability.
   (6) Determine if the passenger was aware that the driver was unlicensed or had only a learner's permit.
   (7) Find out if the passenger had ridden with the driver previously and, if so, how often.

(8) If the named insured was a passenger in his own car, find out how he was injured and whether he intends to press a claim for his injuries. Be discreet.

i. Determine who had control of the vehicle, who directed the route, the driving, starting and stopping times, and other details of the trip.
j. Determine the general condition of the automobile:

(1) Determine the condition of the brakes, steering or other vital mechanical parts that might have contributed to the accident. Find out if the passenger knew or should have known of these defects.
(2) Observe the general condition of the automobile.

k. Determine if the passenger was a minor. If so:

(1) Determine the exact age.
(2) Find out if his or her parents were in the car at the time.
(3) Determine if the minor obtained permission to ride from his or her parents. Obtain details.

7. *Determine if any report was made* to the local or state police department, motor vehicle bureau or other official body. If so, find out the circumstances and obtain a copy.
8. *Develop the factual details:*

    a. Determine the exact date, time and place of the accident.
    b. Determine the direction in which each vehicle was traveling, and name the streets or roads traversed.
    c. Describe all traffic controls, including traffic

policemen, stop or other signs, traffic lights or blinkers, etc.
d. Determine the speed of the insured's vehicle.
   (1) Find out if the speedometer was working properly.
   (2) Find out if there was a governor on the insured's vehicle.
   (3) Determine what gear the car was in at the time of the accident if the car did not have an automatic gearshift. Determine when the driver shifted gears immediately preceding the accident.
e. Determine the estimated speed of the claimant's vehicle. Find out if the driver overheard any comment by the claimant or other witnesses after the accident that would help determine the speed of the claimant's vehicle.
f. Determine the position of all vehicles with reference to traffic lanes, shoulders, and distance from the curb or edge of the road or sidewalk.
g. Determine the position of all cars with reference to the nearest intersecting streets or highways.
h. Describe the physical facts in detail, including such items as weather conditions, road conditions, lighting, and other items specifically outlined in the following section dealing with Physical Facts, such as:
   (1) Find out if the accident occurred during daylight, dusk or night.
   (2) Find out if it was cloudy, foggy, rainy, or snowy.
   (3) Find out if there was a full or partial moon.

(4) Describe the proximity and lighting power of any street or road lights.
(5) Determine if the driver of either car was facing into the sun.
(6) Determine whether approaching headlights blinded either driver momentarily.
(7) Determine what headlights were in operation.
(8) Determine if windshield wipers were in operation.
(9) Learn if the windshield or either side window was obstructed.
(10) Learn if there was any obstruction to the approach to the scene of the accident or to any of the vehicles.
(11) See section on Physical Facts for further details.

i. Determine as nearly as possible the point at which the driver first observed the claimant or adverse vehicle.
j. Determine how far away the pedestrian or adverse vehicle was when first seen.
k. If a pedestrian was involved, obtain description as follows:

(1) Determine the colors of the clothes worn.
(2) Determine what type of clothes they were.
(3) Find out if the pedestrian was carrying an umbrella.
(4) Find out if the pedestrian was carrying any packages or other objects or animals.
(5) Find out if the pedestrian had his or her hat pulled down or coat collar up so as to obstruct vision.

l. Obtain a complete description of the movements of the pedestrian or adverse vehicles

immediately preceding, during and after the impact, with distances and positions placed as exactly as possible.
m. Obtain the exact position of the pedestrian or vehicles immediately after all motion had stopped.
n. Determine if either driver sounded the horn.
o. Determine if either driver attempted to swerve or slow down. If not, find out why.
p. Determine if any other action was taken by any of the parties involved to avoid the accident when danger was first perceived.
q. Find out if any arm or mechanical directional signals were given immediately before the accident.
r. Determine if skid marks were made by any of the vehicles involved. If so, describe the direction and other details.
s. Determine the exact point of impact on the vehicles in relation to each other and to the scene of the accident.
t. Learn if any pertinent remarks were made by anyone immediately after the accident, including any admissions of fault.
u. In accidents involving bus or trolley passengers, obtain the following information:
  (1) Find out if the passenger was boarding or leaving the vehicle, by what door, and if the door was in the process of opening or closing.
  (2) Determine if the passenger was seated, walking or running toward or away from the vehicle.
  (3) Find out if the claimant tripped or stumbled before or while entering or leaving the vehicle.

(4) Determine if any other passenger preceded or followed the claimant.
(5) Determine if the bus made a sudden stop or was involved in any other unusual movement.
(6) Determine if the driver gave any warning.
(7) Find out if there were any warning signs on display.
(8) Determine approximately how many other passengers were aboard.
(9) Find out if any of the passengers witnessed the accident and get their names and addresses if possible.

9. *Injuries:*

   a. Obtain the names and addresses of all persons injured or allegedly injured.
   b. If possible, obtain the age, marital status, occupation and dependency of all persons injured.
   c. Describe the injured (tall, short, obese, pallid, etc.).
   d. Describe any visual evidence of injury:

      (1) Give the exact location of any cuts, bleeding or other evidence of injury.
      (2) Describe the nature of any complaints of injury. Were they apparently sincere or did the complaints seem to involve malingering?
      (3) Did the injured make any outcries or show any other evidence of pain?

   e. Determine if first aid was given at the scene and if so, by whom. Determine if any comment was made by such attendant.
   f. Determine if the injured was taken from the scene and, if so, where, by whom and how.
   g. If the injured were occupants of the insured's vehicle:

(1) Describe their exact position and seating arrangement in the vehicle immediately preceding the accident.
(2) Determine their relationship to the driver.
(3) Where pertinent try to find out about any previous disabilities or medical history.

10. *Property damage:*
    a. Obtain description of the damaged vehicles:
        (1) Name, address and registration information of all owners and drivers.
        (2) Year, make, model and serial numbers of all cars.
        (3) Colors and other distinguishing features.
        (4) General condition.
    b. Obtain description of the damage in detail:
        (1) Point of impact.
        (2) Extent of damage, listing all damaged items individually.
        (3) Extent of apparent previous damage not attributable to present accident because of:
            (a) Extensive rusting.
            (b) Irreconcilable location of damage.
            (c) Obvious previous wear and tear.
    c. Determine if the cars were able to move away under their power after the accident.
    d. If any car involved in the accident was towed away, find out where it was taken.
    e. In pedestrian accidents:
        (1) Obtain description of any scratches, dents, scrapes or other marks on the insured's vehicle, showing the point of

impact and corroborate by an inspection of the vehicle.
 (2) Obtain immediate close-up and distant photographs of insured's car, where necessary.
f. Obtain description of damage to all personal belongings (luggage, packages, clothing, jewelry, glasses, etc.).
g. Obtain complete description of any damaged property which was being transported.

11. *Witnesses obtained from insured:*

    a. Obtain the names and addresses of all people in the insured's car:

     (1) Determine their locations in the car.
     (2) Determine their reasons for being in the car.
     (3) Determine their relationship to the driver or the named insured.

    b. Find out if the named insured or his driver obtained the names and addresses of anyone in any other vehicle involved in the accident.
    c. Determine if the named insured or driver obtained the names and addresses of any outside witnesses. If there were witnesses whose names or addresses were not obtained, try to get any information that might help in locating them.
    d. Determine if any pertinent remarks or comments were made by any of the witnesses.
    e. Determine if a police officer witnessed the accident or if any police officer obtained the names of any witnesses. If so:

     (1) Obtain the names and numbers of the policemen, home addresses if possible, and precinct numbers.

(2) Determine if any traffic or other charges were made against any party involved in the accident. Get details.

(3) Determine if there were any police, motor vehicle, or coroner's hearings and obtain details.

(4) Find out if any tests were made to determine intoxication of any of the involved parties and, if so, get details.

D. **Claimant's Investigation**

This section is devoted to the information which must be obtained from the claimant. Wherever possible and permissible under the law or code of ethics, a signed statement should be obtained from each claimant and, in particular, from the drivers of all adverse vehicles. Many points to develop in the investigation obviously cannot or should not be incorporated into any signed statements. This is matter of judgment.

From the following suggestions, take what is necessary to develop the investigation of the case under consideration.

1. *Claimant's background information and introductory matter:*

    a. Name and all previous names or aliases under which the claimant was ever known, including the maiden name of married females.

    b. Present address and, if warranted, any previous addresses in order to check with Index Bureau reports.

    c. Age, general appearance and impression made by claimant. This should include any information on the claimant's moral character, honesty, reputation, industriousness, intelligence, education and other factors that might bear on his or her sincerity and impression as a witness.

d. Physical condition or possible deformities which might have a bearing on the accident as follows:

    (1) Intoxication or alcoholic consumption:

        (a) Determine the nature of the drinks.

        (b) Determine how many were taken, when and where.

        (c) Try to determine whether the driver felt the effects of any such drinking.

    (2) Drugs, pills or other narcotics. Get all details.

    (3) Generally weakened condition due to illness.

    (4) Fatigue or lack of sleep:

        (a) Determine how long the claimant had been driving before the accident.

        (b) Find out his starting time. Determine the distance driven including point of departure, route and destination.

        (c) Determine what rest the claimant had immediately preceding the last driving.

    (5) Physical infirmities such as:

        (a) Heart disease.

        (b) Fainting spells, blackouts or dizziness.

        (c) Epilepsy.

        (d) Defective hearing.

        (e) Defective eyesight. Find out if the claimant needed glasses, and if he or she was wearing them.

(6) Physical deformities such as:
- (a) Crippled or prosthetic devices which the claimant was either wearing or should have been.
- (b) Amputation of a limb or other extremity.
- (c) Extreme overweight.
- (d) Unsteadiness due to old age or infirmity.

e. Business, employment or military service that might interfere with appearance at time of trial.
f. Possible criminal record.

2. *Claimant's marital status and dependency:*
   a. Name, age and dependency status of wife.
   b. Names, ages and dependency status of all children.
   c. Marital status, including details of previous marriages, divorces or widowhood. If necessary, obtain copies of records of all previous marriages, separations, divorces, children by former marriages, and other pertinent birth and death records.

3. *Employment history:*
   a. Names and addresses of all present employers.
   b. Names and addresses of previous employers where pertinent, and time employed by each.
   c. Exact nature and duties of employment.
   d. Salaries received, including regular salary, commissions, overtime, tips, board and lodging or other remuneration of any kind.
   e. Time and exact earnings lost as a result of the accident.

4. *Educational background:*

a. Name and address of present school being attended.
b. Names and addresses of previous schools, if applicable, to obtain background information.
c. Obtain years or grades in attendance and previous marks.
d. Determine the exact time lost from school as a result of the accident.
e. Review checklists on the investigation of claims involving minors.

5. *Pensions, insurance or welfare help:*

Obtain details and check information where warranted, concerning past or present help received from:

a. City, state or federal relief or benefits, including social security.
b. Private or public pensions of any kind, including any private charities.
c. Disability benefits of any kind.
d. Workmen's Compensation benefits. Obtain name of carrier and check this out.
e. Medical payments coverage on automobile policy. Obtain name of carrier and interview.
f. Accident and health insurance. Obtain name of carrier and check this out, including Blue Cross or other medical plan.

6. *Driver's experience:*

a. Driver's or chauffeur's license or learner's permit and how long obtained.
b. Find out if the driver was required to wear glasses and, if so, whether he was wearing them at the time.
c. Find out if the claimant's driver had any recorded or unrecorded traffic violations. Get details.

- d. Find out if the claimant's license was ever revoked or suspended and, if so, get the details.
- e. If the claimant or his or her driver was a learner, determine if he or she was accompanied by a properly licensed driver. Find out if the driver had a learner's permit.
- f. If possible, determine previous accident record, with dates, locations and other details if pertinent.
- g. Check periodically, to determine whether claimant has been involved in any accident since the one under investigation.

7. *Driving distractions:*
   - a. Find out if the driver was watching something or someone.
   - b. Find out if the driver was talking to someone in the car or otherwise distracted.
   - c. Find out if the driver was daydreaming.
   - d. Find out if the driver was smoking and, if so, whether this distracted him or her.
   - e. Determine if the driver was worried or under emotional strain.
   - f. Determine if the driver was in a hurry and, if so, why.
   - g. Find out if the driver was familiar with the area in which he or she was driving.
   - h. Determine if there was a dangling object in front or behind the windshield.
   - i. Determine if the radio, C.B. or recorder was in operation.

8. *Claimant passengers:*

   Interview all passengers in the claimant's car separately and, where warranted, obtain a signed statement from each including:
   - a. Relationship of the passengers to the driver or the named insured.

b. Exact seating arrangement and positions immediately preceding the accident.
c. Reason for making the trip.
d. Exact nature of the trip:
    (1) Determine for whose benefit the trip was being made.
    (2) Determine at whose request it was being made, and get details.
e. Exact nature of any contributions toward expenses.
f. Control of vehicle and manner of driving, route to be taken and destination.
g. Determine who invited the claimant to ride. Determine if he or she would be considered a guest in jurisdiction.
h. Determine if the claimant had ever ridden with the driver before. Determine the claimant's knowledge of driver's ability as such.
i. Determine it any objections were made by anyone concerning the driver or his or her driving and if there were any outcries or admonitions.
j. Complete details concerning any alcoholic consumption, intoxication, or use of any pills or drugs.

9. *Claimant pedestrians:*

In claims involving pedestrians, determine:

a. Whether claimant's attention was distracted at time of the accident because of:
    (1) The weather (rain, snow, sleet, ice, fog, etc.).
    (2) A slip, trip, stumble or because claimant was running.
    (3) An umbrella, package, animal or other object which claimant was carrying.
    (4) Watching someone or something.

AUTOMOBILE LIABILITY & PROPERTY INVESTIGATIONS

    (5) Daydreaming or preoccupation for any reason.
    (6) Worry or other emotional stress or illness, or being unusually tired.
  b. What kind of clothes the claimant was wearing:
    (1) Find out if they were drab and blended in with the scenery.
    (2) Determine if the claimant had a hat over his or her eyes.
    (3) Determine if the claimant had his or her collar up enough to interfere with vision.
    (4) Determine if any part of the claimant's clothes created a tripping hazard.

10. *Determine if the claimant made any report* to the police, motor vehicle bureau or coroner. Find out if any official hearing of any kind was conducted and get the result.
11. *Report on claimant's economic status* and financial responsibility.
12. *Determine the insurance carriers for any claimants* that may become co-defendants or who may be primarily liable.
13. *Develop the factual details:*
    a. Obtain the exact date, time and place of the accident.
    b. Determine the direction in which each vehicle was traveling and the names of the streets or roads traversed.
    c. Describe all traffic controls including traffic policemen, stop or other signs, traffic lights, blinkers, etc.
    d. Determine the speed of the claimant's vehicle:
        (1) Determine if the speedometer was working properly.
        (2) Find out if there was a governor on the claimant's vehicle.

(3) If the gearshift was not automatic, determine what gear the claimant's car was in. Find out if the driver shifted gears immediately before the accident.
e. Determine the estimated speed of the insured's vehicle as described by the claimant.
f. Determine the position of all vehicles with reference to traffic lanes, shoulders, and distances from the curb, edge of the road and nearest intersecting streets or roads.
g. Describe all other physical facts in detail, including such items as weather conditions, road conditions, lighting and other items specifically outlined in the following section dealing with Physical Facts.
h. Determine as nearly as possible at what point the claimant or his driver first observed the insured or adverse vehicle.
i. If the claimant was a pedestrian, obtain complete description as follows:

(1) Learn if the claimant is tall or short, and if he or she was visible or should have been. Find out if there were any obstacles to visibility.
(2) Determine the colors of the clothes worn.
(3) Find out if the claimant was carrying an umbrella, package or other object, or an animal.
(4) Find out if the claimant had a hat pulled down or a coat collar up so as to obstruct vision.

j. Obtain a complete description of the movements of the claimant or adverse vehicles immediately preceding, during and after the impact, with distances and positions placed as exactly as possible.

k. Obtain the exact positions of the pedestrian or vehicles immediately after all motion had stopped.
l. Determine if either driver sounded the horn.
m. Determine if either driver attempted to swerve or slow down. If not, find out why.
n. Determine if any other action was taken by any of the parties involved to avoid the accident when danger was first perceived.
o. Find out if any arm or directional signals were given before the accident.
p. Determine if skid marks were made by any of the vehicles involved. If so, describe their length and direction.
q. Obtain the exact point of impact on the vehicles in relation to each other and to the scene of the accident.
r. Try to learn if any pertinent remarks were made by anyone immediately before or after the accident, including any admissions of fault.
s. *In accidents involving bus or trolley passengers* or vehicles, obtain the following information:

   (1) Determine if the claimant was boarding or leaving the vehicle. If so, find out by what door and whether it was in the process of being opened or closed.
   (2) Determine if the claimant was seated, walking or running toward the exit doors.
   (3) Determine if the claimant was walking or running toward or away from the vehicle.
   (4) Determine if the claimant tripped or stumbled before, during or while entering or leaving the vehicle. Find out if any physical hazards on the bus might

have contributed to the claimant's injury.

(5) Determine if any other passenger or prospective passenger preceded or followed the claimant and if names and addresses were obtained.
(6) Determine if the bus made a sudden stop or was involved in any other unusual movements. Describe in detail.
(7) Find out if the driver gave any warning and if any warning signs were on display.
(8) Determine approximately how many other passengers were aboard.
(9) Find out if any of the passengers witnessed the accident and if their names and addresses were obtained.

14. *Medical information to be obtained from the claimant:*

Wherever possible, written authorization to receive medical information should be obtained from the claimant at the earliest possible time. Enough copies should be obtained so that they may be presented to all doctors and hospitals or clinics that attended the claimant.

Attempts should be made to incorporate as much of the medical information as is applicable in the statement. Information obtained should include:

a. Detailed description of all objective (noticeable) evidence of injury.
b. Detailed account of any unconsciousness, giving exact duration.
c. Complete list of subjective complaints (those not accompanied by noticeable evidence of injury), when first developed, and their duration.

AUTOMOBILE LIABILITY & PROPERTY INVESTIGATIONS

- d. Medical assistance rendered at the scene of the accident.
- e. Details concerning any first aid treatment and by whom given.
- f. Name of hospital or doctor to whom the claimant was taken immediately after the accident.
- g. Name and address of family physician who subsequently treated the claimant.
- h. Name and address of any specialists who were called in for consultation and treatment.
- i. Dates of all visits to physicians, specialists, hospitals, clinics, etc., and dates of visits made to the claimant's home by doctors, nurses or medical technicians.
- j. Dates of admission to and discharge from any hospital, sanitorium, rest home, etc.
- k. Information concerning X-rays. By whom taken, when and how. Give details.
- l. Details concerning any operations or casts.
- m. Details concerning the nature of the treatment or rehabilitation rendered.
- n. Exact duration of confinement to bed and to home.
- o. Exact duration of disability from working.
- p. Exact nature of any present complaints.
- q. Description of any scars or disfigurements. If possible, obtain snapshots or photographs.
- r. Details of previous medical history where applicable:
    - (1) Family history, including inherited tendencies or weaknesses, and history of family deaths which might have had a connection with the present or future disability of the claimant.
    - (2) Names and addresses of all doctors and hospitals that were involved in the treat-

ment of previous serious ailments that might have some connection with the present disability.
(3) List of previous operations that might be applicable including details of previous X-rays taken.
(4) Details concerning any previous protracted treatments for mental or physical disability that might be applicable.
(5) History of previous diseases such as heart or lung disease which may have been aggravated as a result of the accident.
(6) History of previous ailments or diseases which might have left aftereffects such as scarlet fever, rheumatic fever, measles, mumps, etc.
(7) History of any previous diseases which might affect healing in any manner such as tuberculosis, syphilis, gonorrhea, diabetes, etc.
(8) Special emphasis on previous injury to eyes, ears or members of the body that may have impaired complete function or contributed to the cause of the accident.
(9) Previous dental history if applicable.
(10) History of any previous extensive physical examinations such as those made by life insurance companies, armed forces, private companies for employment purposes or school examinations if warranted.

15. *Property damage:*

   a. Obtain description of the damaged vehicles as previously outlined, including name and

addresses of owners, year, make and model of vehicles, color, license number and general condition.
   b. Obtain description of damage in detail as previously outlined, including point of impact, extent of damage and location, extent of previous damage or wear and tear, etc.
   c. Determine if the cars were able to move under their own power after the accident.
   d. If any car involved in the accident was towed away, learn where it was taken.
   e. Obtain description of damage to all personal belongings including luggage, clothing, jewelry, glasses, etc.
   f. Obtain description of any damaged property which was being transported.

16. *Witnesses obtained through claimant:*
   a. Obtain the names and addresses of all people in the claimant's car. Determine their relationship to the driver, their locations in the car and their reasons for being in it.
   b. Find out if the claimant or his or her driver obtained the names and addresses of anyone who might have witnessed the accident. Get description of any witnesses whose names may not have been obtained.
   c. Determine if any outcries or pertinent comments or remarks were made by any witnesses.
   d. Find out if a police officer witnessed the accident or obtained the names and addresses of any witnesses. Get the name, address, precinct number and police number where warranted.
   e. Find out if any tests were made to determine intoxication.
   f. Determine if any traffic violation or other charges were made against any party involved

in the accident and the nature of such charges. Were there any police, motor vehicle or coroner's hearings and, if so, get copies.

E. **Medical Investigation**

The writer recognizes the fact that obtaining medical information today is very difficult. Lest the reader laugh out loud at some of the suggestions for the investigation of the medical aspects of a claim or suit let me hasten to state that such information would be the ideal, if it could be obtained. Nevertheless, the investigator should not assume a defeatist attitude. It is still possible to get much information if intelligence and persistence are applied to the investgation, and if permission has been granted by the claimant or his representative.

If the matter is in suit, it may become necessary to obtain vital medical information by deposition or interrogatories. Ideally, the following information should be obtained:

1. *Detailed information from the claimant* as outlined in the previous section "C. 9. Injuries."
2. *Attending doctor's report.* Information obtained from the attending doctor should be signed by him whenever possible. Whatever the form, the information should include:
    a. *Personal and descriptive data concerning the claimant:*
        (1) Date, time and place of the initial examination.
        (2) Name, address, age, weight, height, occupation and marital status.
    b. *History of the accident.* This should include as much information as can be obtained concerning the time, place and manner in which the accident occurred, as reported to the doctor by the claimant.

c. *Previous medical history* where applicable, with special emphasis on any condition which would have any bearing on the disability or any possible effect on the manner in which the accident happened. Review the outline entitled "Medical information to be obtained from the claimant."
d. *Details concerning the initial examination,* including results of any X-rays or laboratory tests, consultant's or other medical reports.
e. *Treatment rendered,* including the type and dates of office and home visits.
f. *Diagnosis.* This should include a detailed account of the doctor's findings concerning injury, ailments and disability, with special emphasis on trauma.
g. *Prognosis.* This concerns the estimated disability and the possibility or probability of ultimate partial or complete recovery. Determine if the doctor believes that there will be any partial or permanent disability.
h. *Conclusions and recommendations.* Here, an attempt should be made to get the doctor to comment on recommendations concerning future treatments, operations, or further hospitalization that may be necessary, as well as any other details that might affect the medical picture.
i. *Diagrams.* Drawings of various parts of the body are usually imprinted on the opposite side of medical report forms which most companies use, in order to enable the doctor to show scars or to indicate the location of fractures, burns, cuts or other injuries.
j. *Doctor's bill.* The doctor should always be requested to indicate the amount of his bill up to the time of the report. He should also be

requested to give an estimate of the possible future medical expenses.

3. *Hospital records:*

    Wherever possible, a complete transcript of the hospital records should be obtained. A wealth of information can sometimes be obtained from records that would not appear in any abstract sent by a hospital. The records usually contain the following information:

    a. *Admission information.* Beside the regular admission information, there may be Welfare Board reports concerning financial background of the claimant, police reports, an itemized list of the clothes and possessions of the claimant at the time of admission, condition of the clothes and other valuable information.
    b. *History of the accident* as given by the claimant, police, or other attendant at the time of admission.
    c. *The examination reports by attending doctors* and interns, X-ray reports, notes and instructions by such doctors or interns, details concerning treatments, pathologist's and laboratory reports, and of great importance, *nurses' notes.*
    d. *Diagnosis and prognosis* of the various attending physicians, surgeons and specialists, including date and circumstances under which the patient left the hospital. Wherever warranted, interview attending doctors, interns and nurses personally, if possible.

4. *Physical examination:*

    Physical examination of the claimant should not be ordered indiscriminately. The following factors

should be given serious consideration before ordering or attempting to get a physical examination:
  a. *Determine the purpose for such examination.* If the purpose is merely to corroborate information obtained from the claimant, the hospital records or the reputation of the attending physican together with the information he gives, may be sufficient.
  b. *Determine the type of examination that is needed.* The ordinary examination that involves relatively minor injuries should usually be made by a general practitioner. However, if there are allegations of a nature that might have to be refuted at trial, or if there is any doubt about the allegations, it is advisable to get an examination by a qualified specialist. In choosing the specialist, consideration must be given to his standing in the profession and to the impression he would make on a jury.
  c. *Determine the time when the examination is to be made.* Ordinarily, where protracted disability is involved, the examination should be made after the longest healing period possible. Where fraud or malingering is suspected, however, it may be advisable to obtain the physical examination as soon as possible. This is a matter of judgment, depending upon the allegations of the injury and disability and an appraisal of the claimant's integrity.
  d. *The examining physician should be furnished with all of the medical information available before he makes his examination.* This should include, whenever available, attending doctor's reports, hospital records, X-ray and laboratory reports, and whatever other information might be pertinent to the examination. The

examining physican should, whenever possible, personally examine previously-taken X-rays, or point out the need for them.

    e. *Information which the examining physican should include in his report* corresponds for the most part with the information that should be obtained from the claimant's attending physician and which has previously been outlined in "Medical information to be obtained from the claimant."

5. *Additional interviews.* Whenever pertinent and whenever the seriousness of the accident warrants it, interviews should be sought with the ambulance attendant at the scene of the accident, the attending physican or intern at the hospital, hospital nurses, dentists, chiropractors or others that might be able to give valuable information.

The compensation carrier and the insurers that have reported previous Index Bureau reports should also be interviewed.

6. An effort should be made, wherever warranted, to *determine if malpractice of any kind was evident or probable* that could have been committed by any of the doctors, surgeons, nurses, technicians or the hospital. If so, obtain as many details as possible.

F. **Physical Facts**

This is a term used to designate the physical conditions at the scene of an accident. Not only must the physical facts be determined by the investigation, but evidence in the form of signed statements, photographs, diagrams, reports, etc. should be obtained in order to be able to prove the actual conditions in the trial of the case being investigated.

The physical facts will of course vary greatly with the type of accident under investigation. The investigator should

AUTOMOBILE LIABILITY & PROPERTY INVESTIGATIONS 39

follow whatever leads he may need from the following suggestions:

1. *Complete description of the scene of the accident:*
    a. Determine which roads or highways are main arteries, which are secondary, and which one had the right of way.
    b. Observe the general area and describe whether it is urban, suburban, rural, business, factory, etc.
    c. Determine the exact widths of the streets or roads.
    d. Determine the number of traffic lanes and whether they were marked. Find out if there was a center traffic island. Describe, giving width, height of curb or separation and other pertinent data.
    e. Determine if the street had sidewalks and give dimensions. If a road was involved determine if it had berms or shoulders. Determine width, depth and type of any ditches.
    f. Describe all marks on the street, road or other areas, resulting from the accident, such as:
        (1) Debris from the vehicles such as broken glass, broken parts of the car, scattered contents of the vehicles, etc.
        (2) Stains such as oil slick, anti-freeze, blood, etc.
        (3) Gouges and skid marks, giving depth, length, direction, measurements with reference to the area and exact location.
    g. Determine if the street or road is straight or curved, level or inclined, or dead-end. Give directions and degrees.
    h. Describe the paving of the road, whether con-

crete, macadam, asphalt, brick, cobblestone, gravel or dirt. Were they flat or crowned?
  i. Determine the general condition of the roads. Were they dry, wet, slippery, icy, etc.? Were they smooth, rough, bumpy, rutted, etc.? Describe in detail. Find out if they had trolley tracks and, if so, what was their condition.
  j. Determine the locality with respect to general visibility and list obstructions such as parked cars, buildings, trees, shrubbery, etc.

2. *Weather conditions and reports:*
   a. Determine if it was snowing, raining, foggy, misty, etc., at the time of the accident.
   b. Find out if the windshield wipers were working properly.
   c. Determine if the side window visibility was obstructed, if it was down, and if the windshield or windows were steamed-up or frosted.
   d. Determine if snow tires or chains were used or necessary.
   e. Where necessary, obtain weather report from nearest weather station.

3. *Traffic controls:*
   a. Determine if there were any traffic controls at the scene of the accident (police officer, traffic lights or signals, stop signs or other warning signs). Find out if they were visible and in proper working conditon. Give exact locations and details.
   b. Determine if the scene of the accident was within a hospital or school zone. If so, were proper signs posted?
   c. Determine if local ordinance gives either driver the right of way.
   d. Determine if there was any violation of an ordinance or traffic regulation.

AUTOMOBILE LIABILITY & PROPERTY INVESTIGATIONS 41

4. *Lighting.* Obtain complete details as follows:
   a. Determine if it was daylight, nighttime, dusk, cloudy, foggy, moonlight, etc.
   b. Determine if bright sunlight interfered with the vision of either driver. Determine the position of the sun to indicate in which direction it was shining.
   c. Determine if headlights were on or necessary, and, if so, were they bright, medium, dim, parking or fog lights.
   d. Find out if approaching headlights were blinding, and if traffic was heavy. Determine if both vehicles had tinted glass, or if the drivers were using pull-down sunshades.
   e. Describe the road or street lights in detail. Give their power and location as nearly as possible.
   f. Determine if flares were used:
      (1) Find out if they were required by local, state or federal law.
      (2) Find out if they were needed because of night or road conditions.
      (3) Find out if they were available and, if so, exactly where they were placed. Determine if the placing was proper and if it conformed with legal requirements.

5. *Condition of the vehicles:*
   a. Determine their age and general condition.
   b. Obtain detailed information concerning any defective equipment that might have contributed to the accident, such as:
      (1) Brakes, steering mechanisms, defective tires.
      (2) Speedometers, governors, horns.
      (3) Headlights, directional signals, wind-

shields, windshield wipers or windshield obstructions.

c. Determine whether state inspection was required and if in order. Determine when and where made.

6. *Witnesses' possible vantage points.* Describe the scene of the accident with respect to the location of any houses or other buildings from which possible witnesses might have seen the accident. Follow up by neighborhood investigation in order to locate any witnesses.

7. *Diagram.* Draw a complete diagram of the scene of the accident including all pertinent information previously listed, and in particular:

   a. Measurements of streets, traffic lanes, shoulders, and any others that might have a bearing on the accident.
   b. Position of all vehicles and pedestrians before, during and after the impact.
   c. Distances of vehicles from intersections, curb lines, shoulders, lights.
   d. Position of skid marks, gouges, debris, lights.
   e. Location of all obstructions to vision such as trees, buildings, parked cars, etc.
   f. Location of vantage points of possible witnesses.
   g. Position of all traffic controls or signs.
   h. Compass indication showing "north."
   i. Legend at bottom of diagram should include key to scale, designation of all objects to be identified, the date and time of the accident and when the diagram was drawn.

8. *Photographs and snapshots.* Photographs and snapshots should be taken, where possible, before any change has occurred in the scene or object being

photographed. Where necessary, photographs should be made of the vehicles to show the point of impact and the extent of the damage, as well as of the scene of the accident. Types of photographs can, where advisable, include:

   a. Commercial photographs.
   b. Snapshots.
   c. Aerial photographs.
   d. Panorama shots and enlargements.
   e. Police photographs.
   f. Newspaper photographs.

9. *Other prepared evidence:*

   a. Movies.
   b. Surveys and plats.
   c. Laboratory and engineering reports.
   d. Advertising catalogues and instructional material.

10. *Hearings and hearing reports:*

    a. Police, sheriff's or state trooper's reports:

       (1) Interview all officers.
       (2) Obtain any special reports made by the Homicide Squad or concerning intoxication or drug use.
       (3) Determine if any charges were made against anyone.

    b. Determine whether a criminal hearing will be or has been held. If so, decide upon the advisability of obtaining transcripts or attending as an observer.
    c. Obtain Motor Vehicle report and determine whether there will be a Motor Vehicle hearing. If so, decide on the advisability of obtaining a transcript of the hearing if any, or attending as an observer.

d. Obtain autopsy report, coroner's report or transcript, if any.
e. Obtain complete newspaper accounts that may contain leads to witnesses or further investigation.

G. **Witnesses' Investigation**

This section is devoted to the information which must be obtained from outside witnesses (other than the parties directly involved in the accident). Here again, wherever possible, a signed statement should be obtained from the witness. Suggested leads for inquiry are:

1. *Identification and background.* Obtain:
    a. Name and address. If present address is temporary, obtain permanent address or that of a close relative or friend through whom the witness can always be located.
    b. Age, general appearance and characteristics for the purpose of evaluating the effect of the witnesses' testimony at trial, such as:
        (1) Mental attributes (bright, stupid, incoherent, irrational, articulate, etc.).
        (2) Personality (well-poised, likeable, modest, loud, irritating, aggressive, etc.).
        (3) Sincerity (apparently honest, shifty-eyed, positive, vacillating, etc.).
        (4) Education. Indicate whether witness' language and subject matter bear out allegations of schooling.
        (5) Physical appearance (sloppily- or loudly-dressed, physically dirty, immaculate, etc.).
        (6) Physical defects (poor eyesight, poor hearing, etc.).

AUTOMOBILE LIABILITY & PROPERTY INVESTIGATIONS 45

   c. Employment, including name and address of employer and job or position held.
   d. Driving experience.
2. *Location of and reason for witness' presence:*
   a. Learn the exact location from which the witness viewed the accident.
   b. Check to see if the scene was actually visible from the alleged vantage point.
   c. Find out if the witness was a pedestrian or a driver or passenger of a vehicle.
   d. Find out from which direction the witness approached the scene of the accident.
   e. Determine why the witness was allegedly there. Find out where he or she was going. Try to find out if there is any reason to doubt the witness' credibility.
   f. Determine in what direction the witness was looking.
   g. Find out what first attracted the attention of the witness to any of the parties or objects involved in the accident.
   h. Find out if the witness was alone. Obtain the names and addresses of, or leads to, any other witnesses.
3. *Factual details:*
   a. Obtain the date, time and place of the accident.
   b. Determine the direction in which each vehicle or pedestrian was traveling and how far away they were when first seen.
   c. Describe the vehicles and or pedestrians and obtain all details concerning their location at the time.
   d. Describe all traffic controls, including traffic policemen, stop signs or other traffic signs, traffic lights, blinkers, etc.

e. Estimate the speed of each vehicle.
f. Find out if the witness overheard any comments made after the accident that might help to determine fault.
g. Determine the position of all vehicles with reference to traffic lanes, shoulders and distances from curb or edge of the road.
h. Obtain the position of all cars with reference to the nearest streets or highways.
i. Describe the physical facts in detail as previously outlined, including such items as weather conditions, road and lighting, obstructions to visibility, etc.
j. Obtain a complete description of the movements of the pedestrian or vehicles immediately preceding, during and after the impact, with distances and positions placed as nearly as possible.
k. Determine if either driver sounded the horn.
l. Find out if any arm or directional signals were given.
m. Determine if skid marks were made by any of the vehicles. Give length and direction.
n. Determine if there were any other stains or debris marks that could help to locate the exact position of the cars at the point of impact.
o. Learn if any pertinent remarks were made by anyone immediately after the accident involving fault.
p. In accidents involving bus or trolley passengers, see paragraph 8 under "Insured's Investigation" for details.

4. *Injuries:*

   a. Obtain description of all persons allegedly injured.

b. Obtain description of their positions in the vehicles.
c. Obtain description of all visual evidence of injury.
d. Find out if the witness overheard any comments or groans that would indicate injury or degree of pain.
e. Obtain details concerning first aid given at the scene of the accident and by whom administered.

5. *Property damage:*
   a. Obtain description of the automobile damage:
      (1) Point of impact on each vehicle.
      (2) Extent of the damage to each vehicle.
      (3) General condition and extent of previous damage or wear and tear observed by the witness.
   b. Determine if the cars were able to move away under their own power after the accident. If not, find out where the vehicle or vehicles were taken.
   c. Obtain description of damage to personal belongings such as luggage, clothing, jewelry, glasses, etc.
   d. Obtain description of any damaged property which was being transported.

6. *Neighborhood canvass—Discovering the unknown witness.*

In a serious accident of questionable liability, nothing is more important in the investigation than an immediate attempt to locate any outside (impartial) witnesses. Leads may be obtained from the following sources:

   a. Insured, driver or anyone in his or her car.

b. Claimant, claimant's driver or anyone in the claimant's vehicle.
c. Police report or police officers who made the report.
d. Motor Vehicle report of all parties involved in the accident.
e. Hearings, such as Traffic Court, Motor Vehicle, criminal or coroner's inquest.
f. Other witnesses to the accident who may have recognized someone in the immediate vicinity, or who may be able to describe someone who lives nearby.
g. Neighborhood stores that may have been open at the time of the accident. Since shopkeepers usually know the people in the area, this is ordinarily an excellent source for leads.
h. Private homes facing, and in the area of, the accident.
i. Apartments facing the scene of the accident. A canvass should be made of all apartments in the building that have windows facing onto the scene of the accident, where warranted.
j. Bus and trolley drivers who may have witnessed the accident. These men are usually very difficult to track down. However, where the seriousness of the accident warrants, it might pay to be present at the scene, at the same hour, and question passing drivers. Sometimes the claim department of a bus or trolley company will help to locate a driver or passenger witness.
k. Ambulance attendants or nurses.
l. Park department crews, firemen, gas department workers, street cleaners or repair men, garbage collectors or other municipal or public utilities employees.

m. News vendors, delivery men, milkmen or other delivery or driver employees that may have been working in the area, or that may make regular deliveries in the area.

H. Special Damages

All special damages should be checked carefully where the amount involved warrants it, as follows:

1. *Lost time and earnings.* It is important to remember that the claimant is entitled to take-home pay only.

   a. *Where employee is salaried:*

      (1) Check employer's payroll record. Verbal corroboration by a clerk, or even a letter from someone in the employer's office may sometimes be open to question.

      (2) Check exact dates of absence from work carefully.

      (3) Check the exact amount of the lost earnings. The employer may have paid all or a part of the employee's salary.

      (4) Determine the amount of the regular salary rate.

      (5) Determine the average amount of overtime for that particular time of the year.

      (6) Determine the average amount of commissions for that particular time of year.

      (7) Make an estimate of the average tips and other gratuities including board and lodging.

      (8) Determine whether the injury has necessitated a change of job or employment.

      (9) Determine whether the injury has necessitated claimant's going on part-time work.

      (10) Check with the compensation carrier, all lost time and medical expenses.

b. *Where the claimant is self-employed:*

   (1) Request permission to check income tax returns, including Federal, State, and City, if any.
   (2) Check social security tax if possible.
   (3) Get permission to examine business books and accounts.

2. *Automobile property damage:*

   In handling claims involving property damage only, the investigator should make absolutely certain that there is no bodily injury involvement. Obtain signed statement where advisable. In all cases:

   a. *Determine the amount of the property damage:*

      (1) Obtain competitive estimates or bills from reputable repair shops.
      (2) Check damage personally and compare with estimates where warranted.
      (3) Obtain an appraisal of the damage where warranted.

   b. *Check all bills or estimates carefully concerning possible:*

      (1) Replacement of parts not damaged in the accident.
      (2) Replacement of parts where the damage was caused by ordinary wear and tear.
      (3) Charge made for new parts although used parts were actually installed.
      (4) Overcharge on parts.
      (5) Labor overcharge.
      (6) Duplication or overlapping of labor items.
      (7) Inclusion of previous damage.
      (8) Incorrect addition.

c. *Obtain parts discount where possible.*
d. *Obtain deduction for depreciation* where possible and warranted.
e. *Arrange for repairs instead of replacement* of parts if warranted. Because of high labor costs, this is admittedly of questionable value today.
f. *Where repairs have already been made, be doubly careful when checking out bills.* If there is any doubt:

   (1) Obtain an appraisal and have the appraiser or yourself check the allegedly replaced parts by:

      (a) Examination of all parts which were allegedly replaced.
      (b) Examination of the books and records of the repair shop concerning replaced parts.

g. *Determine loss of use where applicable:*

   (1) Find out if replacement expense was necessary.
   (2) Determine if replacement expense was kept at a minimum.
   (3) Determine the reason for the replacement expense.
   (4) Obtain bills and check for authenticity and reasonableness. Be highly skeptical of bills from friends or relatives.

h. *In total losses:*

   (1) Determine the general condition of the car before the accident.
   (2) Determine what accessories were part of the car such as radio (AM or FM,

C.B.), air conditioning, radial tires, special wheels, etc.
  (3) Learn the market value of the car and its accessories before the accident.
  (4) Determine the salvage value by competitive bids and make proper deduction for the salvage.
3. *Other property damage.* Always be conscious of possible salvage, depreciation or betterment and replacement or repair where warranted.
   a. Clothing (torn, stained or otherwise destroyed).
   b. Jewelry (watches, rings, necklaces, pins, etc.).
   c. Luggage and contents.
   d. Packages or bundles being carried or transported.
   e. Glasses, false teeth, hearing aids.
   f. Merchandise, samples or other contents of car or truck.
4. *Medical expenses.* Check all bills for authenticity and reasonableness where warranted.
   a. Obtain attending doctor's, surgeon's or other specialist's or dentist's bills.
   b. Obtain all nurses fees.
   c. Determine the amount of hospital, clinic, sanitorium, rest home or similar bills.
   d. Obtain the cost of ambulance bills or other bills for transportation.
   e. Determine the amount of X-ray bills.
   f. Determine the amount of bills for rehabilitation services including all therapists.
   g. Get the amounts of any laboratory bills not listed on the hospital bills.
   h. Obtain bills for any prosthetic devices, wheelchairs, or similar apparatus.

i. Determine the amount of the bills for medicines and other prescriptions.
5. *Fatal claims.* Obtain:
    a. Funeral expenses.
    b. Cost of burial plot or mausoleum or cremation.
    c. Cost of tombstone.
6. *Expected future monetary loss.* Such loss, in order to be given proper consideration, must be reasonably probable considering the claimant's age, education and general economic status:
    a. Expected future lost earnings.
    b. Expected future lost increases.
    c. Expected future lost earning capacity.
    d. Possible future medical expense, including convalescent costs.
7. *Pain and suffering.* Determine the allegations concerning pain and suffering. In fatal claims, determine as closely as possible the length of time from the moment of impact until the claimant died and the length of time that the claimant was conscious.
8. *Loss of services or support:*
    a. Determine if there was any loss of services by a wife or child, including loss of consortium if alleged.
    b. Determine whether there were any dependents and how they were affected by the claimant's injury or death.
9. *Cosmetic disfigurement.* Determine whether there was any facial or other ordinarily visible disfigurement that might be noticeable when wearing a low-cut gown or bathing suit. Such disfigurement will have greater value in a young unmarried female.

CHAPTER II

Additional Automobile Investigations

A. **Automobile Medical Payments Investigation**

Ordinarily, this type of claim does not call for a detailed investigation. However, where there is reason to suspect padding or fraud, remember that the company is entitled to obtain signed statements, medical reports and physical examination. Medical payments coverage is diminishing in importance as "no-fault" legislation continues to grow, but the rate of growth indicates that medical payments coverage will continue to be an important part of the automobile policy for some time to come.

In any event, in dealing with this coverage, information should be developed along the following lines:

1. *Coverage information:*
    a. Determine whether the vehicle is properly covered under the policy. Check the ownership of the vehicle and compare it with the policy declarations.
    b. Make sure that the date of the accident falls within the policy period.
    c. Check the name or names of the insured against the name or names designated on the policy.
    d. Make sure that there is medical payments on the vehicle involved in the accident and check the limits.
    e. Determine whether the vehicle was being driven with the permission of the insured.
    f. If the policy covers the *individual,* determine

whether there is any primary coverage on the *vehicle.*

2. *Factual details:*
    a. Determine if the claimant was *in* the car.
    b. Determine if the claimant was *upon* the car. Describe.
    c. Find out if the claimant was *entering or alighting* from the car. Describe in detail.
    d. Determine if the accident arose out of the insured's or the insured's spouse's occupancy of of the vehicle involved, or out of the occupancy of any other insured.
    e. Find out if the vehicle involved in the accident was driven by an employee of the insured. If so, determine whether the employee was a chauffeur or servant.
    f. Determine if the insured's vehicle was being used as a taxi or otherwise for hire. If so, obtain details in the form of a signed statement.
    g. Determine if the injury was covered under any Workmen's Compensation Act.

3. *Medical information:*
    a. Obtain copies of all doctor's, dentist's or hospital reports.
    b. Where warranted, obtain physical examination to determine the extent of the injury or the effectiveness of the treatment.

4. *Expenses:*
    a. Obtain itemized receipted bills for all medical expenses. Examine them carefully and, if necessary, check for authenticity, reasonableness and apparent necessity.
    b. Determine whether the bills fall within the

ADDITIONAL AUTOMOBILE INVESTIGATION

       medical and/or funeral categories meant to be covered by the policy.
   c. Determine if the bills were *incurred* within one year from the date of the accident.

B. Automobile Non-Ownership Coverage Investigation

The investigation of an automobile non-ownership coverage claims involves the obtaining of all of the information required in the investigation of the regular automobile claim, as previously outlined, plus special items peculiar to this coverage. *Since vehicles owned, hired by, loaned to or registered in the name of the insured are not covered,* the following items must be checked:

1. *Ownership and control of the vehicle:*
   a. Determine in whose name the vehicle is registered.
   b. Find out who has control of the vehicle.
   c. Determine who paid the full purchase price or made the down payment where warranted.
   d. Find out if the vehicle was loaned or hired.
   e. If the non-owned or hired vehicle was a commercial vehicle, find out, in addition to the preceding, how often it is used in the course of the employer's work.

2. *Statement from the owner and operator of the vehicle should be obtained covering:*
   a. All of the points mentioned in the investigation of automobile claims.
   b. By whom the driver was employed, giving the circumstances, dates and scope of employment.
   c. By whom the driver was paid and how.
   d. Determine who directed the driver's activities.
   e. Find out who pays the expenses for the operation of the vehicle and how they are paid.

f. Learn the itinerary followed on the date of the accident, and who prescribed the route.
g. Determine the exact time and location of the last call made before the accident, and location of next proposed call. Determine the exact route taken.
h. Determine all of the activities and places visited the day of the accident by the driver.
i. Obtain a complete description of the accident as previously outlined.
j. Obtain a description of any merchandise or advertising material including samples, that were in the vehicle belonging to the employer.

3. *Statement from the insured covering:*
   a. All the points mentioned previously under "Automobile Liability Investigation."
   b. By whom owner-operator is employed. If independent contractor, secure copy of the contract if written, and the terms, if oral.
   c. How the driver is paid and what deductions are made for social security, state and local taxes, etc.
   d. If the driver is employed by the insured, obtain the hours worked and the nature of the duties.
   e. Who directs the itinerary, or whether it is left to the discretion of the owner-operator. Any restrictions?
   f. From previous operations, determine where the owner-operator would normally be expected to be at the time of the accident.

4. *Corroborate allegations:*
   a. Check itinerary.
   b. Check expense account.
   c. Check payroll and other employer's records.
   d. Check calls allegedly made and determine if

ADDITIONAL AUTOMOBILE INVESTIGATION

the accident was on the direct route to the next call.
   e. Get a signed statement from any witness who may have been in the vehicle with the driver.
5. *Determine existence of any primary insurance on the automobile.* Obtain the name of the carrier, the policy number and the limits of liability. This information must not be incorporated in the signed statements.
   a. If it develops that there is primary coverage on the vehicle, the employer and the insured should both be advised to notify the carrier promptly.
   b. If there appears to be no primary coverage, determine the employer's financial responsibility.
6. *Exercise care in determining whether or not to contact the claimant.* Doing so may sometimes lead to a premature injection of non-ownership insurance into the picture.

C. **Automobile Physical Damage Investigation**
1. *Identify the vehicle and determine whether it is properly covered.*
   a. Note the mileage and general condition.
   b. Inspect the damage carefully.
   c. Determine the point of impact and compare with the accident report.
   d. Check apparent cause of damage against the insured's allegations.
2. *Make sure that there have been no material misrepresentations in the policy declarations:*
   a. Obtain a signed statement from the insured outlining all of the facts if there is any doubt.
   b. Obtain a signed statement from the agent or

broker concerning the information that was furnished to him when the insurance was purchased, if warranted.
3. *Obtain information concerning the purchase of the vehicle where necessary:*
   a. Determine the actual cost to the insured.
   b. Determine the date of purchase.
   c. Determine whether the car was new or used at the time of purchase.
   d. Determine the method of payment.
   e. Determine the name and address of the seller of the car.
4. *Check the existence of any liens,* mortgages or other encumbrances on the vehicle and determine if they are listed on the policy or by endorsement.
5. *Make a complete investigation of the accident if necessary,* especially where subrogation possibilities exist. In addition to the regular investigation, determine whether the third party has insurance and, if possible, the name of the insurer and the limits of the policy. If there is no insurance, try to determine the financial responsibility of the third party.
6. *Determine the amount of the loss or damage* by obtaining competitive estimates, by personal inspection or by survey by an appraiser.
   a. Take advantage of all parts discounts.
   b. Take depreciation where warranted.
7. *Furnish the insured with a blank proof of loss form* and inform him that he must complete and return it within the specified time.
8. *Apply any deductible sum* which may be indicated on the policy, to the settlement figure.
9. *Make sure to include the name of any loss payee* in the settlement draft when settlement has been

ADDITIONAL AUTOMOBILE INVESTIGATION

arranged and particularly where the amount is substantial. The draft should be sent to the agent or broker if this is company practice.

10. *Investigation of total losses:*
    a. Obtain the original bill of sale and other evidence that title is held by the insured.
    b. Obtain assignment of title from the insured to the salvage buyer or company.
    c. Obtain motor vehicle registration certificate or title properly endorsed, where necessary.
    d. Obtain the keys to the vehicle.
    e. Obtain the original insurance policy for cancellation.
    f. Obtain completed proof of loss and subrogation receipt.
    g. Report to the National Automobile Theft Bureau, where warranted, all cases involving total loss due to fire, theft or collision.

11. *Investigation of automobile theft losses:*
    a. Identify the vehicle through the title papers and registration certificate if they are available, including the bill of sale.
    b. If there is any reason to suspect uncertainty of ownership, check the chain of title from the original dealer to the insured in order to be certain that the insured had lawful title to the vehicle.
    c. Obtain a description of the vehicle including its condition when last seen, and a complete list of all accessories. Secure an evaluation of a similar vehicle from several dealers in the locality where the loss occurred. Use the "red book" and similar publications as a general guide.
    d. Make a complete investigation of the facts, as previously outlined, where warranted.

e. Check the financial status of the insured where there is any reason to suspect fraud.
f. Make sure that the theft has been reported to the police even though the vehicle may have been recovered. This is an absolute requirement of the policy and should also be done in cases of the theft of parts of the car or pilferage.
g. Make a report of the incident to the bureaus of which the insurer may be a member.
h. If recovery is made before the loss is paid, the policy provides that the stolen property may be returned to the insured with payment for any damage resulting from the theft.
i. If the stolen vehicle is recovered, carefully check the damage alleged as a result of the theft, against any possible old damage or wear and tear suffered while the vehicle was in the insured's possession.

12. *Investigation of fire losses:*
    a. Obtain a signed statement from the insured concerning all details of his itinerary on the date of the loss.
    b. Obtain details concerning the purchase of the vehicle, including the date, cost, trade-in value, amount of any mortgage due and the amount of any payments that are past due.
    c. Determine the mileage and general condition of the vehicle at the time of the loss, including any defects, and the dates of recent repairs and by whom made.
    d. Determine if any extra equipment, tools or accessories were missing at the time of the inspection by the adjuster or appraiser.
    e. Check for evidence of previous collision damage.
    f. Obtain information concerning the insured's

financial status in cases involving a suspicion of arson.
g. Check into the possible presence of any inflammatory materials that may have been in or around the vehicle at the time of the fire. Get a full explanation for the presence of such materials.
h. Determine if any valuable personal property was burned with the vehicle.
i. *In the event of suspected arson,* obtain a mechanical inspection to determine:
   (1) Whether the gas tank cap shows any sign of tampering or the drain plug at the bottom of the gas tank shows evidence of plier marks recently made, which could indicate that gasoline might have been drained off and used in setting a fire.
   (2) Whether there are any breaks in the gas line from the tank to the fuel pump, or any recent tool marks that might indicate deliberate breaks or disconnections.
   (3) Whether there is any evidence of a short-circuit in the wiring.
   (4) Whether there is any evidence of fire on the front lower part of the motor. Accidental fire in this area can originate only in the fuel pump, carburetor or wiring. Otherwise, the origin might be subject to suspicion.
   (5) Whether any attempt was made to extinguish the fire.

D. **Investigation of Claims Involving I.C.C. or P.S.C. Certificates**
   1. *Legal requirements:*

- a. Determine the limits of coverage required by law.
- b. Check the policy to see if proper filing was made as required by law.
- c. If there is excess coverage, determine if such excess was disclosed in the filing.
- d. Determine whether the trip involved in the accident falls within the confines or requirements of I.C.C. or P.S.C. filing.

2. *Registration and ownership:*
    - a. Obtain the exact name and address of the registered owner.
    - b. Determine if he is also the de facto owner.
    - c. Check the registration of the tractor and/or trailer and the I.C.C. plates or P.S.C. numbers:
        - (1) Determine if the I.C.C. or P.S.C. plates are those of the owner of the vehicle.
        - (2) If not, determine whether the owner has plates of his own, or is required to have them.

3. *Leased trucks:*
    - a. Obtain the name and address of the lessor and lessee and get a copy of the lease.
    - b. Obtain the name and address of the consignor and consignee.
    - c. Determine if there was any previous agreement as to I.C.C. or P.S.C. plates for this operation.

4. *Control of the driver:*
    - a. Obtain the name and address of the driver.
    - b. Obtain the name and address of his ostensible employer.
    - c. Determine the method of salary payment,

registration of employer for Social Security and Unemployment Insurance.
- d. Determine who gave the driver instructions for the trip concerning:
    (1) Points of destination.
    (2) Route to be taken.
    (3) Time limitation and other pertinent details.
- e. Determine who had hired the driver and who had the right to fire him.
- f. Learn the details of the driver's last trip. Find out where he had gone and where he had come from and how long it had taken.
- g. Check the driver's itinerary with the employer and with the people on whom he was supposed to call.

5. Determine whether there is any other insurance involved on either the truck or the trailer.

E. **Investigation of Coverage Problems in Automobile Claims**

The following leads are outlined for the development of an investigation to determine any questionable features concerning the various automobile coverages.

In most of the investigations, there will be little need to develop the information listed under this section. However, when a question of coverage does arise, prompt and complete investigation along the lines suggested is essential. When this is so, review the initial report carefully for every bit of information that might prove useful as a lead in the investigation. Wherever possible, obtain signed statements from all individuals from whom information is obtained concerning a question of coverage. Remember that the problem here is to determine whether the incident reported falls within the policy provisions.

CASUALTY INVESTIGATION CHECKLISTS

1. *Review the application or daily with the utmost care:*
    a. Determine if the date of the accident falls within the policy period.
    b. Check the exact name or names of the insured against the name or names designated on the policy.
    c. Make sure that the vehicle involved in the accident is properly covered under the policy.
    d. Check the limits of liability.
    e. Examine all endorsements to determine which, if any, apply to the reported incident.

2. *Where the alleged date of the accident is close to the inception date of the policy:*

    Make sure that the incident occurred within the policy period. An accident which allegedly happened within a day or two of the inception date of the policy is one that should be checked carefully in order to determine whether the policy had actually been ordered before the accident occurred. If the alleged date of the accident is uncomfortably close to the inception date, the following investigation should be made:

    a. Obtain a signed statement from the insured including:
        (1) The exact date and time when the policy was allegedly ordered.
        (2) The manner in which it was ordered, whether by telephone, mail or otherwise.
        (3) The name of the person from whom the policy was ordered.
        (4) Determine if the policy is a renewal of previous unlapsed coverage.
        (5) Obtain whatever can be recalled con-

cerning the conversations and surrounding circumstances of the order.
- b. Obtain any corroborating material which the insured may have in the form of memoranda, copies of letters, etc.
- c. Obtain a signed statement from the person with whom the original order was placed, covering the same information as outlined in number 1, where warranted.
- d. Check the date stamp of the binder in the agent's or broker's office.
- e. Check any other written notations or memoranda that the agent or broker may be able to produce.
- f. Check the insurance company's records, if necessary, in order to determine the exact date and time when notice was received by the insurer concerning the binder of policy.
- g. Check the date of the accident through police records, hospital records, witnesses, claimant's version or other means that will make the date conclusive.

3. *Where there is a question concerning delayed notice:*
   - a. Obtain a signed statement from the insured, driver or witness giving the details of the accident.
   - b. Obtain a separate signed statement repeating the date, time and location of the accident and include details as to whom, when and how the accident was first reported. If it was reported by telephone, identify the person who took the call and get his or her recollection of the conversation as nearly as possible. Include the reason for the delay, if delay is admitted.
   - c. If the insured was not present at the scene of the accident, get complete information as to

how and when he or she first learned of it, including the name of the person who first gave the details.
d. Obtain a signed statement from the person who first reported the accident to the insured, giving all of the surrounding circumstances and including the exact date and time of the report and the manner in which it was made.
e. Examine the originals and obtain copies of all letters, telegrams or memoranda that corroborate the allegations.
f. If a corporation or business firm is the named insured, obtain a signed statement covering the details of the delayed notice along lines previously outlined, from the person responsible for reporting accidents. In the statement, be sure to identify him or her as such.
g. Signed statements corroborating or denying the allegations concerning the report should be obtained from any alleged witnesses to the reporting.
h. If a broker or agent is involved, a signed statement should be obtained from the person concerned about his or her knowledge of the matter. Original letters and records should be seen and copies obtained both of the receipt of notice and the transmittal to the agent or company. In some jurisdictions there is a difference in the law between the responsibilities of brokers and agents. It is therefore important, in such jurisdictions, to distinguish between the two.
i. Obtain a signed statement or a letter from the agent or his or her repreretatives concerning receipt of notice and its transmittal to the company. Letters and records should be examined where necessary and copies ob-

ADDITIONAL AUTOMOBILE INVESTIGATION 69

tained both of the receipt and transmission of the information.

4. *Where there is a question concerning ownership of the vehicle involved in the accident:*
   a. Determine if the owner is an individual, partnership, corporation, estate, trusteeship, municipality or other entity.
   b. Determine if the owner is someone other than the named insured. If so, obtain details and the reason therefor.
   c. If there is any doubt concerning ownership, develop the following:
      (1) Find out who professes to be the owner.
      (2) Determine in whose name the vehicle is registered.
      (3) Find out to whom the bill of sale was made out.
      (4) Find out who paid for, or is paying for, the vehicle.
      (5) Determine if there has been an attempt at deceit in the ownership of the vehicle because of the age of the owner, the fact that he may have been a member of the armed forces or for any other reason. If so, report this information to the underwriter.

5. *Where there is a question concerning who regularly drives the vehicle named in the policy:*
   a. Determine if the vehicle is driven principally by the owner.
   b. Find out if it is also driven by members of the named insured's family or household.
   c. Find out if the vehicle is driven by employees of the named insured.
   d. Find out how often or how regularly the

vehicle is driven by anyone other than the named insured.
  e. Obtain the ages of all regular drivers of the vehicle.
  f. Determine if the vehicle is regularly driven by a member of the armed forces or by anyone who may possibly be considered as a hazardous risk.
6. *Where there is a question concerning the purposes for which the vehicle is used:*
  a. Determine if the vehicle is used principally for business or pleasure.
  b. If the vehicle is used in the business of the insured, determine whether there is anything questionable about the nature of the business. If so, report this fact to the underwriters.
  c. Determine the average number of miles per year that the vehicle is driven.
  d. Determine where the automobile is principally garaged, if pertinent.
7. *Where there is a question concerning the possibility of uninsured vehicles in the named insured's household:*
  a. Determine how many vehicles are in the named insured's household.
  b. Find out who owns them.
  c. Obtain a description of each vehicle including make, year, model, color, etc.
  d. Find out if the named insured owns or regularly drives any of these vehicles.
  e. Determine if each vehicle is insured and check if necessary.
  f. If any of the vehicles are not insured, make certain that the car involved in the accident is the one covered.

8. *Where there is a question concerning a Commercial Radius Endorsement:*
    a. Determine whether the truck involved is ever driven outside the permissible limits.
    b. If so, find out how often. Obtain the locations as nearly as possible, in writing.
    c. Determine why the truck was outside the permissible limits at the time of the accident. If the truck was on the way to a business call, find out how often such a call is made.
    d. If the scene of the accident was not on the route of a business call, find out where the driver was going and whether he had permission to go there by actual or tacit consent.
    e. Find out if the driver had been specifically forbidden to be in the area of the accident.

F. **Investigation of Uninsured Motorists Claims**

The investigation of claims which fall, or could fall, under the Uninsured Motorist coverage presents some problems which are more complex because first and third party become mixed-up and the ethics in such a situation can become difficult. The highest degree of ethical conduct is necessary in the handling of such cases.

The regular third-party investigation must be made as promptly and thoroughly as possible. In addition, it is essential to determine:

1. Whether there is absolutely no liability insurance coverage available to the driver or owner of the other vehicle.
2. If the other vehicle is insured, whether there is any likelihood that the carrier will deny coverage for any reason.
3. If coverage is denied, whether such denial is justified and likely to stick.

4. Whether there is any other Uninsured Motorist coverage available to the insured, such as:
    a. Another policy issued to the owner of the car.
    b. Another or separate policy issued to the driver.
    c. Possible coverage for someone responsible for the use of the adverse vehicle.
    d. Possible coverage for an injured passenger.
    e. Possible coverage for drive-other-cars, if applicable.
    f. Possible coverage for relatives or members of the same household, if applicable.
5. Whether the injury falls within any workers' compensation, disability benefits or similar law.
6. In hit-and-run cases:
    a. Determine whether it is possible to learn the identity of the driver or owner of the hit-and-run car.
    b. Determine whether the insured complied with the requirements concerning reporting and other duties required by the policy.

CHAPTER III

General or Public Liability Investigation

BUILDINGS, STREETS, AREAWAYS, ETC.

A. **Description and Identification of the Premises:**
 1. *Give the exact location of the accident* including street numbers and any other designation necessary to pinpoint the location.
 2. *Describe the type of building if involved* (one- or two-family house, apartment, store, factory, office building, theatre, etc.).
 3. *Determine the age of the building.* If necessary, obtain the names of the original architect, contractor and builder.
 4. *Determine the general condition of the building or area:*
     a. Find out if the building or area is well-maintained and kept in good repair.
     b. If the building or area is not well-maintained or is in poor condition, make sure to advise the Underwriting Department by means of an appropriate report.
 5. *Determine the use to which the building or area is put:*
     a. Find out if the use is proper in accordance with the facilities offered or the use to which it is put.
     b. Determine if the use is lawful and proper.
     c. Find out if the use is unusually hazardous in any way.

d. Determine if the use creates a nuisance or is in any way objectionable.

6. *Find out if there were any previous accidents* in the building or area and obtain details.

B. **Ownership and Control**

1. Obtain complete and correct name of the insured (individual, corporation, partnership, trade name, estate, trust fund, etc.).
2. Determine what part of the building the insured occupies.
3. Find out how long the insured has occupied that part of the building.
4. Learn if the area or deficiency complained of is completely within the part of the building or area controlled by the insured.
5. If some other tenant may have been involved, obtain a complete list of the tenants occupying the building, that may have been responsible, and try to learn the names of the pertinent insurance carriers.
6. Obtain copies of any leases by or from the insured which may be pertinent to the investigation.
7. Determine if the landlord (if he is other than the insured) controls that portion of the building or area complained of.
8. If the landlord is responsible for the area or portion of the building complained of, determine if he is insured and get the name of his carrier. See that this carrier is notified of the accident promptly and that the landlord is put on notice concerning responsibility.
9. Find out if the rental, cleaning and general maintenance and repair of the building is under the control of an independent servicing agency. If so, obtain name, address and insurer.
10. Determine if the maintenance agency, if any, was

GENERAL OR PUBLIC LIABILITY INVESTIGATION 75

hired by the insured or by someone else. Obtain details.

C. **Coverage**

1. *Review all endorsements carefully* and make sure that the location of the accident is within the territory covered by the policy:
    a. Determine whether the accident occurred inside or outside of the building, or in another area under the possible control of someone other than the insured.
    b. Determine whether the accident occurred on the sidewalk. This may place the scene within the jurisdiction and control of the municipality.
    c. If the accident occurred near a boundary line, make sure it occurred within the boundary of the area controlled by the insured.
2. *Make sure that the accident occurred during the policy period.* See "Investigation of Coverage Problems on Automobile Claims" for detailed checklist.
3. *Determine whether the incident falls within the contractual liability exclusion:*
    a. Learn if the insured entered into any hold-harmless or other agreement assuming any liability for others.
    b. Review the contract or agreement for possible disclaimer and obtain photostat if necessary.
4. *Determine the primary wrongdoer and put him and his insurance carrier on notice* if the insured's liability is contingent.
5. *Determine whether there was any employer-employee relationship or whether Workers' Com-*

pensation was involved. This might bring the incident under a policy exclusion.
6. *Determine whether there was any new construction which might bring the incident within this exclusion.*
7. *Check to see if there was any delayed notice or any other policy violations* that might call for disclaimer. If delayed notice was involved, see "Investigation of Coverage Problems on Automobile Claims," subheading "Delayed Notice" for checklist.
8. *If an edible product was involved, find out if it was consumed on or off the premises.*
9. *Check for possible completed operations:*
    a. Obtain the exact date when the last work was done.
    b. Determine if the job was accepted as completed. If so, obtain any evidence of acceptance that may be available.
    c. Determine if payment was made for the completed job. If so, find out when. Obtain any available evidence of such payment.
    d. Find out if any tools were left at the job site. If so, determine if they were involved in the accident. Obtain details.
    e. Find out if the insured left any uninstalled or unused materials and whether they were involved in the accident. Determine if they were useable or mere debris. Find out if the insured intended to return for the materials, either to take them away or to clean up the area.
    f. Determine if there was any complaint about defective materials or workmanship and whether the insured had to return to correct or repair some condition. Obtain details, including exact dates.
    g. Find out if it was necessary for the insured to

return in order to make adjustments or subsequent inspections, and if he did so. Obtain exact dates and details.
  h. Determine if the operation involved a service or maintenance contract or agreement and, if so, whether the insured returned pursuant thereto. Obtain copy of the contract and all details concerning it.

D. **Insured's Investigation**

Detailed information concerning the incident and surrounding circumstances that bear upon the insured's liability should be obtained from the insured, his rental or maintenance agent, superintendent or engineer of the building, janitor, porter, or anyone else who knows or should know anything about the matter. Signed statements should be obtained from each individual who can contribute material information necessary for the defense of the case. The information to be obtained should cover:

1. *Notice,* actual or constructive:
   a. Determine who was responsible for the general maintenance and condition of the building (superintendent, engineer, agent, janitor, porter, etc.).
   b. Find out if the individual was aware of the condition complained of.
   c. Determine how it came to his attention and when.
   d. Determine how long the condition had been permitted to exist. Obtain exact dates if possible.
   e. Find out if any regular inspections were made and, if so, when and by whom. Obtain copies including dates.
   f. Determine if the condition was open and obvious.

g. If the insured did not know of the condition, find out if he could have known of it had proper inspection been made.
h. Find out if any previous complaints had ever been made about the condition. Determine if there was any record of previous accidents as a result of the condition, or at that particular site.
i. Determine how often the area involved was cleaned and how this was done. Determine if proper safety precautions were taken while cleaning was being done.

2. *Physical Facts:*
   a. Obtain complete description of the defect, obstruction, or other condition which allegedly caused the accident.
   b. Determine the exact location of the condition complained of. Make sure to preserve any evidence by properly marking and controlling the articles complained of, or by obtaining proper photographs of the defect or condition.
   c. Describe the composition of the floor, if it was involved.
   d. Describe the nature and condition of any floor coverings.
   e. Describe the condition of the floor, if involved:
      (1) Determine if it was wet and, if so, whether water or snow was tracked in. Find out how far the location of the accident was from the outside entrance. Describe any other reason or cause for the wet condition.
      (2) Determine if there was any debris on the floor and, if so, obtain details and description.

(3) Find out if the accident involved excessive wax on the floor. (Waxed floors will be discussed separately in more detail.)
(4) Determine if the floor was broken, depressed, rough or defective in any other way.
(5) Determine if the floor was level or sloped. Obtain measurements as nearly as possible, including the degree of the slope.
(6) Find out if it was customary to place a mat at the scene of the accident and, if so, whether it was there at the time. If not, find out why.
(7) If cleaning was being done, determine if proper precautions were taken during and after the cleaning period. Find out if the floor was perfectly dry before people were permitted to walk on it.
(8) Determine if there was any obstruction in the floor area such as signs, tables or other furniture, displays, etc.).

f. Other conditions complained of:

(1) Determine if the condition was a nuisance, or otherwise objectionable in any way.
(2) Determine if a defective object or product was involved and, if so, obtain full details.
(3) Determine if it was defective owing to ordinary wear and tear or to the effect of the weather and natural elements.

g. Determine if faulty construction or a construction defect was involved. If so, follow through as outlined in the checklist for the "Investigation of Construction Claims."

h. Natural lighting:
   (1) Obtain the time of day when the incident occurred.
   (2) Determine if it was daylight, dusk, dark, sunny or cloudy.
   (3) Determine the location of all windows, skylights or other such openings. Describe in detail giving size, type of glass, etc.
   (4) Determine if there was any obstruction to natural light such as curtains, shades, blinds, furniture, display arrangements, etc.
   (5) Determine if the color of the walls or area blended in with the surroundings so as to create a lighting hazard.

i. Artificial lighting:
   (1) Determine if the artificial lighting was in operation and, if it was not, whether it should have been.
   (2) Determine the size and location of all artificial lighting in the area and describe in detail, giving size of bulbs and whether or not they were adequate.
   (3) Find out who controlled the lighting.
   (4) Determine if there was any obstruction to the light reaching the area under investigation. Describe fully.
   (5) Determine if artificial lighting is required by law at the scene of the accident and, if so, whether it was provided and adequate.

GENERAL OR PUBLIC LIABILITY INVESTIGATION

    j. Determine the weather conditions if involved:
- (1) Determine if it was raining or snowing.
- (2) Find out if it was wet and slippery as a result of rain or snow.
- (3) Determine if the wind velocity contributed to the accident.
- (4) Determine if visibility was good and, if not, why.

    k. Obtain complete description and photographs where necessary, of any guards (human or mechanical), warning signs, roped-off areas or warnings of any other nature.

    l. Obtain any photographs that may have been taken by or for the insured.

    m. Obtain any blueprints, sketches or plans that may be available and necessary for a proper defense of the case.

    n. Determine if the scene of the accident was used in common by anyone other than an insured. Obtain details including other insurance.

    o. Building or area violations should be investigated as outlined in the checklist for the "Investigation of Construction Claims."

3. *Repairs:*
   - a. Determine if it was the insured's duty to repair any defects. Check the lease and obtain copy if necessary.
   - b. Determine if any repairs were made, by whom and how.
   - c. Determine when the repairs were made, who ordered them, and why.
   - d. Find out if they were properly made by inspection.

e. Determine if any repairs were made subsequent to the accident, by whom and why.

4. *Information obtained after the accident:*

    a. Find out how the accident came to the insured's attention.
    b. Find out who inspected the scene of the accident immediately after it happened. Obtain signed statements from all parties.

        (1) Determine if the area was clean and dry.
        (2) Find out if lighting was sufficient and proper.
        (3) Find out if there was any defect that contributed to the accident.
        (4) Learn if the claimant indicated the cause of the accident and, if so, whether anyone checked this out.
        (5) Find out if the claimant contributed to the accident in any way and how (high heels, platform shoes, clothing obstruction, etc.).

    c. Obtain information concerning any conversations or admissions that took place immediately after the accident.

5. *Injuries:*

    a. Obtain the name and address of the claimant.
    b. If possible, obtain the age, marital status, occupation and dependency of the claimant.
    c. Describe the injured (obese, wiry, pallid, etc.).
    d. Describe any visual evidence of injury:

        (1) Give exact location of any cuts, bleeding or other evidence of injury.
        (2) Describe the nature of any complaints of injury. Indicate whether they ap-

GENERAL OR PUBLIC LIABILITY INVESTIGATION 83

peared to be sincere or if they seemed to indicate malingering. Give details.
- (3) Determine if the injured made any outcries or showed any other evidence of pain.
- e. Determine if first aid was given at the scene and, if so, by whom (police, hospital attendant, doctor, nurse, passer-by, etc.).
- f. Find out where the injured was taken from the scene of the accident and how transported.

6. *Witnesses:*
   a. Obtain the names and addresses of all people who were with the claimant at the time.
   b. Obtain the names and addresses of any sales people or other employees who witnessed either the accident itself or the scene immediately before or after the accident.
   c. Obtain the names and addresses of bystanders or other witnesses to the accident, including witnesses to the condition of the area at the time of the accident or immediately thereafter.
   d. Obtain the names and addresses of any police officers or other officials, doctors, nurses or anyone else who may have been called to the scene after the accident.

E. **Claimant's Investigation**
   1. *Claimant's background information and introductory matter:*
      a. Obtain claimant's full name and all previous names or aliases under which the claimant was ever known, including the maiden name of any married female claimant.
      b. Obtain the claimant's present address and, if warranted, previous addresses.

- c. Find out the claimant's age and give your impression of the claimant's general appearance.
- d. Indicate what impression the claimant made concerning honesty, reputation, industriousness, intelligence, education or such other factors that might bear on his or her impression as a witness.
- e. Determine the claimant's economic status.
- f. Try to determine if the claimant has a criminal record.

2. *Marital status and dependency:*
   - a. Obtain name, age and dependency status of wife.
   - b. Obtain the names, ages and dependency status of all children.
   - c. Determine the marital status and, if necessary, records of all births, previous marriages, separations, divorces and deaths.

3. *Employment history:*
   - a. Obtain the names and addresses of all present employers and previous employers if pertinent. Determine the time employed by each.
   - b. Determine the nature of work and the duties performed.
   - c. Determine the salaries received, including the regular salary, commissions, overtime, tips, board and lodging, or other remuneration of any kind.
   - d. Determine the time and earnings lost from work.

4. *Education background* if pertinent:
   - a. Obtain the name and address of the present school being attended by the claimant, including year in attendance.

b. Get the names and addresses of previous schools in order to obtain background information if applicable.
c. Get the marks or grades of the claimant.
d. Find out the exact time lost from school as a result of the accident.
e. Review checklists on the investigation of claims involving minors.

5. *Pensions, insurance or welfare help:*

   Obtain details and check the information where warranted, concerning past or present aid received from:
   a. City, state or federal relief or benefits, including social security and unemployment benefits.
   b. Private or public pensions of any kind, including any private charities.
   c. Disability benefits of any kind.
   d. Workers' Compensation benefits. Obtain name of carrier and check it out.
   e. Medical payments coverage on automobile policy. Obtain name of carrier and check it out.
   f. Accident and health insurance. Obtain name of carrier and check it out.
   g. Blue Cross, Blue Shield or other medical or hospital plans.

6. *Physical condition or possible deformities* which might have had a bearing on the accident, as follows:
   a. Intoxication or alcoholic consumption:
      (1) Determine what kind of drinks the claimant consumed.
      (2) Find out, if possible, how many and where taken, and over what intervals.
   b. Find out, if possible, whether drugs or nar-

cotics of any kind were involved and get full details.
c. Determine, if possible, whether the claimant was in a generally weakened condition due to illness or lack of sleep. Find out if the claimant was unduly fatigued.
d. Determine if the claimant had physical infirmities such as:

   (1) Heart disease.
   (2) Epilepsy. Determine if claimant was taking medication.
   (3) Fainting spells, blackouts, dizziness and, if so, whether claimant was taking medication to alleviate such condition.
   (4) Defective hearing.
   (5) Defective eyesight. Find out if claimant was wearing glasses or should have been.
   (6) Weak ankles that turn easily.

e. Determine if claimant had any physical deformities such as:

   (1) Crippled. Find out if the claimant was wearing any prosthetic appliances or whether he should have been.
   (2) Amputation of a limb or other extremity.
   (3) Extreme overweight.
   (4) Unsteady because of infirmity due to old age or infancy.
   (5) Missing eye.

7. *Possible distractions to the claimant:*
   a. The weather (rain, snow, sleet, etc.).
   b. Determine if the claimant was carrying an umbrella, packages or other objects. Find out

how large they were, how heavy, and other details.
- c. Find out if the claimant was watching someone or something.
- d. Determine if the claimant was talking to anyone at the time.
- e. Find out if the claimant was daydreaming or preoccupied for any reason. Learn if he or she was worried or under emotional stress.
- f. Determine if the claimant was in a hurry, and, if so, why.
- g. Find out if the claimant was smoking and whether this may have contributed to the accident.

8. *Obtain previous and subsequent accident records.*

    This is important not only as possible background information on the claimant's honesty, but as a lead for pertinent medical information.

9. *Determine if the claimant's clothes were material to the accident:*
    - a. Find out if the claimant had a hat over his or her eyes.
    - b. Determine if the claimant had his or her collar up over the ears.
    - c. Determine if the claimant was wearing a long dress or coat that might have been a tripping hazard.
    - d. Find out if the claimant's shoes might have contributed to the accident. If so, describe their height, composition of the soles and heels and their general condition. If any evidence is available, see that it is properly preserved.

10. *Nature and purpose of the trip:*
    - a. Determine the reason for making the trip.

b. Determine if the claimant was a guest, invitee, social visitor or trespasser.
c. Determine the route taken by the claimant:
    (1) Find out if this was the usual route and, if not, why it was taken.
    (2) Learn if other routes were available.
    (3) Learn if the claimant was familiar with the route taken and how often he or she had traveled that route before.

11. *Previous knowledge of condition:*
    a. Find out if the claimant had ever been at the scene of the accident before and, if so, how often and when.
    b. Find out if it was necessary for the claimant to pass the scene of the accident in order to get home, to work, to shop, to visit friends or for any other reason.
    c. Determine if the claimant had any previous knowledge of any defect or allegedly dangerous condition. If so, find out why no precautions were taken to avoid the accident.
    d. Determine if the claimant was observant and if he or she saw the condition and tried to avoid it.

12. *Factual details.* Obtain complete information as follows:
    a. Determine the exact date, time and location of the accident. Describe in detail.
    b. Find out if crowding or pushing was involved.
    c. Determine if the claimant slipped, tripped, stumbled, missed a step, failed to step up or down, or whether his or her ankle turned for any reason.
    d. Determine if the condition was open and

GENERAL OR PUBLIC LIABILITY INVESTIGATION 89

   obvious and whether or not there was sufficient light.
   e. Find out if the claimant was looking where he or she was going.
   f. Determine if there was a trap or hidden defect of any kind that was involved in the accident.
   g. Determine if the accident could have been caused by debris, oil spill, water, ice or snow, vegetable matter or obstruction of any kind. Describe in detail.
   h. Describe the direction in which the claimant was going and the manner, whether walking, running, jogging, etc.
   i. Describe the exact position of the claimant immediately before, during and after the fall. Give all details including any outcries.
   j. Determine if a report was made to the police and, if so, obtain a copy.

13. *Blind accidents* (no known witnesses):
   a. Learn from the claimant the name of the person to whom he or she first spoke about the accident and the date and time as closely as possible.
   b. If there was any delay in reporting the matter to the insured, obtain any explanation for such delay.
   c. Check the allegations of injury against the possibility that the claimant might have needed assistance at the scene of the accident. If no assistance was given, determine why.
   d. Check for any evidence of the accident on the claimant's clothes such as dirt, grease, oil or blood stains, etc.
   e. Check the scene of the accident for any possible evidence indicating that the accident had occurred.

    f. Check the background of the claimant with special care in view of the possible questionable nature of the alleged accident.

14. *Medical information to be obtained from the claimant:*

    Written authorization to receive medical information should be obtained from the claimant at the time of the first interview, wherever possible.

    Medical information to be obtained from the claimant should include:

    a. Detailed description of all objective (noticeable) evidence of injury.
    b. Detailed account of any unconsciousness, giving the exact duration.
    c. Complete list of subjective complaints (those not accompanied by noticeable evidence of injury), when they first developed and their duration.
    d. Medical assistance rendered at the scene of the accident.
    e. Details concerning any first aid treatment and by whom given.
    f. Name of the hospital or doctor to whom the claimant was taken immediately after the accident.
    g. Name and address of the family physician who subsequently treated the claimant.
    h. Name and address of any specialists who were called in for consultation or treatment.
    i. Dates of all visits to physicians, specialists, hospitals or clinics.
    j. Dates of visits made by doctors or specialists to the home of the claimant.
    k. Dates of admission to and discharge from any hospital, sanitorium or rest home.

GENERAL OR PUBLIC LIABILITY INVESTIGATION 91

- l. Information concerning X-rays, scan tests or similar examinations. Obtain as full details as possible.
- m. Details concerning any operations or casts.
- n. Details of the treatment rendered.
- o. Duration of confinement to bed and home.
- p. Exact length of disability from work.
- q. Exact nature of present complaints, if any.
- r. Description of any scars or disfigurements. Obtain snapshots or photographs if possible.
- s. Complete details of previous medical history where applicable:
    (1) Family history, including any information that might have a bearing on the present or future disability of the claimant.
    (2) Names and addresses of doctors and hospitals that were involved in previous serious ailments which might have some connection with present disability or allegations.
    (3) List of previous operations that might have some connection with present complaints, with as much detail as possible including information concerning previous X-rays or other tests given.
    (4) Details concerning any previous protracted treatments.
    (5) History of previous diseases such as cancer or heart disease which may have had some effect on the present condition.
    (6) History of previous ailments or diseases which might have left aftereffects such as scarlet fever, rheumatic fever, measles, mumps, etc.

(7) History of any previous diseases which might affect healing in any manner such as tuberculosis, syphilis, gonorrhea, diabetes, etc.

(8) Special emphasis should be placed on previous injury to, or ailment of, the eyes, ears, or to members of the body that may have impaired complete function or that may have contributed to the cause of the accident.

(9) Previous dental history, if applicable.

(10) History of all extensive previous physical examinations such as those made by life insurance companies, armed forces, private companies for employment purposes, or school examinations, if possible.

15. *Witnesses obtained through claimant:*

    a. Name and address of anyone who was with the claimant immediately preceding, during, or after the accident.
    b. Determine if the claimant obtained the names or addresses of anyone who might have witnessed the accident. Interview all such people and obtain signed statements if possible.
    c. Determine if the claimant obtained the names and addresses of anyone who might have observed a condition that allegedly contributed to the accident. Interview them as well.
    d. If there were witnesses whose names and addresses the claimant did not obtain, get his or her best description of them and any leads that might be followed up to help locate them.
    e. Obtain any pertinent comments made by any of the witnesses.
    f. Find out if any police officer witnessed the

accident or obtained the names of any witnesses:

   (1) Obtain the name and number of the policeman.
   (2) Determine the police organization, precinct number and location.
   (3) Determine if any charges or violations were made against the insured or anyone else as a result of the accident.

F. **Medical Investigation**

1. *Detailed information to be obtained from the claimant* as outlined in the previous chapters.
2. *Doctor's report.*

Information obtained from the attending physician should be incorporated in a written report if at all possible. Whatever the form, the information should include:

   a. Personal and descriptive data of the claimant:
      (1) Date, time and place of the initial examination.
      (2) Name and address of the claimant.
      (3) Claimant's age, weight, height, occupation and marital status.
   b. History of the accident. This should include as much information as can be obtained concerning the time, location and manner in which the accident occurred, as reported to the doctor by the claimant.
   c. Previous medical history where applicable, with special emphasis on any condition which would have any bearing on the disability or any possible effect on the manner in which the accident happened. Review the outline entitled

"Medical Information to be Obtained From the Claimant."
d. Details concerning initial examination, including any X-rays, scans or laboratory tests, consultant's or other reports.
e. Treatment rendered, including the type and dates of all office and home visits.
f. Diagnosis. This should include a detailed account of the doctor's findings concerning injury, ailments and disability, with special emphasis on trauma.
g. Prognosis. This concerns the estimated disability and the possibility or probability of ultimate partial or complete recovery with emphasis on any possible partial or permanent disability.
h. Conclusions and recommendations. Here, an attempt should be made to get the doctor to comment on recommendations concerning future treatments, operations, or possible future hospitalization that may become necessary, as well as any other details that might affect the medical picture.
i. Diagrams of various parts of the body are usually imprinted on the opposite side of medical forms which most companies use in order to enable the doctor to show scars or indicate the location of fractures, burns or other injuries.
j. Doctor's bill. The doctor should always be requested to show the amount of his bill up to the time the report is made. He should also be requested to give an estimate of the future medical expense, including his own future bills.

3. *Hospital records:*

   Wherever possible, a complete transcript of the hospital records should be obtained. A wealth of information can sometimes be obtained from hospital records that would not appear in any abstract sent by the hospital clerical department. The records usually contain the following information:

   a. Admission information. Besides the regular admission data, it may contain Welfare Board reports concerning the financial background of the claimant, police reports, an itemized list of the clothes and possessions of the claimant at the time of admission, condition of the clothes and other valuable information. This also includes the extremely valuable history of the accident.
   b. The examination reports by attending physicians and interns, X-ray and scan reports, notes and instructions by interns and doctors, details concerning treatments, pathologist's and laboratory reports and nurses' notes.
   c. Diagnosis and prognosis by the various attending doctors and specialists, including the date and circumstances under which the patient left the hospital. Wherever warranted, interview attending doctors, interns and nurses.

4. *Physical examination.*

   This should not be ordered indiscriminately. The following factors should be given serious consideration before ordering physical examination:

   a. Determine the purpose and the need for the examination. If the intent is merely to corroborate the hospital records or the information given by the attending physician, such records

may be sufficient if the reputation of the attending physician is good.
b. Determine the type of examination that is needed. The ordinary examination concerning injuries of a minor nature, where there is no apparent attempt to exaggerate them, should be made by a general practitioner. However, there may be allegations of a nature that require a specialist's examination. In choosing the specialist, care must be used to choose someone who is not only competent and well-qualified, but who will also be able to make a good presentation in court.
c. Determine the time when the examination is is to be made. Ordinarily, where protracted disability is involved, the examination should be made after the longest healing period possible. Where fraud is suspected, it may be advisable to order the physical examination as soon as possible. This is a matter of judgment, depending upon the allegations of injury and disability.
d. The examining physician should be furnished with all of the medical information that is available before he makes his examination. Where possible, this should include attending doctor's reports, hospital records, X-ray and other reports and anything else that may be pertinent to the examination. The examining physician should, wherever possible, be permitted to personally examine previous X-rays and scans taken. It may avoid the necessity for additional X-rays or scans, or point out the necessity for them.
e. Information which the examining physician should include in his report corresponds, for the most part, with the information that

should be obtained from the claimant's attending physician and which has previously been listed.

5. *Additional interviews.*

   Whenever pertinent or whenever the seriousness of the accident warrants it, the following persons should be interviewed:
   a. Ambulance attendant at the scene of the accident.
   b. Attending physician at the hospital.
   c. Attending interns and residents at the hospital.
   d. Hospital and special nurses.
   e. Dentists, when applicable.
   f. Osteopaths or chiropractors where applicable.
   g. Compensation carrier for complete medical information.
   h. Any leads suggested by Index Bureau reports.

G. **Physical Facts**

The physical facts are so interwoven in every part of the investigation of a public or general liability claim, that to attempt to list them here would be mere repetition of most of the previous sections.

In general, the following should be emphasized:

1. *Obtain a complete description of the scene of the accident* (defects, lighting, control, etc.).
2. *Determine the weather conditions* and obtain weather report where possible and applicable.
3. *Obtain details concerning repairs* if pertinent.
4. *Draw a diagram* of the scene of the accident, where warranted, including all pertinent information previously outlined, and particularly:
   a. Measurements of all pertinent details.
   b. Position of the claimant before, during and after the accident.

c. Position of any defects, debris or other objects or conditions which might have had a bearing on the accident.
   d. Position of windows, lighting and type of lighting, where pertinent.

5. *Photographs and snapshots:*

   These should be taken, where possible, before any change has occurred in the scene or object being photographed. They may include:
   a. Commercial photographs.
   b. Snapshots.
   c. Aerial photographs.
   d. Panorama shots and enlargements.
   e. Police photographs.
   f. Newspaper photographs.

6. *Other prepared evidence:*
   a. Movies.
   b. Surveys and plats.
   c. Laboratory or engineering reports.
   d. Advertising catalogues and instructional material.

7. *Hearings and reports:*
   a. Police reports. Interview all officers and obtain copies of reports where available. Determine if violations were placed against anyone.
   b. Criminal hearings in assault and manslaughter cases.
   c. Autopsy and coroner's reports.
   d. Newspaper accounts that may contain leads to witnesses. Care must be used in giving too much weight to newspaper accounts of factual situations. They are notoriously unreliable.

H. Witnesses' Investigation

This section is devoted to the information which must be obtained from outside witnesses (other than the insured or claimant). Again, checklists will of necessity be general as to the development of factual information since this has already been covered in the insured's and claimant's investigations. They will, however, be specific as to matters pertaining to the witness only.

Here again, a signed statement should be obtained from each witness whenever possible.

Suggested leads for inquiry are:

1. *Identification and background:*
   a. Name and address. If present address is temporary, obtain permanent address or that of a near relative or close friend through whom the witness can always be reached.
   b. Age, general appearance and characteristics for the purpose of evaluating the effect of the witness' testimony at trial if needed:
      (1) Mental attributes (incoherent, stupid, irrational or bright, intelligent, articulate, etc.).
      (2) Personality (well-poised, likeable, modest, or loud and irritatingly aggressive, etc.).
      (3) Sincerity (apparently honest or shifty-eyed, positive or vacillating).
      (4) Apparent education.
      (5) Physical appearance (sloppily or loudly dressed, physically dirty or immaculate, etc.).
      (6) Physical defects (poor eyesight, poor hearing, crippled, etc.).
   c. Marital status if applicable.

d. Military status, to determine availability at trial.
e. Employment, including name and address of employer and job held.
f. Determine if the witness was alone. Obtain the names and addresses of, or leads to, any other possible witnesses known to the witness being interviewed.

2. *Location of, and reason for, witness' presence:*
    a. Learn the exact location and position from which the witness viewed the accident.
    b. Check to see if the scene was actually visible from the alleged vantage point.
    c. Find out from which direction the witness approached the scene of the accident.
    d. Determine why the witness was allegedly there. Find out where he or she was going and where coming from. This may reveal cause to attack the witness' credibility.
    e. Find out in what direction the witness was looking.
    f. Determine what first attracted the attention of the witness to any of the parties involved in the accident.

3. *Factual details:*
    a. Obtain the exact date, time and place of the accident.
    b. Determine how far the witness was from the claimant when first seen.
    c. Have the witness describe the physical facts in detail as previously outlined.
    d. Obtain a complete description of the movements of the claimant immediately preceding, during, and after the accident, with distances

GENERAL OR PUBLIC LIABILITY INVESTIGATION 101

      and positions placed as exactly as possible, as previously outlined.

    e. Find out if the witness overheard any comments made by the claimant that might help determine liability.

4. *Injuries:*

    a. Obtain description of all visual evidence of injury.

    b. Find out if witness overheard any comments or groans that might indicate the extent of the injury or the degree of pain.

    c. Obtain details concerning first aid at the scene and by whom administered.

5. *Obtain description of any property damage* including clothes, jewelry, packages, glasses, etc.

6. *Make a neighborhood canvass* to discover unknown witnesses, where warranted, from the following sources:

    a. Insured, claimant or other witnesses.

    b. Police blotter or officers who made the police report.

    c. Coroner's report.

    d. Neighborhood stores, adjoining offices or building employees.

    e. Private homes or apartments facing the scene of the accident.

I. Special Damages

All special damages should be checked carefully, where the amount involved warrants it, as follows:

1. *Lost time and earnings. Remember that the claimant is entitled to take-home pay only.*

    a. *Where claimant is salaried:*

        (1) Check employer's payroll records.

Verbal corroboration by a clerk, or even in the form of a letter from someone in the employer's office may sometimes be open to question.

    (2) Check the exact dates of absence from work carefully.

    (3) Check the exact amount of the lost earnings. The employer may have paid all or a part of the employee's salary.

    (4) Determine the amount of the regular salary rate.

    (5) Determine the average amount of overtime for that particular time of the year.

    (6) Determine the average amount of commissions for that particular time of the year.

    (7) Make an estimate of the average tips and other gratuities including board and lodging received.

    (8) Determine whether the injury has necessitated a change in job or employment or business conducted.

    (9) Determine whether the injury has necessitated the claimant's going on part-time work.

    (10) Check with the compensation carrier, all lost time and medical expenses.

  b. *Where the claimant is self-employed:*

    (1) Check income tax records if permitted to do so by the claimant, and any other available tax returns.

    (2) Check social security tax if possible.

    (3) Check private books and accounts.

2. *Property damage.*

Be conscious of salvage, depreciation or betterment and replacement versus repair.

    a. Clothing (torn, stained or otherwise damaged or destroyed).
    b. Jewelry (watches, rings, necklaces, etc.).
    c. Luggage and contents.
    d. Packages or bundles being carried.
    e. Glasses, false teeth, hearing aids, etc.
    f. Contents of car or truck (samples, merchandise, etc.).

3. *Medical expenses.*

Check all bills for authenticity and reasonableness.

    a. Obtain the attending doctor's, specialist's and dentist's bills.
    b. Obtain registered and practical nurse's fees.
    c. Determine the amount of the hospital's or clinic's bills.
    d. Obtain the cost of any ambulance charges.
    e. Determine the amount of X-ray, special medical equipment and laboratory charges.
    f. Obtain bills for any prosthetic appliances or surgical apparatus.
    g. Determine the amount of bills for medicines, drugs, and other pharmaceutical supplies.
    h. Find out if there were any travel expenses to and from hospitals, doctors or clinics.

4. *Fatal claims:*

    a. Funeral expenses.
    b. Cost of burial plot or cremation.
    c. Cost of tombstone, vault or urn.

5. *Expected future monetary loss.*

Such loss, in order to be given practical consideration, must be reasonably probable, considering

the claimant's age, education and general economic status.
    a. Determine the expected future lost earnings.
    b. Determine the probable extent of future increases or promotions.
    c. Determine as far as possible, the expected future lost earning capacity.
    d. Find out the estimated future medical expenses, including convalescent costs.

6. *Pain and suffering.*

Determine the allegations concerning pain and suffering. In fatal claims, determine, as far as possible, the length of time from the moment of impact until the claimant died and the length of time that the claimant was conscious.

7. *Loss of services or support:*
    a. Determine if there was any loss of services by a child or wife.
    b. Determine whether there were any dependents and how they were affected by the claimant's injury.
    c. Let the file reflect if any loss of consortium is alleged.

8. *Cosmetic disfigurement.*

Determine whether there was any facial or other visible disfigurement. This will naturally have greater value in a young unmarried female despite its chauvenistic implications.

CHAPTER IV

Some Specific Public Liability Investigations

The basic points of investigation generally required in most public or general liability claims of a serious nature have been covered in the previous chapter. The checklists that follow, therefore, are confined to suggesting avenues of investigations peculiar to the particular and specific types of accidents under which the claim is being made. They are to be used in conjunction with the checklists that have been developed in the previous chapter.

Again, it is obviously impossible to cover all or even most of the situations that may confront an investigator. These checklists are therefore confined to the kinds of accidents most frequently encountered and may be used as a guide to stimulate thinking along proper channels.

A. **Amusement Parks and Fairs**

These cases usually fall into two categories: (1) those in which the claimant is a participant; and (2) those in which the claimant is a spectator. In either event, information must be developed along the following lines:

1. Determine if the insured owns the premises where the accident occurred.
2. Determine if the insured operates or promotes the event involved.
3. Determine who controls and maintains the premises. Obtain copies of all leases, contracts or agreements, if pertinent.
4. If someone other than the insured owns, leases or operates the premises where the accident occurred, determine who they are and put them and their

carrier on notice to take over the investigation and disposition of the claim.
5. Determine if the claimant was a paying spectator:
   a. Find out what kind of a ticket the claimant purchased.
   b. Learn where the claimant sat.
   c. Find out if the area was screened and, if so, whether the screen was adequate and in good condition.
   d. Determine whether the claimant had a choice of seats.
6. Determine whether the premises was constructed and maintained in a manner that can be accepted as reasonably safe by others engaged in a similar business.
7. Determine if the ordinary and usual safety precautions were taken to protect participants or spectators in a manner considered reasonably proper by those engaged in a similar business.
8. Describe the object, contrivance or area complained of:
   a. Determine if it was in proper working order. If not, find out why and who or what caused the defect.
   b. Determine if it was properly constructed.
   c. Find out if all ordinances or statutes were complied with.
   d. Determine if it had proper safety contrivances, screens or barricades and if they were in good operating condition.
   e. Find out if there were any warning signs. Determine if they were necessary and if the claimant paid heed to them.
   f. Determine if the area was clean and dry.
   g. Find out who maintained it. Determine if a concessionaire was involved. If so, get his

SPECIFIC PUBLIC LIABILITY

name and the name of his insurance carrier and put them on notice to take over.

9. Determine if the accident was precipitated by an act of another participant or spectator.
    a. Obtain the name and address and get a signed statement if possible.
    b. Find out if a guard or attendant was present or should have been. If not, find out why.
10. Determine if the claimant was familiar with the area, object or contrivance by reason of previous visits. Find out when these visits were made and how often.
11. Find out if the claimant was aware of the danger and, if so, whether he or she did anything to avoid it.
12. Find out if the danger was obvious, unusual or extraordinary.
13. Obtain the details of the accident.
14. Learn whether the claimant did anything to place himself in a position of unusual jeopardy. Get details.

B. **Animals**

Some jurisdictions have enacted laws that go so far as to impose absolute liability on an owner for the acts of his dog. If this is the situation in a claim which is under investigation, there isn't much that can be done by way of defense. In such an event, determine the extent of the injury and damage and make every effort to reach a reasonable settlement. Although most localities do not go so far, most do have some ordinance or statute governing the responsibility of owners of domestic and wild animals.

This checklist should indicate the avenues of investigation needed:

1. Determine the exact time and location of the incident.

2. Obtain a description of the animal:
    a. Learn the species, breed or variety.
    b. Determine if it is considered as domestic or wild.
    c. Obtain its age, size and color.
    d. Determine its health and general condition.
    e. Find out its nature and reputation (vicious, gentle, snappy, playful, etc.). Check with neighbors.
3. Determine if the insured owns the animal. If not, find out who does and put him and his carrier on notice to take over.
4. Determine if the insured has control of the animal and how he maintains such control.
5. Find out whether the claimant is a guest, invitee or trespasser. Learn if his occupation required him to be on the premises or in the area (mailman, meter reader, salesman, solicitor, relative, friend, customer, trespasser, etc.).
6. Find out if the claimant has been on the premises before and was aware of the presence of the animal.
7. Determine if there was any warning concerning the animal.
8. Find out if the claimant tried to avoid the animal.
9. Determine if the animal was provoked in any way and, if so, how and by whom. Determine whether the claimant struck, threatened or made a sudden movement in front of the animal.
10. Learn what control was being exercised over the animal, if any, at the time and by whom. Find out if the animal was on a leash at the time, or should have been.
11. Determine if another animal or animals were involved and whether they were controlled or running loose. If possible, try to determine the owner of the

SPECIFIC PUBLIC LIABILITY

offending animal and put him and his carrier on notice.

12. Determine if the claimant interfered with the animals in any way and describe in detail.
13. Find out if the claimant was aware of the nature of the animal and its reputation.
14. Determine if the animal was enclosed, caged, chained or tied and, if so, whether such restraint was proper.
15. Determine if the animal was muzzled or should have been, in accordance with local ordinances or statutes.
16. Determine if there was any violation of any other ordinance or statute.
17. Find out if the animal was involved in any previous incident or incidents and whether any previous complaints were made against the animal.
18. Determine if the insured was aware of any previous incidents or complaints indicating possible vicious propensities. If so, find out if he took any precautions to protect the public. Obtain details.
19. Describe the injury in detail (scratch, rip, bite or other wound).
20. Find out if the animal was checked for rabies and whether it had been innoculated. Determine if the health department was notified and if they took any action. Determine if laboratory tests were made.
21. *If the claim involves a dog:*
    a. Determine what ordinances or statutes were pertinent and whether the insured met the legal requirements.
    b. Determine who owned the dog and for how long.
    c. Find out if any control was being exercised over the dog by the insured or if it was allowed to run loose.
    d. Describe the dog, giving breed, age, sex, size, color.

e. Determine the nature of the dog and its reputation.
f. Determine if the dog was involved in any previous incidents or complaints and make a neighborhood canvass to check this out.
g. Determine if the dog was muzzled or should have been.
h. Find out whether the dog was chained or enclosed and, if so, whether it broke out of the enclosure.
i. Determine if the dog was in heat or with puppies.
j. Find out if the dog was provoked in any manner. Find out if it was startled or frightened and why.
k. Find out if other dogs were involved in the incident and, if so, try to obtain the names and addresses of their owners in order to put them and their carriers on notice. Find out if the claimant interfered with the dogs in any way.
l. Determine if warning signs of any kind were posted or should have been. If they were, determine if they were proper and visible.
m. Find out if the claimant was familiar with the dog.
n. Determine if the dog was innoculated for rabies and check this out with the veterinarian. Find out if any tests were made after the accident to determine rabies or any other disease, and whether any action was taken by the health department, police or other appropriate municipal agency.

22. *If the claim involves a saddle horse:*
    a. Find out who owns the horse. If other than the insured, put the owner on notice.

SPECIFIC PUBLIC LIABILITY

b. Obtain complete description of the horse giving age, sex, height, color, breed, etc.
c. Determine how long the insured owned the horse.
d. Determine whether the horse had ever been used for any purpose other than for riding and how long it had been used as a saddle horse.
e. Determine if the horse was hired out for a fee.
f. Find out if horseback riding was part of the services rendered at a hotel or resort for an overall charge.
g. Determine if the horse was owned by, or in the charge of, a concessionaire who is not an insured. If so, determine the insurance carrier and have the owner and the insurer put on notice.
h. Find out, from previous experience, if the horse was gentle, balky, headstrong, nervous, lame or sick.
i. Find out if the horse was well cared for.
j. Determine how often the horse had been used before the accident and how often it is usually ridden.
k. Determine if the horse was in heat and, if so, whether the caretaker knew of this or should have known.
l. Determine what riding experience the claimant had. Find out if the insured or his agent inquired as to the claimant's experience and whether or not the claimant volunteered such information.
m. Determine whether the claimant requested a certain horse or a certain type of horse and whether his request was met. Find out if a mistake might have been made.
n. If no request was made, find out if the horse that was furnished was appropriate for the

claimant, considering his or her riding experience.
o. Determine if any instructions were given concerning the horse or the riding.
p. Find out if any warnings or warning signs were given or on prominent display.
q. Find out if the insured furnished a groom to teach or watch the claimant.

    (1) Find out if a groom was available if needed.
    (2) Check to learn if a groom was requested.
    (3) If a groom was provided, determine if he or she was properly qualified.
    (4) If a groom was not provided, determine if his or her presence might have prevented the accident.

r. Determine if the horse was frightened or startled for any reason, how and by whom or what. Get details.
s. Find out if the horse slipped, tripped or stumbled and if it was walking, trotting or galloping.
t. Determine if the claimant or rider did anything to provoke the horse. Get details.
u. Find out if the horse had proven difficult in the past and whether or not it was involved in any previous incidents.
v. Determine if the accident involved the saddle, reins, bridle, stirrups or other equipment.

    (1) If defective equipment was involved, find out who the manufacturer was, and whether or not he should be put on notice.
    (2) If improper harnessing or saddling was involved, get complete details such as who did the harnessing or saddling, how

and when this was done, how much experience the person had, etc. Get this in writing.
- (3) Find out what type of saddle was being used:
    - (a) Determine if it slipped and, if so, what caused it to slip. Determine if it was tested before the claimant was permitted to mount.
    - (b) Find out if there was a blanket under the saddle.
    - (c) Find out how long it slipped after saddling.
    - (d) Find out if the claimant tampered with or made an attempt to adjust the saddle.
    - (e) Determine if a strap broke and, if so, whether it was old and worn or defective. Determine who manufactured it and the advisability for putting the manufacturer or seller on notice.

C. **Attractive Nuisance**
   1. Find out if the object involved is attractive to children.
   2. Give an opinion as to whether the object is inherently or obviously dangerous.
   3. Find out if the object is visible from the street or area where children usually play.
   4. Determine if the insured knew that children played or congregated in the area. If not, determine whether he should have known and whether or not it was likely for children to have been in the area.
   5. Determine whether the insured or his employees

had ever been warned of the possible danger to children.
6. Find out how long the object had been there and if it had been involved in any previous incidents.
7. Determine if the insured had taken any precautions to avoid danger to children.
    a. Determine if a watchman was on duty or should have been.
    b. Find out if the object was fenced in and, if so, whether it was adequate and in good condition.
    c. Learn if any other precautions were taken and what they were.
8. Determine if the object was placed there or whether the condition was created by the insured.
9. Get all details concerning the child who was injured including his or her age, physical attributes, reputation for behavior, past incidents in which he or she might have been involved and check this by making a neighborhood investigation.

D. **Blasting**
1. Determine the local and state laws concerning blasting and whether or not the insured complied with all requirements.
2. Find out if a permit or license was required and issued for the blasting operation and, if so, obtain a copy.
3. Determine the experience and qualifications of the person doing the blasting.
4. Describe the explosive and give the exact amount of the charge. Find out if the amount was unusual in any way for this kind of an operation.
5. Describe the exact manner in which the charge was placed. Determine if it conformed to ordinary safe practice.

SPECIFIC PUBLIC LIABILITY

6. Determine the method of detonation used and what safety precautions were taken:
   a. Learn the manner of counting the explosives and caps.
   b. Determine who was in charge and whether or not he was qualified, conscientious and properly trained.
   c. Find out if the blasting was done with proper precautions such as the use of mats, the erection of proper warning signs properly placed, and the placement of individual guards where necessary, etc.
7. Determine if vibration tests were made and, if so, obtain a copy.

E. Blind Accidents (Possible Fraud)

Accidents which are not witnessed and are unknown to anyone except the claimant (blind accidents) require intensive investigation. That means the full treatment, plus investigation along the following suggested lines:

1. Make a thorough neighborhood investigation:
   a. For possible witnesses to the alleged accident.
   b. For possible witnesses who will be able to testify that they were at the scene of the alleged accident at the time it was supposed to have happened and who can prove that it never occurred. Take negative signed statements.
   c. For possible witnesses who may have overheard remarks tending to corroborate or deny that the accident occurred.
   d. For possible witnesses concerning the claimant's reputation and character in the area of his present or previous addresses.
2. Detailed information should be obtained from the claimant in the form of a signed statement if possible,

concerning every phase of the alleged accident and injury.
3. Make as complete a check as possible on all of the allegations made by the claimant both as to the facts and the alleged injuries.
4. Obtain a detailed explanation from the claimant for his presence at the scene of the alleged accident:
    a. Determine why he or she was there. Determine whether the reason sounds logical and check.
    b. Determine if the hour was unusual.
    c. Determine whether the claimant could likely have been at that spot in view of his or her employment, school or other regular activities.
5. Obtain details concerning the claimant's background.
    a. General reputation and character.
    b. Financial condition.
    c. Employment history.
    d. Hobbies and sports if pertinent.
    e. Social activities.
    f. Insurance including accident and health policies.
    g. Worker's Compensation.
    h. Police records.
    i. Index Bureau. Make a check on the claimant, witnesses or any other party under suspicion.
6. Make a complete medical investigation including:
    a. Reputation of all attending physicians.
    b. Complete physical examination, including X-rays if called for.
    c. Complete hospital records if any.
7. Make a complete investigation of all alleged special damages as previously outlined.
8. If called for, have an undercover investigation made of the physical activities of the claimant including:

SPECIFIC PUBLIC LIABILITY 117

    a. Photographs.
    b. Movies.
    c. Statements made to neighbors, friends, others.
    d. Reputation of the attorney representing the claimant.

F. **Boiler Explosions**
1. Determine whether the incident is covered by the policy:
    a. Check for products coverage.
    b. Check for completed operations.
    c. Check for boiler exclusions.
    d. Determine if there is coverage for the boiler itself.
2. Describe the boiler in detail, including:
    a. Age, years in operation and condition.
    b. Determine if it is proper for the job it was supposed to do.
    c. Determine the method of firing and the fuel used.
    d. Determine the make, manufacturer and installer.
    e. Obtain the serial and other pertinent identification numbers.
    f. Determine the size and capacity.
    g. Determine its construction and metallic composition.
    h. Find out if it is a high or low pressure boiler.
3. Determine who owns the boiler.
4. Find out who maintained and had charge of it. If leased, obtain a copy of the lease or report on any verbal agreements. If the boiler is not owned or operated by the insured, put the responsible party and insurer on notice.
5. Determine what inspections were made or necessary:

a. Learn when the last municipal or state inspection was made and obtain copy of the report.
b. Obtain details concerning any inspections made by the insured before and after the accident:
    (1) Find out how often they are made.
    (2) Determine when the last inspection was made before the accident and obtain a copy of any report that may have been made.
    (3) Obtain copies of the reports of any inspections made after the accident.
    (4) Determine the advisabiity for an engineer's inspection to determine the cause of the explosion.
6. Determine whether the boiler was properly installed:
    a. Find out who made the installation and all details.
    b. Learn who inspected it after installation if pertinent.
7. Determine if proper instructions for use and maintenance were issued.
8. Determine if faulty equipment was involved. If so, see that the manufacturer, installer or anyone else responsible is put on notice. Check equipment such as:
    a. Valves:
        (1) Determine the make, type and manufacturer.
        (2) Find out if it was properly set.
        (3) Find out if it was in proper position.
        (4) Learn whether it was adequate.
        (5) Find out if it was faulty in any way.
    b. Pressure gauge:

SPECIFIC PUBLIC LIABILITY

       (1) Determine its make, type and manufacturer.
       (2) Find out if it was vacuum or steam.
       (3) Determine if it was high or low pressure.
       (4) Find out it it was broken or defective in any way. If so, put the manufacturer or his insurer on notice.
    c. Find out if the accident involved a defective or broken fire box or nozzle. Follow through as suggested above.
    d. Determine if the explosion involved a rusted, corroded or cracked boiler jacket. If so, follow through as suggested above.
    e. Find out if the explosion or break involved any other defective or broken part or parts and follow through as suggested above.

9. Determine if the explosion or break was a result of improper supervision:

    a. Find out who hired the attendant and the surrounding circumstances.
    b. Find out if he was properly qualified. Determine his previous training and experience.
    c. Determine if the attendant was required to have a license or certificate and, if so, whether he had one.
    d. Determine what investigation the insured made in order to determine the qualifications of the attendant.

G. Carbon Monoxide

1. Determine the owner of the heater, stove or apparatus involved in the accident.
2. Determine if the insured was aware of any defect in the appliance.
3. Find out if any previous complaint had been made about the appliance:

- a. Interview and obtain signed statements from previous occupants who had used the appliance and whether they had any trouble with it.
- b. Determine if the insured or his employee made any inspections of the appliance before permitting it to be used. Find out when the last inspection was made. Find out whether a subsequent inspection should have been made.

4. Describe the appliance in detail:
    - a. Make, model and manufacturer.
    - b. Age and general condition.
    - c. Type of operation, whether manually lighted, C.P., pilot light, etc.
    - d. Find out if the appliance had the American Gas Association or other seals of approval.
    - e. Determine the type of gas used (bottled, natural, etc.).

5. Obtain an engineer's inspection to determine if the appliance was defective in any way:
    - a. Determine who installed the appliance or apparatus and obtain signed statement concerning the installation:
        - (1) Find out if the installation was proper.
        - (2) Find out whether the installer had any required license or certificate.
        - (3) Determine if the installer was properly qualified by reason of training and past experience.
        - (4) Find out who authorized the installation.
        - (5) Determine if the installation complied with all local and state laws.
    - b. Find out if the appliance or apparatus itself was defective or broken:

SPECIFIC PUBLIC LIABILITY 121

   (1) Try to determine who broke it or caused the defect.
   (2) If fairly new, determine whether the manufacturer and the distributer should be put on notice.
  c. Find out if the appliance had proper vents.
  d. Determine if change of temperature affected the operation of the appliance.
  e. Obtain carbon monoxide tests to determine the degree of concentration.
6. Find out who last connected the gas:
  a. Determine if any test was made before the gas was turned on. Get details.
  b. Determine if the meter reading was unusual.
  c. If the gas company was involved, consider the advisability of putting them on notice.
7. Investigate the possibility of suicide or death from other possible causes:
  a. Obtain death certificate.
  b. Obtain copy of coroner's report if any.
  c. Obtain copy of autopsy report if any.
  d. Check carefully for any notes or letters that may have been written shortly before the incident.
  e. Check to see if an attempt was made to seal any openings, including doors and windows.
  f. Find out, if possible, whether there was a suicide motive such as ill health, mental or financial stress, marital trouble, etc.
  g. Try to find out if the claimant used sleeping pills and whether he or she had taken any on the day of the incident.
  h. Try to determine the amount of life insurance involved.

8. Describe the physical facts carefully:
    a. Obtain complete dimensions of the room, building, apartment or other enclosure.
    b. Determine the location and size of all openings including doors and windows.
    c. Describe, in detail, the position and location of the appliance or apparatus and the position of the claimant.
    d. Draw a detailed diagram incorporating the above.
9. Review any articles on the subject published by the National Safety Council, U.S. Government, gas companies, consumers groups including research outfits, etc.
10. Obtain and review all advertising, descriptive or instructional pamphlets or bulletins put out by the manufacturer.

H. **Ceiling Cases—Falling Plaster**
1. Determine who owns, occupies or manages the building.
2. Find out who maintains it and put them on notice, including their insurer, if it is not maintained by the insured or an employee of the insured.
3. Determine who is responsible for repairs. Obtain a copy of the lease.
4. Find out the age of the ceiling and, if warranted, the name of the contractor or subcontractor, architect or individual. If pertinent, find out if the installation met all legal requirements and if the workmen were qualified and properly chosen. Put on notice anyone who may have been at fault.
5. Check the composition of the ceiling. Determine if it was plaster, plaster board, celotex, cork, etc. If the ceiling was plastered:
    a. Find out if it was lathed, how, and how nailed.

SPECIFIC PUBLIC LIABILITY

    b. Determine the number of coats and how thick the plaster was.

    c. Determine if the method used was in conformance with ordinary good practice.

6. Determine if the insured or his agent received any notice of previous defects:

    a. Determine if any regular inspection was made of the ceiling.

    b. Determine if there was any noticeable sagging.

    c. Find out if there were any visible cracks and whether any plaster was missing.

    d. Find out if any occupants ever complained about the ceiling and whether a portion of it had ever fallen before.

7. Determine if previous repairs were ever made to the ceiling:

    a. Find out when the last repairs were made and by whom.

    b. Determine the extent and location of the repairs.

    c. Find out who ordered them made.

    d. Determine if the repairs were proper and adequate.

    e. Find out what other repairs had ever been made to the ceiling and by whom.

8. Determine the cause of the falling ceiling if possible.

    a. Obtain an inspection from a properly qualified person.

    b. Determine if drying heat had any effect on the ceiling.

    c. Find out if any heavy work or nailing had recently been done over the area or near it. Determine if proper precautions were taken to avoid damaging the ceiling and, if not, put on

notice anyone who might have been responsible for damaging or weakening the ceiling.
   d. Determine if any heavy equipment had been installed above the defective area, such as heating, ventilating, or air conditioning equipment, lighting fixtures, etc.
9. Describe the piece that fell giving its weight and dimensions. Preserve the object for evidence if possible.
10. Determine the reason for the claimant's presence:
   a. Find out why the claimant was in the premises.
   b. Find out why the claimant was at that particular spot.
   c. Determine whether the claimant was an invitee, social visitor, licensee or trespasser.

I. **Construction Cases**

Construction or contract cases are among the more difficult investigations that claim investigators encounter. This is chiefly due to the physical difficulty in locating and interviewing witnesses and other interested parties and because conditions are apt to change overnight. Unless you get that photograph today, it may be too late.

Then, there is the problem of determining the liabilities of the owner, contractor and subcontractors. The contracts themselves are often ambiguous. Sometimes, required insurance may not have been purchased. Occasionally there is controversy as to which policy is primary and what the percentage of contribution should be.

Here are some leads that might be helpful in this kind of an investigation:

1. Read the policy and every endorsement carefully.
2. Determine if the insured is the owner, principal, architect, general contractor or subcontractor. Obtain names and insurance carriers for all parties.

SPECIFIC PUBLIC LIABILITY

    a. Find out who controlled the operation.
    b. Determine who supervised the actual work.
    c. Obtain the name of the individual who gave instructions and directions, how they were given and through whom.

3. Obtain copies of all contacts and get signed statements concerning any verbal agreements.
4. Obtain copies of specifications if necessary.
5. Determine if the work was unusually hazardous. Describe.
6. Find out if the workmen were experienced:

    a. Determine if they were licensed, if licensing was required. If not, find out why.
    b. Determine if the workmen were properly supervised and obtain details.
    c. Find out if the workmen were engaged in any unusual practices and, if so, why.

7. Describe the tools and equipment used:

    a. Find out who furnished them.
    b. Determine if they were proper for the work to be done.
    c. Determine whether they were in proper working order.
    d. Find out how old they were, how long they had been in use and how cared for.
    e. Determine if they were regularly inspected before being given to a workman and when, how and by whom. Determine when they were last inspected. Find out if any defects were noted, or should have been, upon proper inspection.
    f. Determine if any repairs were made to the tools, when, by whom and how. If defective and not repaired, find out why.
    g. Determine who furnished the work clothes,

uniforms or other personal equipment, if pertinent.
8. Determine what safety measures were taken and by whom. Find out if signs, barricades, walkways and overhangs were erected if needed and whether lanterns or other lighting was properly placed.
9. Determine if all safety regulations were observed and, if not, why.
10. Learn if special safety equipment was available and used, and, if it was not, why.
11. Obtain progress sheets giving the exact dates and locations where specific work was being done, if applicable.
12. Obtain any progress photographs which may have been taken, if applicable.
13. Obtain any report from the first aid station.
14. Obtain full details and medical reports from the compensation carrier.
15. Arrange for immediate photographs before the condition has been changed substantially.
16. Learn if plans were properly filed with the building department of the locality and whether they were approved.
17. Find out if a permit was granted to do the construction and, if so, obtain a copy of it.
18. Learn if the job was done in accordance with the plans, specifications and building permit. Find out if it conforms with the building code. If necessary, have this checked out by an architect.
19. Find out if periodic inspections were made by any building department. If so, determine if any violations were ever filed against anyone involved. Obtain details.
20. Determine if a certificate of completion was issued and, if so, obtain a copy. If not, find out why.
21. Find out if the Federal Government was involved in any way. If so, obtain a copy of the government

SPECIFIC PUBLIC LIABILITY 127

inspector's report (F.H.A., Housing Project, H.U.D., etc.).
22. Put on notice everyone who might possibly be involved.
23. If a pre-existing condition in a finished building is alleged to be structurally defective:
    a. Determine whether the structure or portion of it which is being complained of conforms with local and state building requirements.
    b. If not, determine if the building was erected before such requirements were established.
    c. Find out if any part of such requirements or laws are retroactive in respect to fire prevention or for any other reason.
    d. Determine if the complaint involved new construction on an old building. Be careful about possible policy exclusions.
    e. Determine if repairs were involved. If so, find out if they were made merely to conform with the old original structure. Watch for possible violations.

J. **Crop Dusting**
   1. *Determine who controlled the spraying:*
      a. Learn who did the actual spraying.
      b. Find out who ordered the spraying done.
      c. Determine if the pilot was an employee and, if so, get the name and insurance carrier of the employer.
      d. Learn how payment for the work was arranged.
      e. Find out who directed the work, exactly what directions were given, and how.
      f. Determine who owned the plane and equipment used.
      g. If possible, obtain a copy of any contract or the terms of any verbal agreement.

    h. Apply all tests outlined in the section on independent contractor to determine whether the relationship was that of employer-employee or independent contractor. If the pilot was an independent contractor, and was not the insured, arrange to put him on notice.
2. *Determine the exact area sprayed* and draw a diagram showing the area and location of allegedly damaged vegetation. Obtain aerial photographs if advisable.
3. *Determine the cause of the crop failure* or vegetation damage as follows:
    a. Learn the condition of similar crops, trees or other vegetation in that area, which were unaffected by the spraying.
    b. Find out if there was a drought during the period of the spraying.
    c. Determine if poor farming methods were used in the affected area.
    d. Find out if sufficient fertilizer was used and, if so, whether it was the right kind.
    e. Learn whether plant disease affected the vegetation.
    f. Determine if insect infestation affected the vegetation.
    g. Find out if the age or inherent delicate nature of the trees, crops or plants created or helped to create the condition complained of. Determine the average life of such trees or plants and compare with the age of the allegedly damaged trees or plants.
    h. Arrange for an inspection of the trees, crops or plants and get a report from:
        (1) Agricultural expert from a local college, university or grange.
        (2) County or state agricultural agent.

SPECIFIC PUBLIC LIABILITY

    i. Find out if the equipment used was defective in any way. Get details.

4. *Arrange for chemical analysis* of the compound used for the spraying and determine its exact components and concentration. The report should comment on its destructive qualities, if any.
5. *Preserve a sample of the compound* as evidence if necessary.
6. *Determine the purposes for which the compound is ordinarily used.* Find out if it was properly used and in the right concentration.
7. *Determine the manner in which the compound was applied* (railroad car, airplane, motor spray, hand-spray, etc.).
8. *Determine what precautions were taken* to avoid damage to neighboring crops or plants:
    a. Determine if the direction of the wind and the wind velocity were checked.
    b. Determine how close were the crops or plants that were damaged to the spraying that was done.
    c. Determine how much nozzle pressure was used.
    d. Find out the concentration used.
    e. Determine whether the precautions taken were those ordinarily taken by others in similar situations and conditions.
9. *Determine if the sprayers were competent and experienced.*
10. *Determine whether the compound was properly labelled* and, if not, put the packer and/or manufacturer on notice.
11. *Determine whether the compound was changed or tampered with* as follows:
    a. Find out from whom it was purchased.

  b. Find out how it was packaged and by whom.
  c. Learn if it was repackaged by someone else, who it was and his insurance carrier.
  d. Find out if anyone could have tampered with the compound before or after delivery. Get details.
  e. Try to learn if there might have been any reason for changing the compound.
  f. If anyone other than the insured might be involved, consider the advisability of putting them on notice.

K. **Doors**
 1. *Describe the door in detail:*
  a. Whether wood, glass, composition, etc., or combination. If wood, whether plywood or solid. If metal, the type. If glass, whether or not it was "unbreakable" or shatterproof, etc.
  b. The hinges, whether swinging, door check, revolving, etc.
  c. Size and weight if pertinent.
  d. Direction of opening.
  e. Dimensions, if pertinent.
 2. *Determine if the door or hinges were defective in any way.*
 3. *If the door was transparent:*
  a. Find out if the door handles were plainly visible.
  b. Determine whether there was any other marking or indication to show the presence of the door.
  c. Determine the exact composition of the door.
  d. Make shatter tests if pertinent and obtain complete information concerning its breaking and shattering qualities.

SPECIFIC PUBLIC LIABILITY 131

4. *If the door was the swinging type:*
    a. Determine if they swung too easily or if there was too much tension.
    b. Describe if the doors were transparent.
    c. Describe if it was a one-way entrance or exit.
    d. Determine if there was any way of warning anyone who was approaching from the opposite direction if pertinent.
    e. Learn whether any warning signs were posted.
5. *If the door was revolving:*
    a. Determine how much pressure was needed to start the door revolving.
    b. Find out how long the door continued to revolve after pressure was released.
    c. Describe the approach to the door and the door exit in detail if pertinent.
    d. Learn whether a doorman was in attendance or whether he should have been.
    e. Find out if the doorway was constructed in such a manner as to create danger of wedging to hands or feet.
6. *Determine if the door saddle was involved* and, if so, describe in detail.
7. *Determine whether injury was caused by sudden opening or closing.* If so, get details in the form of a signed statement from the responsible party if possible.

L. **Elevators**
1. *Determine the exact location* of the elevator involved, and the exact location of the accident.
2. *Give a complete description of the elevator* including diagram and photographs were necessary:
    a. Find out the kind and make.

- b. Determine whether it was a passenger or freight elevator.
- c. Find out the size, capacity and lifting weight.
- d. Obtain details concerning its mechanical or automatic operation.
- e. Learn what automatic devices it had.
- f. Determine the age of the elevator.
- g. Find out what type of operation it had. Describe.

3. *Describe the actions and qualifications of the operator:*
    - a. Obtain the age and physical condition of the operator:
        - (1) Determine when he had his last physical examination, and obtain the results.
        - (2) Determine if there were any medical or physical defects that may have interfered with the proper operation of the elevator and get details.
    - b. Find out the length of employment and previous experience as an operator.
    - c. Determine the operator's previous employment and accident records. Determine if there were any previous complaints.
    - d. Learn if the operator did anything or failed to do anything that might have been involved in the accident.
    - e. Find out if the operator took any applicable precautions or preventive measures to avoid the accident or to lessen its severity.
    - f. Determine what floor the claimant entered or alighted from the elevator.
    - g. Learn the height or depth at which the elevator stopped above or below the floor level.

4. *Determine control of the elevator as follows:*

SPECIFIC PUBLIC LIABILITY 133

    a. Find out who hired the operator.
    b. Determine if the owner had a maintenance contract for the operation of the elevators. Obtain the name of the maintenance company and put on notice, if applicable.
    c. Find out if the owner leased the entire building. If so, find out if the tenant had an elevator maintenance contract and get details.
    d. Put on notice anyone who might be directly or indirectly involved, such as an elevator service or maintenance company, manufacturer of the elevator, installer of the elevator, building maintenance agency, owner or tenant of the building, lessee or anyone else.

5. *Determine the cause of the deficiency if any:*
    a. Find out if the elevator doors were involved:
        (1) Describe their type and mechanics of operation.
        (2) Find out if they can be accelerated or slowed by hand.
        (3) Determine what closing pressure they exert.
        (4) Find out if they were properly closed.
        (5) Learn if a mirror was attached to the elevator and, if so, whether it was used.
        (6) Determine if the elevator can be in motion while the doors are open.
        (7) Learn if they were open while the elevator was in motion.
        (8) Find out if the shaft door can be opened when the elevator is not at floor level. If so, determine what precautions were taken to avoid opening the door at the wrong time.
    b. Determine if the defect was due to natural

wear and tear. Determine the condition of the elevator and its component parts.
- c. Find out if the breakdown of the machinery, cable, doors or other parts could have been foreseen and get details.
- d. If there was a defect, determine if it was known or unknown. If unknown, determine if it could have been discovered upon proper inspection.
- e. Learn if improper operation was involved in any way.
- f. Find out if any safety devices were missing or inoperative.
- g. Determine if the elevator was overloaded or overcrowded:
    - (1) Find out if the elevator dropped suddenly.
    - (2) Find out on what floor it last stopped and how many floors it fell.
    - (3) Determine if there was any unusual noise before the elevator dropped.
- h. Determine if a passenger was responsible or involved in any way. Get details.
- i. Determine if any debris was on the elevator door, if pertinent, and describe fully.
- j. Determine if there was any defect in the elevator floor, if pertinent.
- k. Determine if there was a mat or other covering on the elevator floor and describe its condition in detail if pertinent.

6. *Obtain inspection details as follows:*
   - a. Determine when the last inspection by the building department or proper local authority was made before the accident. Get copy of report if possible.
   - b. Determine if it was inspected by such agency

SPECIFIC PUBLIC LIABILITY 135

after the accident and when. Get copy of report if possible.
c. Interview the inspectors and try to get a signed statement.
d. Determine if any violations were filed, when and, if so, whether the condition was corrected, when and by whom. Follow through with copies of reports and signed statements.
e. Obtain the previous accident and breakdown record of the elevator from the elevator or maintenance company.
f. Obtain the name of the insurance carrier other than that of the insured and interview.
g. Find out when the last service inspection was made before and after the accident, and get copy of any report if possible.
h. Obtain a copy of any service contract if possible.
i. Interview the service man and obtain a signed statement from him.
j. Find out what inspections were made by the building superintendent or engineer:
   (1) Determine if any inspections were made before the accident. If so, find out when and how often.
   (2) Determine if any inspections were made after the accident and when. Obtain copies of any reports that may be available and get signed statements if pertinent.
k. Consider the advisability of an examination of the elevator by an impartial expert.

7. *Witnesses:*
   a. Obtain the names and addresses of everyone in the elevator, if possible, and interview and obtain signed statements from them.

b. If the names are not known, obtain the number of people in the elevator as closely as possible and their descriptions, as leads for identification. Follow through as indicated.

c. Canvass the building in an effort to locate any witness and interview if found.

M. **Entrances and Lobbies**
1. *Determine the exact location of the accident.*
2. *Draw a diagram of the scene* including all details as previously outlined.
3. *Determine if the owner or tenant is responsible for for the maintenance* of the area involved. If the insured is not responsible, see that the proper person and his insurer are put on notice.
4. *Determine if there is any defect in the area* complained of:
    a. Describe the defect in detail, if any.
    b. Determine how it was or could have been created.
    c. Try to find out who created it and when. If applicable, put the responsible party and his insurer on notice.
    d. Determine if any repairs were made before or after the accident and get all details such as whether the repairs were adequate, by whom made, in what manner, etc.
5. *Determine if there was any debris* that allegedly contributed to the accident. Check thoroughly as previously outlined.
6. *If a slippery condition is alleged:*
    a. Determine what allegedly caused the slipping.
    b. If rain or snow was involved, or could have been, obtain a weather report.
    c. Determine the composition of the floor in the

SPECIFIC PUBLIC LIABILITY 137

   area. Review the checklists involving floor accidents.
   d. If the accident warrants it, arrange for skid tests.
7. *If crowding is alleged:*
   a. Determine what precautions are usually taken to avoid overcrowding and jostling and whether these were taken at the time.
   b. Determine if the crowds were unusual due to a sale, holiday or for any other reason.
8. *If stairs were involved,* review the checklists outlined in the section entitled "Stairways" in this chapter.
9. *Check to see if lighting conditions were adequate.*

N. **Escalators**
1. *Review the checklist on "Elevators" covering service, maintenance, control and inspection.*
2. *Obtain complete description of the escalator* as follows:
   a. Determine in which direction it was going.
   b. Find out if the handrail was properly synchronized with the movement of the steps.
   c. Find out if the movement was smooth or jerky.
   d. Determine the exact speed of the escalator.
   e. Obtain all measurements including the height, width and depth of the steps and the height of the handrail.
   f. Describe the landing platform.
   g. Examine the handrail carefully to determine if a finger or an object such as clothing could get caught in it.
3. *Describe how the accident happened:*
   a. Find out if the claimant was getting on or off.

b. Determine if a child was involved:
   (1) If so, was he or she attended properly.
   (2) Learn if an adult was in front of or behind the child to help him on or off.
   (3) Find out if there was any horseplay.
c. Determine if the claimant was holding onto the handrail.
d. Find out how the claimant was standing.
e. Determine if the claimant was running on, off or up and down the escalator, or otherwise acting improperly.
f. Find out if the claimant was jostled or pushed.
g. Find out if there was any sudden cessation of power.

4. *Determine how the claimant was injured.* Describe in detail.
5. *If a foreign substance was involved,* make the usual investigation as previously outlined, for foreign substance claims.
6. *Determine if an attendant was present.* If so, interview him or her for all details.
7. *Find and interview anyone who was with the claimant at the time.*
8. *Follow up on other aspects of the investigation* concerning witnesses, etc., as previously outlined.

O. **Falling Objects**
   1. *Determine from where the object fell.*
   2. *Determine the exact spot where the object landed.*
   3. *Find out the name of the owner and tenant* and obtain the name of all insurance carriers.
   4. *Describe carefully the object that fell,* giving measurements and weight.
   5. *Learn who owned the object.*
   6. *Determine what caused it to fall.*
   7. *If the object that fell was a piece of the building:*

SPECIFIC PUBLIC LIABILITY

   a. Determine who owned, leased or was in control of the building.
   b. Find out how old the building was.
   c. Determine when the area was last inspected.
   d. Find out if this was the first time such an incident occurred.
   e. Determine when the area was last repaired, if ever.
   f. If repaired, find out who did it, how, and whether properly done. Determine the insurer and consider advisability of putting on notice.
   g. Determine the general condition of the building.
   h. Find out if weather factors were involved.
8. *Learn if the area had been blocked off* before the accident. Obtain all details and determine if adequate.
9. *Determine if a protective shed was erected* and, if so, if it was properly built and adequate.
10. *Determine if warning signs or guards were properly posted.*
11. *In construction cases:*
    a. Determine if the floors above were properly covered.
    b. Find out who was working above. Obtain the names and insurers of all contractors, subcontractors and employees who might have been involved.
    c. Find out who was most likely to have used the object that fell.
12. *If the object fell in a store;*
    a. Determine how it was stacked.
    b. Find out if it was caused to fall by some other person and, if so, try to obtain his or her name and address.

c. Find out if the object was stacked in the line of traffic or otherwise improperly placed.

P. **Floor Accidents**

1. *Determine the exact location of the condition complained of.* Make sure to preserve any evidence by proper means. Draw diagrams and take photographs if necessary.
2. *Obtain any blueprints, sketches or plans that might be of help in the defense of the case.*
3. *Describe the construction of the area involved:*
    a. Determine the composition of the floor, whether wood, cement, marble, terrazzo, linoleum, asphalt tile, regular tile, etc.
    b. Determine if the surface was level or sloped. If sloped, give the degree and direction.
    c. Determine if the floor was smooth, rough or depressed.
    d. Describe any defect in the floor and give its exact measurements.
    e. Describe any other defect that may have contributed to the accident.
4. *Describe the condition of the floor:*
    a. Find out if it was wet. If so:
        (1) Find out how the water got there.
        (2) Determine if the water was tracked in.
        (3) Find out how far from an outside entrance the location of the alleged accident was.
    b. Determine if any obstructions were on the floor that might have contributed to the accident (low or sharp counters, boxes, displays, merchandise, etc.).
    c. Find out if any debris was on the floor. Obtain details and description if pertinent.

SPECIFIC PUBLIC LIABILITY

    d. Find out if the floor was sagging or broken and obtain reasons, measurements, notice, repairs, etc., if pertinent.
    e. If cleaning was being done, determine if proper precautions were taken during and after the cleaning period.

        (1) Determine if the area was blocked off or should have been.
        (2) Find out if it was perfectly dry before people were permitted to walk on it.

5. *If the accident allegedly involved waxed floors,* determine:

    a. When the floor was last waxed.
    b. By whom and, if not by the insured, obtain the name of the insurer.
    c. The name of the wax product and all available printed matter concerning its use.
    d. Find out who manufactured it and who insured the manufacturer. Consider putting them on notice.
    e. How the floor was prepared for waxing.
    f. If necessary, obtain a chemical analysis of the wax.
    g. Whether friction tests should be made by a properly qualified engineer, of the floor before waxing, after waxing and after buffing.

6. *Describe the nature and condition of any floor coverings* such as carpets, rubber mats, paper, etc.

    a. Determine if it was customary to place a mat at the scene during the time when the accident occurred, because of wetness due to rain or snow. If so, determine whether it was in place at the time or should have been. If not, find out why.

7. *Determine if the complaint involved other conditions:*
    a. Find out if an alleged defective object or product was involved and describe in detail.
    b. Find out if any defect was due to ordinary wear and tear or to the effect of the weather and other natural elements.
    c. Determine if faulty construction or a construction defect was involved. If so, follow through as outlined in the checklist for the "Investigation of Construction Claims."
    d. Find out if the condition might have resulted from faulty repairs and, if so, follow up as indicated previously.
    e. Determine if defective, improper or insufficient lighting was involved. If so, follow through as previously suggested in the investigation of "General Liability Claims."
8. *Determine if the scene of the accident was used in common* with anyone and, if so, obtain details and put on notice if appropriate.

Q. **Liquor Law Liability**
    1. Determine whether the jurisdiction involved has enacted dram shop or liquor liability legislation and, if so, become familiar with it.
    2. Determine whether drinking or intoxication was the direct or proximate cause of the accident. Make a complete investigation of the accident as previously outlined.
    3. Determine whether the customer had automobile liability insurance and, if so, make every attempt to get the automobile carrier to take over.
    4. As nearly as possible, find out when the customer entered and when he or she left the insured's establishment.

SPECIFIC PUBLIC LIABILITY 143

5. Determine the quantity and nature of the drinks which were consumed.
6. Determine, if possible, whether the customer had visited any other tavern or tap room, or had imbibed any other liquor before or after that taken at the insured's establishment. If so, seek contribution or attempt to have someone else take over.
7. Find out if the customer was or appeared to be intoxicated at the time he or she entered the insured's place.
8. Determine if the customer became intoxicated while at the insured's place.
9. Find out if the customer was under the legal age:
    a. Determine if the insured inquired as to the customer's age.
    b. Determine if the insured requested or received any purported proof of the customer's age.
10. Determine if the sale of liquor was illegal in any other way.
11. Find out if the owner or manufacturer can be brought into the picture under the particular statute applicable.
12. Determine whether a bond has been issued to the insured in addition to the liability policy. If so, determine whether an attempt should be made to try for contribution.

R. **Machinery Claims**
   1. *Determine who owns the machinery.*
   2. *Determine who controls the machinery.* If it is leased, obtain a copy of the lease or rental agreement.
   3. *Obtain copies of all instructional and advertising material.*
   4. *Determine whether the machine could be considered as inherently dangerous:*
       a. Describe the machine in detail and obtain

sketches, blueprints and photographs if warranted.
   b. Determine if it was being properly operated.
   c. Determine if it was being operated by a properly qualified person. If not, find out if the insured should have known this.
   d. Find out who supplied the operator, how obtained and what previous experience he or she had.

5. *Determine if the machine was defective or worn:*
   a. Learn if the insured knew of the defect, or should have known on proper inspection.
   b. Find out what inspections and tests were made before and after the accident and the results.
   c. If necessary, have the machine inspected by a properly qualified engineer.
   d. Determine the advisability of putting the manufacturer on notice.

6. *Determine if the claimant was aware of his or her danger:*
   a. Find out if the claimant had been properly warned.
   b. Determine if the situation required any warning.
   c. Find out how long the claimant had worked with or near the machine.
   d. Determine if the claimant took any precautions to avoid danger and, if not, why.

7. *Determine if guards or warning signs were necessary,* and, if so, whether they were present. If not, find out why.

S. **Playgrounds**

   1. *Determine ownership and control:*

SPECIFIC PUBLIC LIABILITY 145

    a. Find out if the insured is a charitable or semi-charitable organization.
    b. Learn if the charitable defense is available under the insured's policy.
    c. Find out if the claimant or claimant's parents pay a fee for the use of the playground or equipment by way of tuition or in any other way.

2. *Determine the nature and manner of supervision:*
    a. Learn how many supervisors or teachers were in attendance.
    b. Find out if the supervisors were adequate in number considering the number of children.
    c. Find out how the supervisors or teachers are chosen.
    d. Learn how much experience they had.
    e. Determine the age of the attendants and whether they might have been too young or too old to handle the situation.
    f. Determine if the attendants paid proper attention to their duties at the time of the accident.
    g. Find out if the use of the equipment was in accordance with commonly accepted good practice.
    h. Learn whether any unusual effort or strain was required of the claimant. If so, obtain full details.

3. *Determine if the playground or equipment was defective,* worn or unsafe for any other reason:
    a. Identify and describe in detail the exact area or piece of equipment involved and draw a diagram and obtain photographs if warranted:
        (1) Find out how old it was.
        (2) Determine how hard it was used and if it had undergone unusual stress.

(3) Determine its general condition.
(4) Obtain all of the details concerning its operation.
   b. Find out who erected or constructed the equipment and who manufactured it.
   c. Determine if it had a latent defect and, if so, consider putting the manufacturer or erector on notice.
4. Determine if the insured had previous notice of defective or dangerous condition:
   a. Find out if anyone had ever complained about the condition or the equipment before the accident. Get details.
   b. Find out if regular and proper inspections were made in an effort to detect any unsafe conditions, and, if so, find out why.
   c. If inspections were made, find out how they were done, by whom made, and how often.
   d. Determine when the last inspection was made and what was found.
   e. Determine if any previous accidents were involved with this same equipment and whether any previous repairs were made. Obtain complete details.
5. *Determine if any other child or adult was responsible* in any way for the accident:
   a. Find out if the area was overcrowded.
   b. Determine if there was any jostling, pushing or horseplay.
6. *Find out if the claimant's disobedience or willful conduct contributed to the accident.*
7. *Determine if the claimant was rightfully and properly on the premises or equipment at the time.*

T. **Pollution Claims**

Even more than in other cases, an investigation of claims involving allegations of pollution must include a complete

SPECIFIC PUBLIC LIABILITY

investigation of the physical facts involved. In such cases, it is essential that a determination be made of the exact nature of the alleged pollution, its duration, the extent of the contamination or alleged contamination, and all other aspects of the physical facts. The following checklist will suggest avenues to be investigated.

1. Determine if there was actual damage to tangible property belonging to the plaintiff and others.
2. Determine if the insured's plant or operation has any public or economic value to the area in which it is located.
3. Determine how many people are employed at the plant or operation.
4. Determine if there was any reasonable way to abate the pollution and if the insured made any sincere attempt to remedy the condition. Get complete details.
5. Determine who came into the area first and if the plaintiff moved into the area fully aware of the condition.
6. Find out if the plant or operation conforms to all federal acts or state or local laws and all regulatory agency requirements. Learn if any violations have ever been filed against the insured by any of these agencies or whether previous serious complaints have been made. Get full details.
7. Determine whether the insured has specific permission to pollute or to discharge the wastes if such were involved.
8. Find out if the insured was invited to build a plant or operate in the area by local, state or federal governmental agencies of any kind.
9. Determine whether the insured's operation was vital to the defense or welfare of the government or otherwise vital.

U. **Porcelain Handles**

Porcelain handles on bathroom fixtures, doorknobs and other equipment went out of style quite a few years ago. Nevertheless, enough of them remain in use to warrant this checklist.

1. *Examine the broken handle carefully:*
    a. Determine the necessity for an examination by a specialist to learn if the handle was struck by a hard object or had previously been cracked or otherwise damaged.
    b. Determine if the handle was loosely fitted or defective in any other way.
    c. If warranted preserve the handle and pieces for use as evidence.
2. *Determine how old the porcelain handle was.*
3. *Interview and obtain signed statements from the maintenance supervisor and cleaning help:*
    a. Determine if any instructions were ever given to check the handles.
    b. Find out who makes these inspections, and how often they are made.
    c. Determine when the last inspection was made before the accident and by whom.
    d. Find out if there was any report of previous defects in the handles and get complete details.
4. *Determine the general condition of the hotel,* apartment building or other building involved, and, especially, of the plumbing and plumbing fixtures.
5. *Determine the condition of the remaining porcelain handles* or faucets:
    a. Find out if the broken porcelain handles or faucets are being replaced by metal or plastic ones.
    b. Determine how many porcelain handles are

SPECIFIC PUBLIC LIABILITY 149

      left and, if advisable, notify the underwriting department.

6. *Determine how long the claimant occupied the room before the date of the accident.*
7. *Determine if the claimant made any previous complaints.*
8. *Locate and obtain signed statement from previous occupants* of the room concerning the condition of the faucet handles if possible and warranted.

V. **Road Construction**

1. *Determine who controlled the area,* whether general contractor, subcontractor, or state or municipal highway department.
2. *Describe the area under construction* in detail, draw detailed diagram and obtain photographs:
   a. Describe the condition of the road.
   b. Determine the width of the passing lanes and describe.
   c. Describe the defect complained of, giving exact measurements.
   d. Describe the length of the road area under construction.
3. *Determine how long the construction had been in progress* at the time of the accident.
4. *Determine whose duty it was to erect and maintain proper barriers or flares.* If not the insured, consider request to take over:
   a. Determine if barriers were erected.
      (1) Find out if they were adequate and proper. Describe in detail.
      (2) Describe how they were erected.
      (3) Describe exactly where they were erected.
      (4) Learn how far from either side they were visible.

(5) Describe their condition immediately before the accident.
(6) Determine whether they conformed with all legal requirements.
(7) Determine if flares were required or customary.
(8) If they were required, find out if they were put up.
(9) Determine if proper warning and speed signs were erected and, if so, whether they were at a proper distance from the danger area.
(10) Determine if a watchman or flagman was required or needed, and, if so, whether he was present.

b. *Determine if the barricades were checked:*

(1) Find out if they were checked regularly.
(2) Determine when they were last checked before the accident and by whom.
(3) Find out if they were in proper order and confirm this in a signed statement by the proper person.

5. *Determine if there was any detour or bypass:*
   a. Find out if such detour or bypass was needed.
   b. If there was such a detour, find out if it was properly marked for day and night traffic.
6. *Obtain complete diagrams and photographs* showing the condition at the time of the accident.
7. *Obtain reports from the state highway* or appropriate municipal departments.
8. *Determine whether there was any outside interference* with the visibility of the area or barricades:
   a. Determine if weather conditions interfered in any way:

SPECIFIC PUBLIC LIABILITY

      (1) Learn if high winds blew the barriers down or affected the flares.
      (2) Find out if heavy rain interfered with visibility or created an unusually dangerous condition.
      (3) Find out if the sun obstructed vision.
   b. Determine if vegetation, ascending hill or condition of the topography obstructed the view.

9. *Make an effort to obtain signed statements from others who used the road* that day or night concerning the condition and visibility of the area and the barricades.

W. Sidewalk Claims

1. Obtain the exact location of the accident.
2. Obtain a complete description of the defect or obstruction complained of.
3. Describe the composition of the sidewalk, whether cement, brick, stone, dirt, wood or whatever.
4. Describe the general condition of the sidewalk.
5. Determine the exact location of the building line, the private property boundary and the boundaries of adjacent landowners.
6. If necessary, make a complete diagram, with measurements, and take photographs. Obtain copies of any available photographs showing the condition before the accident.
7. Determine whether the sidewalk is privately or publicly owned.
8. If it is private, determine if an easement is involved. Obtain details.
9. If the municipality is involved, see that is is properly notified in time, since many cities require formal written notice within a definite time period.
10. Determine who or what caused the defect, condition, or obstruction complained of.

11. Learn if the insured derives any benefit from the act which allegedly caused the defect. Obtain details.
12. If the condition was dangerous, see if any attempt was made to guard or barricade the area. Describe in detail.
13. Determine how long the condition complained of existed before the accident.
14. Determine who owned the abutting property when the defective condition was created.
15. Find out if any attempt was made to correct the condition:

    a. If so, determine if the corrections or repairs were made properly.
    b. Determine who made the repairs.
    c. Find out how they were made and by whom. Learn who ordered them made.

16. Learn who was in control of the abutting property at the time of the accident.
17. Find out if a building or highway department violation was placed against the abutting owner, and obtain a copy.
18. Determine if any repairs or corrections were made in compliance with any violation.
19. Learn if any warning signs were placed around the defect or alleged condition.
20. Find out who originally constructed the sidewalk if possible.
21. See if the defect involved trees or tree roots:

    a. If so, determine who planted and maintained the trees.
    b. Find out who owns them.

22. *If cellar doors, coal holes, sidewalk hoists, gratings or other items of a like nature are involved:*

    a. Give their exact location and make sure that

SPECIFIC PUBLIC LIABILITY

they are within the proper property boundaries.
- b. Determine whether the object or objects are in good condition and were properly installed.
- c. Determine if bars or barricades were in their proper place. Describe in detail with measurements.
- d. Determine whether their presence and installation were in accord with local ordinances.
- e. Find out if proper precautions were taken and warnings given as to the openings of cellar doors (bells, personal attendants, etc.).

23. *In Snow and Ice Cases:*
    - a. Describe the slope of the sidewalk.
    - b. Determine if the ice was caused by leaking water.
    - c. If so, find out if it was due to a defective rain spout, plumbing or other defective object or part.
    - d. If snow was involved, find out when the last snowfall stopped.
    - e. Determine if the entire walk was covered and to what depth.
    - f. Determine if the snow was smooth or ridged, fluffy or hard-packed.
    - g. Find out if snow covered ice or if ice formed over the snow.
    - h. Find out if there was any defect of the sidewalk under the snow or ice.
    - i. Obtain a weather report.
    - j. Determine if an attempt was made to clean the the snow and ice from the sidewalk, by whom, when and how.
    - k. Find out if it was properly cleaned. Determine if it was piled so that melting snow would

dribble onto the sidewalk and create an icy hazard if it froze.
- l. Find out the details concerning any municipal or other local ordinance concerning the cleaning of snow and ice from the sidewalk.
- m. Determine if a claim is being made against the city, municipality or other local governmental agency. If so, obtain any available information from such agency. Determine whether such agency should be put on notice, if this has not been done.

X. **Sporting Events**

These events may be subdivided into two categories, namely (1) those in which the claimant was a participant and (2) those in which the claimant was a spectator. Apply whatever is pertinent from the following checklists.

1. Determine who owns the premises.
2. Determine who operates or promotes the event.
3. Learn who is responsible for the maintenance of the premises.
4. Find out who controls the premises. Obtain copies of all leases, contracts or agreements.
5. *Determine if the claimant was a paying spectator:*
    a. Find out what kind of a ticket he or she purchased.
    b. Determine where the claimant sat.
    c. Find out if the claimant had a choice of seats.
    d. Determine if the seat was protected by screening or if it was walled off. If so, determine if it was in good condition.
6. *Describe the object, contrivance or area allegedly defective:*
    a. Determine if it was properly constructed.
    b. Determine if the contrivance was proper for the event, and if it was in good working order.

SPECIFIC PUBLIC LIABILITY

    c. Determine if it was properly maintained.
    d. Find out if there were any warning signs and whether the claimant paid heed to them.
7. Determine if a guard or attendant was present or should have been. If not, find out why.
8. Determine if failure or defect was due to the intervention of someone else. If so, obtain names and details if possible.
9. Find out if the claimant was ever there before, when and how often.
10. Learn if the claimant was aware of the danger.
11. Determine if the danger was unusual or extraordinary.
12. Learn how the claimant was injured. Get all details.
13. Find out if the claimant did anything to place himself in a position of jeopardy. Get all details.
14. Get details concerning notice, i.e., if proper inspections were made and, if not, why.
15. *In golfing accidents:*
    a. Determine if the claimant was a participant, caddy or spectator.
    b. Find out if the claimant was on the course for any other reason, legitimate or otherwise.
    c. Determine if the claimant was outside the course either as a pedestrian or in an automobile, and get details.
    d. Determine if the claimant was new at the game.
    e. Determine the exact position of the claimant and why he or she was there.
    f. Determine the exact position and actions of the insured.
    g. Find out if the insured looked to see if anyone was in his or her line of play.
    h. Determine if the insured cried "fore" or gave any other warning before or after he or she hit the ball.

i. Find out if the claimant was aware of the danger, or should have been.
j. Find out if the claimant saw the ball as it was hit or after it was in flight.
k. Determine if the claimant moved after or immediately before the ball was hit.
l. Find out what club the insured used and whether it was proper.
m. Learn whether the ball was hooked or sliced, and whether it went straight or rebounded.
n. In addition to the statements of the insured and the claimant, signed statements should be obtained from those who were playing with the insured, the caddies, if any, and any other witnesses.

Y. **Stairways**

1. *Obtain complete description of the stairs:*
    a. Determine the composition and construction of the steps.
    b. Determine the height, width and depth of the stairs.
    c. Find out if all steps are of equal height and depth.
    d. Determine the number of steps and locate as nearly as possible the exact location of the accident.
    e. Determine the condition of the steps, i.e., new, worn, slippery, firm, abrasive, wobbly, uneven, etc.
    f. Find out if the steps had any covering and, if so, describe its composition and condition.
    g. Find out if the steps had nosings and describe in detail.
    h. Determine if the stairway was straight, curved, winding or unusual in any way.

SPECIFIC PUBLIC LIABILITY 157

    i. Determine the locations and describe the landings, giving exact measurements if warranted.
2. *Describe the handrail:*
   a. Determine if there was a handrail, or whether there should have been and describe in detail.
   b. Pay special attention as to how such handrail was fastened, and of what it was composed.
   c. Determine its condition and whether it was firm.
   d. Describe the handrail in detail, giving exact measurements including height and accessibility.
3. Determine if the construction of the stairway and rail conformed to local and state building code requirements.
4. Find out if there was any obstruction on the stairway and describe in detail.
5. Learn who was responsible for the lighting of the stairway and follow through as previously suggested in matters of lighting sufficiency.
6. Find out if the stairway was used in common and who else used it. Determine responsibility for maintenance and put on notice anyone other than the insured, who may have been responsible.
7. Check inspection and notice. Find out if regular inspections of the stairs were made, how often cleaned, by whom, and similar details.
8. *Information to be obtained from the claimant:*
   a. Determine the exact location from which the claimant allegedly fell, between which floors and on exactly what step.
   b. Find out what type of shoes he or she was wearing and obtain complete description.
   c. Determine whether the claimant was carrying anything.

d. Find out what caused the claimant to trip, stumble, slip or otherwise lose his or her balance.
e. Determine whether a handrail or the lack of it was involved and, if so, review the checklists previously outlined for accidents involving handrails.
f. Determine how the claimant fell, whether backward or forward, and all other details.
9. Locate and interview possible witnesses as previously outlined.

Z. Swimming Pools

1. Determine who owns the pool and how it is maintained, as previously outlined.
2. If it is not a private pool, find out who operates it and is responsible for its maintenance. Obtain a copy of the lease if pertinent and put on notice anyone other than the insured who may have been responsible for the condition which allegedly caused the accident.
3. *Describe the pool:*
    a. Determine if it is in good condition.
    b. Determine its length, width and depth at both ends.
    c. If pertinent, find out if the shallow end is roped off or if any other precautions were taken to safeguard children.
    d. Find out where the ladders were located and how they were constructed and maintained.
    e. If pertinent, describe the ledge and ledge grip, if any.
    f. Determine if the pool has a stairway leading into it and describe in detail including handrails.
    g. If pertinent, determine the composition of the walkway around the edge of the pool and

SPECIFIC PUBLIC LIABILITY 159

whether or not it was slippery. If so, determine if any precautions were taken to avoid slipping.

4. *Describe the diving board:*
   a. Determine if it was clean and free from debris or slime.
   b. Find out how high it was, and how long.
   c. Describe the stairway, ladder or other approach in detail.
   d. Determine if it was properly balanced.
   e. Learn its exact composition, construction and covering. Determine the condition of the covering if pertinent.
   f. Learn who manufactured and who erected the board, and put on notice if warranted.
   g. Determine if any warning signs were posted, and, if so, whether they were visible from the direction of approach. Describe in detail.
   h. Find out if the claimant simply lost his or her her balance and fell off accidentally. Find out what diving experience the claimant had.
   i. Learn how familiar the claimant was with the board.

5. *Determine if life guards or other attendants were present:*
   a. Find out if they are required by law, and, if so, whether the proper number were present.
   b. Learn what experience and training they had.
   c. Find out how old they were, their physical condition and mental stability.
   d. Determine how the guards were chosen.

6. Determine if the claimant paid an admission fee. If not, find out if the claimant was properly on the premises. Obtain complete details.

7. Learn if there was any horseplay or if the claimant

contributed to the incident in any way. Get all details.
8. Find out if the claimant could swim and how well.
9. Determine if drinking and/or intoxication or drugs were involved.
10. *Determine if artificial respiration or other lifesaving efforts or devices were involved,* and, if so, get full details, such as:
    a. How soon it was done.
    b. Whether it was effective.
    c. Whether it was properly done, and, if not, why.
    d. Whether any machinery was involved, by whom used, and if it was in proper working condition.
11. Take photographs and have inspections of all equipment involved in the accident made by properly qualified specialists.
12. Determine if an autopsy was made, and, if so, obtain copy.
13. Obtain signed statements from those who previously used the pool or diving board and found them safe and in good condition, if this was so.
14. Obtain signed statements from any witnesses as previously outlined.

AA. **Tenancy Claims**
1. Determine the type of tenancy:
    a. Yearly or month to month.
    b. Written or oral.
    c. Find out if a sublease was involved.
2. Obtain a copy of the lease or the terms of any oral agreement.
3. Determine how long the claimant lived at that location.
4. Determine if the flat, apartment or premises was in good condition.

SPECIFIC PUBLIC LIABILITY

5. Find out who was responsible for its maintenance and when it was last repaired or redecorated. Determine what work was done, by whom, and at whose direction.
6. Determine if the premises was properly inspected before occupancy, by either the tenant or landlord.
7. Find out if any inspection was made after repairs had been completed and by whom.
8. Determine if periodic inspections are made:
    a. Find out when and by whom, and if the landlord had the right.
    b. Learn whether any complaints had been made.
9. Determine the general condition in addition to the specific complaint.
10. Find out if the defect or condition complained of could have been caused by other tenants or by outsiders.
11. Find out if the condition or defect was open and obvious.
12. Determine if the defect or condition was known to the tenant, or could have been known on proper inspection.
13. Determine who controlled the area complained of.
14. Determine if the area was used in common with other tenants, and, if so, by whom. Get details.
15. Determine if notice of the defect or condition was given to the insured, by whom, and when.
16. Learn if any violation of local or state law was involved and get details and copies of any reports that may be available.
17. Determine whether there was any ill-feeling or trouble between the tenant and the landlord or janitor if pertinent.
18. Learn if the tenant ever threatened to make trouble for the landlord or janitor.

19. Determine if the tenant paid the rent regularly and on time, and whether any back rent was due.
20. Find out if the claimant was a desirable tenant.
21. Determine if any action was started or threatened to dispossess the tenant.

AB. Theatres and Auditoriums

1. *Determine ownership and control* in accordance with previous outlines.
2. *Describe the premises in detail:*
    a. Determine the degree of slope in the aisle or the steepness of the stairs.
    b. Determine if there was any handrail or whether there should have been.
    c. Determine the condition of the aisle or stairway as suggested in previous outlines.
    d. Describe the seating arrangement and the seats, if pertinent.
    e. Determine if the runners and carpeting were in good condition.
3. *Describe the lighting conditions:*
    a. Determine if the theatre was dark at the time.
    b. Find out if there were any aisle or seat lights.
    c. Determine if the contrast from the outside was great.
    d. Learn if the claimant waited until his or her eyes became adjusted to the light change.
4. *Determine whether there were any ushers in attendance:*
    a. Find out if an usher was present at the time of the incident, or should have been.
    b. Find out if the usher offered to help and whether such an offer was accepted. Get all details.
5. *Follow through on physical facts,* witnesses and other details as previously suggested.

CHAPTER V

Investigation of Products Liability Claims

The investigation of products liability claims can tax the imagination, ingenuity and mental versatility of the claimsperson. For one thing, aside from those accidents which occur in restaurants, the claims mostly arise out of what are known as "blind accidents," or those to which there are no witnesses other than the claimant and his or her relatives or close friends.

For another thing, a products liability claim may involve any one of a vast variety of unrelated products; the claimsperson may have to learn much in a short time about fields which are entirely new to him. Products claims, for instance, involve not only drugs, cosmetics, food products and beverages, but also vehicles and other mechanical devices, ladders and tools, electrical appliances, insecticides (with or without pressure containers), dyes and paints, home permanents, pressure cookers, gas, oil and electric stoves, matches, inflammable gases such as butane, and other products too numerous to mention.

The insured may be the manufacturer, wholesaler, jobber, distributor, retailer, or maintenance, repair and/or service agency. It is important to remember that the defect complained of may have been produced anywhere along the line from the manufacturer down to and including the consumer.

The quickest way to learn about a product manufactured by the insured is to call on the insured and make a thorough inspection of his plant under the guidance of someone who can properly explain the various processes after reading all of the available advertising and instructional material and manuals available. Such calls serve not only to familiarize the claimsperson with the information he or she must have, but permits him or her, when a claim is presented, to make arrangements for obtaining specific information in the shortest possible time and with the least amount of friction. Such calls also afford the opportunity to make arrangements for handling claims a matter of public relations.

Often, products liability claims do not involve serious injury. In many instances it is more a matter of outraged dignity than of actual damages. A courteous, considerate and understanding claimsperson who calls on the claimant in the capacity of representative of the firm which his company insures can very often nip a claim in the bud by offering to replace the allegedly defective product (and hope that the defect, if any, is not repeated).

Very often, the alleged defect is nothing more than something that is quite natural or inherent in the product such as salmon crystals which may be mistaken for glass, burnt cracker dust which may be mistaken for rodent excrement, or things of a similar nature.

A tactful explanation, sincere regret for the misunderstanding, and the offer of several cans or packages in replacement for the one that was allegedly defective, will very often turn a a prospective claim into good publicity.

There are, however, occasions when a claim or claims can involve many individuals who may have sustained serious injuries or death, or where the property damage may be very extensive with considerable consequential loss of business. In such cases every lead must be explored, every contract reviewed and all advertising and technical instructional material carefully examined to determine where the ultimate responsibility lies, and to put the wrongdoer on notice if the wrongdoer is other than the insured. The insurance carrier for such wrongdoer must be brought into the picture as soon as possible.

In view of the possible diversity, it is obviously impossible to outline the investigation for every product that might be made the subject of a claim. The following checklists must therefore deal in generalities which it is hoped will give leads to the investigator.

A. Coverage

1. Obtain complete and correct name of the insured and insured's legal status (individual, corporation, partnership, trade name, estate, trust, etc.) and compare it with the policy declarations.
2. Make sure that the policy contains products liability coverage and check to see if the policy contains a retailer's endorsement, and what kind.
3. Obtain the names of all jobbers, retailers, wholesalers, distributors and any others that may have been involved, to see if they are covered by the insured's policy or if they are also insured in the same company.
4. Determine whether the incident falls within any of the policy exclusions or if there was a breach of a policy condition.
5. Determine the primary wrongdoer and put him and his insurance carrier on notice if the insured's liability is secondary or contingent.
6. If an edible product was involved, determine whether it was consumed on or off the premises and if properly covered.

Description and Identification of the Product

1. Determine the name of the product.
2. Determine the name and address of the manufacturer.
3. Determine the names and addresses of all retailers, jobbers, wholesalers and distributors that may be involved.
4. Obtain the names of the insurance carriers for the manufacturer, retailers, jobber, wholesaler and distributor, if applicable.
5. Obtain a complete description of the product. Get copies of all advertising, descriptive and instructional material, including blueprints where applicable.

6. *Describe the general condition of the product:*
    a. Determine if it was defective in any way.
    b. Determine if it was contaminated or deteriorated.
    c. Determine if it was inherently dangerous.
    d. Determine the age of the product and how it was stored.
7. *Describe the label:*
    a. Determine if the label properly identified the product.
    b. Determine if it conformed with all legal requirements, such as the Pure Food and Drug Act.
    c. Determine if it contained proper and prominent warnings.
8. Determine if packaging was proper and obtain samples of labels and packages.

C. **Insured's Investigation**

1. Obtain the name and address of the person who purchased the article.
2. Determine where the purchase was made and whether from the retailer, jobber, wholesaler, etc.
3. If pertinent, obtain the name and address of the sales person who sold the article and interview.
4. Obtain the exact date of the purchase and corroborate by checking the sales slip or other records.
5. Determine when the product or article was delivered, by whom and how.
6. Determine the exact price of the article and whether it was charged or paid for in cash, and by whom.
7. Determine if the product was asked for by trade name.
8. Learn if the sales person recommended the product and obtain details of any conversation between the sales person and the purchaser.

9. If the article was not purchased by the claimant, determine how it was obtained by him or her, from whom, and when.
10. Find out what complaint was made about the product, when it was made, and by whom.
11. Find out if the alleged defect could have been caused by ordinary wear and tear.
12. Describe the defect in detail and determine if it was natural to the product, like a fishbone in canned fish.
13. Determine if the alleged defect could have been caused by the claimant or someone other than the insured.
14. Find out what tests were made to determine the safety of the product. Describe in detail.
15. *Find out what became of the article:*
    a. Determine if the evidence was properly preserved.
    b. Determine if it was properly identified.
    c. Find out how much of the product was used.
16. Try to obtain possession of the product for the purpose of taking laboratory tests, chemical analysis, bacteriological counts, etc., but try to make sure that the tests will not destroy its usefulness as evidence, if possible. If the nature of the product will be changed by any essential tests, it may be advisable to obtain the claimant's permission in writing, if possession was relinquished provisionally.
17. Obtain other packages or jars of the product from the same batch or carton, for the purpose of comparison examination and analysis.
18. Determine if there is any evidence of improper use of the product.
19. Use your imagination to think of ways in which, through improper use, the product could have become in the condition complained of and follow through on investigation.

20. Obtain the names and addresses of all who consumed the product or had anything to do with it. Check them all for injury or illness attributable to the product.
21. Determine if the product conformed with all applicable federal, state and local laws or ordinances.
22. Describe the methods of storing and handling from the factory to the purchaser.
23. *Obtain complete details concerning the manufacture,* canning, packing or bottling, including inspection, testing, wrapping or capping, etc.:
    a. Describe the package in detail.
    b. Determine if it was properly sealed.
    c. Determine if the package could have been refilled or otherwise tampered with.
    d. Find out if the product was sold in the original wrapper.
    e. Find out if it was received by the insured in the same wrapper.
    f. Describe the label and box or can markings, including any code marks for identification.
    g. Check the coding to determine the packer (if other than the insured) and put on notice if warranted.
24. Obtain details concerning transportation if applicable, including a description of all places where tampering might have occurred.
25. Where warranted, check organizations such as the Association of Safety Engineers, the American Standard Association, the National Safety Council, Consumers Union, Consumers Reports, Ralph Nader's organization and other consumer groups for any available information concerning the product.
26. *If glass or other sharp object* was alleged to have been taken into the mouth:

PRODUCTS LIABILITY CLAIMS

    a. Obtain the object for examination or get a detailed description of it.
    b. Determine if it was inherent to the product such as food crystals mistaken for glass.
    c. Find out if there was any evidence of bleeding.
    d. Determine if there were any outcries or other evidence of injury or illness.

27. *If the product was mechanical in nature:*
    a. Determine its general condition as heretofore outlined.
    b. Find out how old it is and what kind of use it has had.
    c. Get the defective part inspected by an expert. See if metal fatigue was involved.
    d. If the defect was in a part not manufactured by the insured, find out who did manufacture it and put on notice.
    e. Determine if the claimant was familiar with the product and its use.
    f. Determine if proper care had been used in the maintenance of the product.
    g. Check scientific and engineering indices of technical articles that apply to the product.
    h. If warranted, check the U.S. Patent Office through a patent attorney to get details concerning the inventor's or manufacturer's allegations concerning the product.

D. **Claimant's Investigation**

1. *Claimant's background information:*
    a. Claimant's name and all previous names or aliases under which the claimant was ever known, including the maiden name of any married female claimant, for Index Bureau reasons concerning previous accidents or injuries.

b. Present address and, if warranted, previous addresses.
c. Age, general appearance and impression made by the claimant. Include any available information concerning the claimant's character, honesty, reputation, industriousness, intelligence, education or other such factors that might bear upon his or her impression as a witness.
d. Economic status.
e. Military status if applicable.
f. Possible criminal record.

2. *Marital status and dependency:*
    a. Name, age and dependency status of wife or husband.
    b. Names, ages and dependency status of all children.
    c. Marital status, including details and, if warranted, records of all births of children, previous marriages, separations, divorces and deaths.

3. *Employment history:*
    a. Names and addresses of all present employers.
    b. Names and addresses of previous employers if pertinent.
    c. Time employed by each.
    d. Nature of work and duties performed.
    e. Salaries received, including regular salary, commissions, overtime, tips, board and lodging, or other remuneration of any kind.

4. Claimant's educational background if pertinent, as outlined in the investigation of general liability cases.
5. Pensions, insurance or welfare help received by the claimant, if pertinent, as previously outlined.
6. Claimant's physical condition or possible deform-

ities which might have had a bearing on the case, as previously outlined.
7. Possible distractions to the claimant, as previously outlined, such as the weather, drugs or alcohol, smoking, emotional stress, etc.
8. Obtain previous and subsequent accident records.
9. *Factual details:*
   a. Determine the exact date, time and location of the accident.
   b. Obtain a description of the accident in detail.
   c. Obtain the name and address of the person who purchased the article or product.
   d. Determine where the purchase was made.
   e. Find out from whom the purchase was made, and whether it was the retailer, jobber, wholesaler or manufacturer.
   f. Identify the sales person who sold the article.
   g. Obtain the name and address of the person for whom the purchase was made, if not for the buyer.
   h. Obtain the exact date and time of the purchase.
   i. Obtain the date and time of delivery.
   j. Find out how it was delivered and by whom.
   k. If the article was not purchased, determine how it was obtained by the claimant.

      (1) Determine from whom it was obtained.
      (2) Find out exactly where it was obtained.
      (3) Find out exactly how it was obtained.

   l. Determine the price paid for the product.
   m. Find out who paid for it and how.
   n. Determine if the product was asked for by trade name.
   o. Learn if the sales person recommended the product and obtain details concerning the conversation between the seller and the buyer.

p. Learn when and how the alleged defect was first discovered.
q. Describe the defect in detail and whether it was natural to the product, like a fishbone, chicken bone, etc.
r. Determine if the claimant was familiar with the product and how often he or she had previously used or eaten it.
s. Determine what became of the remaining product.
t. Try to obtain possession of the product for the purpose of examining and testing it as previously outlined.
u. Find out how the product was used or consumed and whether it was examined before being used. Determine if it appeared in good condition.
v. Determine if the product was used properly or if it was abused in any way.
w. Obtain the names and addresses of all who consumed the same product or had anything to do with it.

    (1) Determine what else was eaten at the same time.
    (2) Find out what was eaten at prior or subsequent meals and how long an interval was involved.
    (3) Determine how many people ate the same things.
    (4) Try to determine the common factor. (Food eaten by all of the people who became ill.)

10. *Medical information* to be obtained from the claimant:

    a. Determine when the first complaint of illness

or injury was made and when first manifested. Get details.
b. Find out what the injury or illness or reaction consisted of.
c. Determine how many people suffered the same symptoms.
d. If glass or a sharp object was involved, see item 26 under "Insured's Investigation."
e. Determine what medical assistance was given at the scene of the injury or illness.
f. Obtain the name of the doctor or hospital where the claimant was taken immediately after the injury or illness.
g. Obtain the name and address of the family physician who subsequently treated the claimant, including identification of any specialists or consultants called in.
h. Obtain, as closely as possible, the dates of treatment.
i. Obtain information concerning X-rays:

(1) By whom taken, when and where.
(2) What parts of the body were X-rayed.
(3) What the X-rays showed.
(4) Whether they are available for review.

j. Obtain details of any operations for review.
k. Obtain duration of confinement to bed and home.
l. Obtain the exact length of disability from work.
m. Obtain the exact nature of any continuing complaints or disability.
n. Obtain description of any scars or disfigurements. Get snapshots or photographs, if possible.
o. Obtain details concerning claimant's previous

medical history, if applicable, as listed in the investigations previously outlined.

11. *Witnesses obtained through claimant:*
    a. Obtain the names and addresses of anyone who was with the claimant immediately preceding, during or after the incident, or who might have witnessed it. Interview them and obtain signed statements where possible.
    b. Obtain claimant's best description of any possible witnesses whose names are not known. Try to locate and interview them.

E. **Medical Investigation**

1. Obtain local health department report and examination where possible and pertinent.
2. Obtain detailed medical information from the claimant as previously outlined.
3. Obtain doctor's report as previously outlined.
4. Obtain hospital records as previously outlined.
5. Obtain physical examination if necessary, as previously outlined.

F. **Special Damages**

1. *Check claimant's lost time and earnings:*
    a. Check employer's payroll records.
    b. Check exact dates of absence from work.
    c. Check exact amount of lost earnings.
    d. Determine the amount of the regular salary rate.
    e. Determine the average amount of overtime for that particular time of the year.
    f. Determine the average amount of commissions for that particular time of the year.
    g. Make an estimate of the average tips and other gratuities including board and lodging.

h. Determine whether the injury or illness has necessitated a change of job or employment.
i. Determine whether the injury has necessitated claimant's going on part-time work.
j. Check all lost time and medical expense with the compensation carrier, if involved.

2. *Where the claimant is self-employed:*
   a. Check income tax returns where available, including federal, state and local.
   b. Check social security records if available.
   c. Check any other tax or license returns that may be made available.
   d. Examine private books, records and accounts.

3. *Medical expenses:*
   a. Obtain attending doctor's, specialist's or dentist's bills.
   b. Obtain registered and practical nurse's bills.
   c. Determine the amount of any ambulance charge, hospital or clinic bills.
   d. Determine the cost of X-rays, laboratory bills and the expenses for any other tests or scans.
   e. Determine the amount of bills for drugs, medicines, medical appliances, prosthetic devices, etc.
   f. Determine whether there were any travel expenses from the scene of the accident or to and from visits to the doctor and hospital or clinic.

4. *Fatal claims:*
   a. Determine the funeral expenses.
   b. Determine the cost of burial plot or crypt.
   c. Determine or estimate the cost of a tombstone.

5. Determine whether there was any conscious pain and suffering.

6. Check possible loss of support.
7. Check possible cosmetic disfigurement.

CHAPTER VI

Some Specific Products Liability Investigations

A. **Automobiles**

Negligence has been accepted as creating liability on the manufacturer or assembler of automobiles for many years. This has subsequently developed, in some jurisdictions, to the acceptance of the doctrine of strict liability for design as well as for manufacturing or assembling errors.

More and more jurisdictions are also holding that there is a further duty to produce vehicles that are crash resistant and free of defects that may make it unsafe for passengers or the driver after an impact occurs.

The effect of recall letters on the liability of a manufacturer for admitted defects can also be a complicated matter that might either aid in the defense, or be used with deadly effect by the plaintiff.

The investigation of products liability claims involving automobiles can affect the designer, manufacturer, assembler, sales agency and repair shop. The following checklist is meant to guide and stimulate the imagination of the investigator.

1. Obtain the name of the manufacturer of the part complained of.
2. Obtain and determine the conditions of the contract between the automobile assembler and the manufacturer of the subcontracted part.
3. Find out what tests were made by the parts manufacturer and the assembler before or after installation.
4. Determine where, when, how and by whom the part was installed. The individual, of course, cannot usu-

ally be determined, but it may be narrowed down to a small group including the inspector of that unit.
5. Find out if there were any previous complaints concerning the part or its operation.
6. Find out if the automobile company made any attempt to call in the defective part or parts, or issued any notice or warning concerning them. Determine if the purchaser of the automobile received such notice or if it only went to the sales agencies. Obtain copies of any recall or warning letters.
7. Find out if there was any mention of the defective part in any of the instructional material given to the purchaser, or in any of the advertising matter or manuals. If so, get copies.
8. Determine whether or not the allegedly defective part part was vital to the safe operation of the vehicle.
9. Determine whether the alleged defective part was obvious or hidden.
10. *In checking possible brake failure,* it is important to determine the following:
    a. When the plaintiff purchased the automobile.
    b. How many miles it was driven safely.
    c. Whether the car was purchased new or used.
    d. If it was ever involved in a collision before the accident under investigation.
    e. When the brakes were last adjusted and inspected and by whom.
    f. If the adjustment could have been improper.
    g. The system of brakes that was installed.
    h. If there was a defect in the brake mechanism or lining.
    i. If there was a system of double brakes, and if the secondary system worked properly.
11. Find out if bad or careless driving played any part in the accident.

SPECIFIC LIABILITY INVESTIGATIONS

B. Bottling Claims

One of the most common types of products liability claims involves the manufacture, sale and distribution of carbonated bottled beverages. Flying glass fragments can and have done a lot of harm. It is seldom that an explosion of this kind occurs without some sharp change in temperature together with an external bruising or contact with hard objects.

While cases involving alleged foreign substances in bottled beverages do not usually result in serious injury, the number of these claims has reached major proportions. They require the careful and prudent attorney for the plaintiff and the defendant to take care in order to determine that the allegations made by the plaintiff are factual. In cases alleging foreign substances, it is particularly important to check the manner in which the bottles were cleaned before they were filled and capped.

Quite often, there is an allegation of swallowing glass particles allegedly dislodged as a result of defective capping. Such cases should be viewed with a great deal of skepticism, since it is very difficult to dislodge small particles of glass from a bottle containing liquid until all of the liquid has been drained from it.

If a broken bottle or foreign substance is involved, the following checklist should be helpful:

1. *Obtain the bottle fragments for examination.* Assure the claimant or his attorney that these fragments will not be disturbed and will be returned in the same condition in which they were released. Proper laboratory examination can determine:
    a. Whether some outside force was applied to the bottle that may have nicked or cracked it causing weakening sufficient for it to shatter.
    b. Whether there was a defect in the bottle that made it weaker than normal.

      c. Whether there was a defect in the cap or in the capping process.
2. If necessary, determine the manner in which the bottle was handled and stored by all previous parties from the manufacturer to the consumer.
3. Obtain report on previous similar accident from parties anywhere along the line between the consumer and the manufacturer.
4. Determine where the claimant stored the bottle and whether it was kept near artificial heat or in the sunlight.
5. Obtain a description of the sound of the explosion and the manner in which the flying fragments separated, and check this out with an appropriate expert.
6. *In mouse claims,* determine the advisability of:
      a. Autopsy to determine whether there was any liquid in the lungs of the mouse.
      b. X-ray, to find out if any bones were broken. These are two means that are almost foolproof in helping to determine whether the mouse was pushed into the bottle after it was dead or if it actually drowned in the liquid.
7. *Complete description of the bottling process,* including:
      a. Temperature and pressure control.
      b. Use of returned bottles and their cleaning and inspection before and after filling.
      c. Capping process.
8. Find out if a no-return bottle was used and, if so, whether this is common practice.
9. Learn the name of the manufacturer of the bottle from the code markings and put on notice if it is not the insured.

C. **Crop Dusting or Spraying**

While the laws governing the responsibility of an independent contractor or the owner of crops for liability to

SPECIFIC LIABILITY INVESTIGATIONS

others varies depending upon the state statutes, our concern in products liability is principally with damage caused by an allegedly defective product used in the dusting or spraying.

Nevertheless, since it is sometimes difficult to separate the two, the following checklist will, of necessity, contain much of the information previously outlined in discussing this type of claim under the "General Liability" section.

1. Obtain a copy of the contract between the owner of the crops and the person or firm that performed the crop dusting. If the contract was oral, obtain as many details as possible. Find out what specific directions were given and by whom. Determine how payment was made, who owned the equipment, and other details that could establish whether the ones performing the work were independent contractors.
2. Determine the applicable local laws or state statutes and whether they were complied with.
3. Find out if any preliminary testing was made to insure safety to other plants and to animals or humans.
4. Determine if any warnings were issued and how.
5. Find out the exact weather conditions with particular emphasis on wind velocity and drift. Determine if weather conditions were properly checked in advance, and whether or not a sudden, unexpected and unpredicted wind was instrumental in causing the damage.
6. Determine the exact nature and inherent danger of the insecticides used. Find out whether or not any other product of a less dangerous nature could have been used as effectively. Determine whether the product was properly labeled and packaged, and arrange for a chemical analysis of the compound to deter-

mine its nature, ingredients and concentration. Preserve a sample of the compounds so that it may be used in evidence if advisable.
7. Find out from whom the compound was purchased.
8. Determine the method of application and whether or not it was in accordance with ordinary prudent standards. Determine whether or not the application or the applicator was defective in any way and find out whether the operator or pilot confined himself within the proper area. Find out if the operators and pilot were experienced and competent, and get full details.
9. Investigate the condition of similar plants or crops ouside the range of contamination, but in the same general area. Find out if harm might have been due to causes other than dusting, such as drought, poor farming methods, insufficient or improper fertilizer, plant disease, insect infestation, age, general condition of the soil or of the delicate nature of the crops themselves.
10. Have an inspection made of the injured plants, trees or crops by an expert agriculturalist.
11. Check the local agricultural agent, local agriculture college, and all similar sources of information. Obtain copies of any reports that may have been made.
12. Check the past record of the dusting outfit to determine if they were a responsible company or individual.

D. **Drugs and Cosmetics**

This is, today, an extremely sensitive area not only because of consumer group activity, but because of the changing law in the courts. Overpromotion, for instance, has been held to nullify the effects of warning statements in some instances. Testing requirements have been greatly increased.

1. Determine when the drug or cosmetic was first

SPECIFIC LIABILITY INVESTIGATIONS

placed on the market and what previous experience the manufacturer has had with it.
2. Determine what tests were made by the manufacturer.
3. Find out if the product was compounded by the insured. If there was an error in the compounding, and if the compounding was done by someone other than the insured, put them and their insurer on notice.
4. Find out if the product had ever been recalled and, if so, get complete details.
5. Determine from whom the insured purchased the ingredients.
6. Obtain the formula, if possible.
7. Determine the method of manufacture or compounding:
    a. Check the general sanitary conditions.
    b. Check the quality and qualifications of the personnel, including the supervisors.
    c. Check the adequacy of inspections of both the plant and the product.
8. Obtain samples from the same batch or carton complained of, and have such samples analyzed and tested.
9. Determine whether the product complies with all applicable pure food and drug laws and whether it received the approval of the federal Food and Drug Administration.
10. Determine if there have been any comments or tests made on the product by organizations such as Consumers Union, Consumers Reports, Ralph Nader's organization or others of a similar nature.
11. Determine if the product was subject to the regulations of the Federal Trade Commission and, if so, whether it complied with any such regulations.
12. Find out if any restraining order of any kind was ever

issued against the product by any governmental or medical authorities.
13. Find out if any professional papers or articles have been written about the drug and, if so, obtain copies.
14. Determine what literature or advertising material may have been distributed to doctors, retailers and pharmacists, or the general public concerning the product. Find out what other advertising was done and if such advertising might be considered as over-promotion.
15. Determine what experience the manufacturer or compounder has had with the product since it has been on the market. Find out if any previous complaints were made and, if so, get details.
16. Find out if any side effects or allergies were involved.
17. Determine what action, if any, the manufacturer or compounder took as a result of previous complaints.
18. Inspect the label carefully and determine:
    a. If the instructions for use were clear, adequate and prominent.
    b. If proper warnings were prominent, if required.
    c. If the label honestly portrayed the product.
19. Determine if the product was properly packaged:
    a. Determine if there was any danger from the method in which the product was packaged.
    b. Determine if the package contributed to the possible deterioration of the product.
    c. Find out if the packaging was so defective as to permit tampering without detection.
20. Determine who prescribed or recommended the drug or cosmetic and whether prescribed instructions were followed. Get details as to when it was first prescribed, how often the drug was taken, and in exactly what quantities. If recommended, find

SPECIFIC LIABILITY INVESTIGATIONS

out if the claimant followed instructions for its use on the label or package.

21. Determine if the claimant was unusually allergic to certain otherwise harmless ingredients in the product. Find out if allergy or other sensitivity tests were made or suggested, before or after usage.
22. Find out if the doctor gave any warnings concerning possible side effects. Find out when manifestations of side effects or allergic reactions were first noticed and in what manner. Determine whether any other drugs or combination of products taken internally, like alcohol, aspirin, barbiturates, tranquilizers, etc., could have affected the end result, and get complete details.
23. Find out if the drug or cosmetic was tampered with in any way before being used and, if so, get details.
24. If noxious vapors were involved, find out if there was a warning concerning proper ventilation for use, and if such warning was heeded. Get full details surrounding the use of the product.
25. Determine if the claimant's reaction was unusual and if such reaction was reported to his doctor. Find out if any countermeasures were taken, and get full details.
26. Find out what previous experience the claimant's doctor had with the drug and how it came to his attention.

E. **Electrical Appliances**

1. Determine if the product is approved by the Underwriters Laboratories and other such organizations.
2. Find out if the wiring was adequate and proper.
3. Determine whether there was a possible overload.
4. Determine whether voltage and amperes were proper.
5. Find out if the proper current was being used (A.C. or D.C.).

6. Determine whether the automatic controls were in proper working condition. Check the thermostat and the breakers or overload switches.
7. Determine whether the cord was defective.
8. Determine whether the plug was defective or the connections improper.
9. Find out if the appliance was permitted to be overheated.
10. Determine if proper instructions were issued with the appliance and get copies:
    a. Find out if the claimant observed instructions for grounding.
    b. Find out if the claimant observed instructions for proper insertion of a three-pronged plug.
    c. Find out if other instructions were properly followed for the use of the appliance.
11. Determine if the claimant attempted to repair the appliance. Find out if he or she worked on it while it was connected or plugged in.

F. **Food Contamination or Foreign Substance**

1. Obtain the exact date, time and place of the incident.
2. Determine the exact nature of the food and beverages consumed.
3. Determine what food or beverages were consumed immediately or shortly before or after the food complained of.
4. Determine the ingredients and make tests to find out if contamination or defect was the responsibility of someone other than the insured. If so, see that the responsible party is put on notice to inform its insurer and to take over.
5. Determine when the insured bought or made the food.
6. *Determine how the product was kept:*
    a. Learn the general conditions concerning cleanliness.

SPECIFIC LIABILITY INVESTIGATIONS 187

    b. Determine if the product should have been refrigerated, and, if so, whether it was done properly.
    c. Get details concerning the transportation of the product, if applicable.
7. *If consumed off the premises:*
    a. Determine all the details concerning purchase, storage, delivery, and, if applicable, put on notice those that might be involved.
    b. If applicable, determine how long the claimant had the product in his or her possession before consumption and what refrigeration it got.
    c. Find out who was with the claimant at the time of consumption and whether he or she partook of the food or drink.
    d. Make the usual investigation concerning food and beverage claims as heretofore suggested.
8. *If a canned product* was involved:
    a. Determine if the can was swollen before being opened.
    b. Find out if the product had a peculiar odor or color.
    c. Obtain the code marks of the packer from the can and put the packer and its carrier on notice, if applicable.
    d. Find out how long the claimant had the can in his or her possession before opening.
    e. If the can was already opened, find out if the food was consumed directly from the can and how long and under what conditions it was kept.
9. Determine if the product conformed to all pure food and drug laws.
10. Obtain health department reports.

11. Have laboratory tests made to determine the bacteria count, if applicable.
12. *If a foreign substance* was involved:
    a. Examine the objectionable object to determine if it was indigenous to the product.
    b. Review the checklists previously given on this subject.
13. Determine the exact date and time of the onset of symptoms and obtain a description of them. If there was vomiting, determine the duration and contents. Find out if there was any diarrhea.
14. Check the claimant's prior medical history to determine whether or not a chronic ailment may have been involved. Find out if pregnancy, known to the claimant or not, may have been involved.
15. As previously indicated, determine the others who ate the food complained of and interview if possible. Try to determine if there was a common factor which may have caused the problem.
16. *Make a complete investigation concerning the processing and serving of the food:*
    a. Check for cleanliness.
    b. Learn how and for how long the food was cooked.
    c. Determine exactly what went into the dish.
    d. If frozen food was involved, determine from whom it was purchased and put on notice if warranted. Find out if the frozen food was refrozen after defrosting.
    e. If a steam table was involved, determine how long the food was on the steam table and at what temperatures the food was kept.
17. Determine if the claimant was on medication that might have affected him or her if combined with certain foods or alcohol.

SPECIFIC LIABILITY INVESTIGATIONS 189

G. **Inflammables**
 1. Determine whether the product conformed to all applicable regulatory laws:
    a. *Contents.* Determine if it had the Fire Department seal of approval and if this was necessary.
    b. *Label.* Determine if proper instructions were given on the label or container. The same for proper warnings.
    c. *Transportation.* Determine if the product was properly transported.
 2. Determine if laboratory tests were made to determine the flash point of the product.
 3. Compare the labeling and the flash point with other products of a similar nature on the market.
 4. Obtain a copy of the Fire Marshall's report.
 5. Find out if anything was mixed with insured's product:
    a. Determine if a thinner was required.
    b. Determine if anything was used as a mixer.
 6. Find out if the claimant followed instructions on the label.
 7. *Determine if the product was subjected to heat of any kind,* whether natural or artificial:
    a. Determine how it was applied, if artificial and for how long.
    b. If natural, determine how the product was stored and where. Find out if there was an unusual amount of sunlight or if there was an unusual storage confinement.
    c. Determine if it was necessary for heat to be applied.
    d. Find out if there was any warning against the application of heat on the label or container.
    e. Determine if sparks caused ignition and get details.

8. Obtain weather report if applicable.
9. Determine if proper ventilation was used or needed.
10. Keep in mind the possibility of arson and point the investigation toward a determination if warranted.
11. Request help in the investigation and defense from any association of manufacturers of the product involved.

H. **Motorcycles, Mopeds and Snowmobiles**

Motorcycles, mopeds and snowmobiles, because of the special skill and care required in their operation, produce a relatively higher percentage of accidents than do automobiles.

Many of the allegations concerning defective parts or design are made in an effort to cover up negligence in the operation of the vehicle. Accordingly, in addition to the usual investigations heretofore suggested in "Products Liability" claims, here are some further leads:

1. Determine if there was a defect in design or in the product itself, as heretofore outlined.
2. Learn if the claimant was aware of such defect.
3. Determine what maintenance care had been given to the vehicle, and if it was proper according to instructions.
4. Find out if the claimant was familiar with its proper operation.
5. Determine how long the vehicle was in the claimant's possession and how often he or she used it. Check the operator's driving experience on this type of vehicle.
6. Check the previous accident record of the operator.
7. Check the claimant's reputation for careful driving.
8. If the claimant was inexperienced, find out what instruction the claimant obtained in the operation of the vehicle. Get details concerning its duration and adequacy in view of the claimant's apparent intelli-

SPECIFIC LIABILITY INVESTIGATIONS 191

gence, and learn if the claimant felt that it was sufficient.
9. Obtain copies of all instructional and maintenance material, as well as warranties and advertising.
10. If there was a defect try to find out if the accident would have happened had it not been present.
11. *Make the usual investigation concerning the terrain and driving, as previously outlined under "Automobile" investigation.*
12. Determine whether the vehicle met all federal, state and local governmental and consumer requirements.

I. **Percussion Caps**
  1. *Determine if the cap was owned by the insured:*
      a. Find out if the insured was working in the area.
      b. Find out if the insured used dynamite in the area, when and how often.
      c. Learn the insured's method of marking the caps.
      d. Determine how it was identified.
      e. Determine if this was the type of cap used by the insured.
  2. *Determine the facts concerning the handling of the caps:*
      a. Determine how they are stored.
      b. Find out how they are transported.
      c. Find out how they are accounted for and the method of counting.
      d. Find out if the distribution was properly supervised, by whom, how, and if written records were kept. Get copies of all available records.
      e. Learn what precautions were taken to avoid theft or pilferage.
      f. Find out what special precautions, if any, were

taken to keep the caps from getting into the hands of children.

3. *Determine if the claimant contributed to the accident:*
    a. Find out if heat was applied to the cap.
    b. Determine if the cap was struck by a hard object.
4. *Find out if the cap was defective.* If so, find out who manufactured it and put them and their carrier on notice to take over the investigation and defense.

J. **Power Mowers**

The invention of the power mower was a boon for home owners and negligence lawyers. Even today, after years of improvements, the power mower is a product that must be handled with a great deal of care. The following are a few suggestions for the investigation of this product:

1. *Obtain a complete description of the mower:*
    a. Determine the name and manufacturer or assembler.
    b. Find out how old it is and observe its general condition.
    c. Find out how much use it got and what care and conditioning it got.
    d. Determine who manufactured the motor and any component parts that might have been involved in the accident.
    e. Find out if it is a two- or four-cycle motor and what horsepower it has.
    f. Determine whether is is self-propelled.
    g. Find out if the shield is low enough to give proper protection.
    h. Find out if the mower has an automatic recoil starter.
    i. Determine if it is belt-operated.

SPECIFIC LIABILITY INVESTIGATIONS

j. Describe whether it is reel or rotary type. *If rotary:*
   (1) Determine if the blade was properly attached.
   (2) Find out if the blade or connecting bolt broke.
   (3) Determine if the guards were in good order.

2. Determine if the gasoline tank was bulged or split.
3. Determine whether the gasoline line was flexible or rigid:
   a. Find out if it broke or became disconnected.
   b. If applicable, determine if gasoline spilled over the motor.
4. *If the mower was electrically powered:*
   a. Find out if the motor burned out.
   b. Determine if the cord was cut and, if so, how.
   c. Find out if the cord or plug was defective. Describe.
   d. Find out if the mower was being operated in the rain or whether the mower or plug got wet otherwise.
5. Find out if the design of the mower meets the requirements set by the Association of Safety Engineers and similar organizations. If warranted, have the machine examined by a specialist.
6. Make sure that the mower meets all local, state and federal guidelines.
7. Obtain records of previously reported accidents and complaints concerning the machine. Get details.
8. Obtain copies of all advertising, instructional and warranty material that may be available. Find out if exaggerated claims such as "absolutely safe" were made.

9. Get copies of all warnings in print and determine if verbal instructions or warnings concerning the operation were given by the retailer.
10. Obtain copies of reports by consumer organizations such as Consumers Reports, Consumers Union, Ralph Nader's organization, etc.
11. Find out if the operator was familiar with the operation of the mower and how long he had used it or a similar model.
12. *Obtain complete details concerning the manner in which the mower was used:*
    a. Find out if the injured or the operator used care to avoid the injury.
    b. Determine if the operator was pushing uphill or downhill.
    c. Find out if the mower was being forced over some obstruction.
    d. Determine if the mower was being pulled backward.
    e. Find out if the operator was running or walking too fast.
    f. Determine if the operator removed or disregarded the guards on the mower.
    g. Determine if the claimant was smoking while filling the tank, if applicable.
    h. Find out if smoking, alcohol or drugs contributed to the accident in any way.
    i. Find out if the operator slipped, tripped or stumbled.
13. *If a bystander was involved:*
    a. Find out if the blade hit a stone or other object.
    b. Find out exactly where the injured was at the time and why he or she was there.
    c. Check the area to determine whether it was rocky, strewn with debris, or otherwise hazardous.

SPECIFIC LIABILITY INVESTIGATIONS   195

   d. Determine if any precautions were taken, or warnings given, in an effort to avoid the accident.
   e. In a case of this kind, it is especially important to have the mower examined by a specialist to see if all safety shields were in place, that the blade was tight, and that the machine had not been tampered with.

K. **Pressure Spray Containers**

While pressure spray containers are being banned in certain localities because of ecological factors, it may be a long time before they are no longer a problem in the handling of products liability claims. I have, accordingly, made some suggestions for the investigation of claims involving this product.

1. Make the usual investigation concerning the manufacture, distribution and retailing of the product.
2. *Determine from the claimant and witnesses exactly how the accident happened:*
   a. Find out if the product was properly used, handled and stored in accordance with instructions.
   b. Determine if the claimant or anyone else misused the product or was negligent in its use.
   c. If a child was involved, try to find out if the accident was due to improper supervision of the child. Determine if the product should have been kept out of reach of the child.
3. If possible, obtain the allegedly defective product and have it examined by the insured, and, if necessary, by an outside specialist, to determine the cause of the explosion or other defect. Make sure that the examiner does not alter the condition so that it

becomes useless as evidence unless absolutely necessary.
4. Obtain another can from the same retailer which belonged to the same batch for comparison examination.
5. Determine what warning or precautionary wording was contained on the product. Describe how prominent this was, and how easy to read.
6. Find out who manufactured, assembled, filled and distributed the product and whether the defect, if any, was in the manufacture, filling or shipping of the product. If others than the insured might be involved, see that they are put on notice.
7. Determine if the product could be considered as inherently dangerous and, if so, whether its manufacture, assembling and distribution was in accord with all possible regulatory laws and ordinances. Get copies of all such laws and ordinances.
8. Obtain copies of any pertinent printed matter which may have been issued concerning the product.
9. Obtain past history concerning previous incidents and what action, if any, was taken to correct defective conditions previously brought to the attention of the manufacturer. If no action was taken on previous complaints, find out why.
10. Find out what testing had been done before marketing the product and whether any governmental approval was required and obtained.

L. **Trichinosis**

1. *Determine whether the insured's product contained the trichinae:*
    a. Obtain all available health department reports:
        (1) Previous inspections of products and the plant.
        (2) Results of laboratory and other tests

SPECIFIC LIABILITY INVESTIGATIONS

that were made after the onset of symptoms.
   b. *Make independent laboratory tests if necessary.*
   c. *Describe complete manufacturing process:*
      (1) Describe what precautions were taken to avoid infestation.
      (2) Find out if the product or any of its ingredients are cooked and, if so, for how long and at what temperatures.
      (3) Find out if the product is cured or smoked and, if so, for how long and under what conditions.
      (4) Find out if the product is pickled and, if so, in what kind of solution and for how long.
      (5) Determine if the product is refrigerated and, if so, when and at what degrees. If it is not refrigerated, determine if it should have been and why it was not.

2. *Try to determine whether the insured's product was the one responsible for the trichinosis:*
   a. Find out when and where the insured buys his or her pork products and casings. If pertinent, put the seller of the defective part on notice.
   b. Determine exactly when the product was purchased by the claimant, and from whom.
   c. Determine exactly when it was eaten.
   d. Inteview everyone who ate some of that same batch and determine whether others were affected.
   e. Find out if the trichinosis might have come from some other product.
   f. If possible, have tests made on other products that might have been involved.

g. Find out what other retailers or wholesalers bought the insured's product and check to see if any cases of trichinosis developed in the other areas.
3. *Find out if the product was cooked by the claimant before being eaten:*
   a. Find out exactly who did the cooking.
   b. Find out how long it was cooked and under what heat and conditions.
4. *Determine whether the product and its manufacture complies with all legal requirements* including any guidelines set by the Food and Drug Administration, consumer organizations and industry associations.

CHAPTER VII

Investigation of Claims
Under Professional Liability Policies

The investigation of claims arising out of professional liability policies, commonly known as malpractice claims, obviously requires some specialized knowledge of the professional field involved in the claim. The handling of medical professional claims, for instance, requires a greater knowledge of basic medical terminology than does the handling of other types of negligence claims.

Professional liability claims may also involve practitioners such as insurance agents or brokers, beauticians, undertakers, or others besides actual professional practitioners in the accepted meaning of the term.

Aside from some degree of technical knowledge, as previously mentioned, there is nothing particularly complicated or mysterious in this type of investigation.

Certain fundamentals of the law concerning professional liability must be constantly borne in mind. The investigation will be geared to the precept that a professional man or woman is held to the same degree of care and skill as is usually shown by other reputable people in the same profession. In this day of immediate communication, the location of practice is becoming less important than it was in the past in measuring negligence. The investigator must also make sure to determine whether the professional person involved had enlarged in any way the scope of his or her responsibility by making a guarantee of cure or implying a cure by irresponsible words or actions. Bad results do not necessarily imply negligence amounting to malpractice.

Since the vast majority of malpractice claims fall within the province of the physicians, surgeons, pharmacists, nurses and other medical practitioners, the outlines for investigation will stress medical malpractice. In many instances, an investigator who is concerned with a professional liability claim involving some other profession can substitute basic principles of investigation without too much orientation.

It must always be remembered that in most professional liability policies, one of the conditions of the policy requires the permission of the insured before any settlement may be negotiated. It is, therefore, essential that the investigator or attorney representing an insurance company establish a close liaison with the insured and keep him or her advised of all discussions and negotiations with the claimant or the attorney.

The claimsperson must be wary of the information obtained from the insured because of personal involvement, and must, accordingly, check information given by the insured wherever possible. It is not unknown for a doctor to have tampered with his own, or even hospital, records.

In medical malpractice, an excellent tool for obtaining information on the background, education, specialties and other useful information is the American Medical Association Directory. Another source for obtaining information are local state and national medical associations, societies and committees.

Generally speaking, the following lists will help in obtaining the necessary basic information.

A. **Coverage Information**
   1. Make sure that the incident is within the terms covered by the policy.
   2. Check for possible delayed reporting.
   3. Check to see if the previous carrier for the insured might be involved in overlapping coverage.
   4. Check to see if the insured carries excess or umbrella coverage that might apply.
   5. If applicable, check any coverage that might apply to co-defendants or previous physicians.

6. Consider the necessity for excess ad damnum and/or reservation of rights letters, if applicable. (See applicable sections of *Successful Handling of Casualty Claims* by Pat Magarick.)

B. **Insured's Investigation**
   1. Obtain the complete name, address and age of the individual, association, partnership, hospital, clinic or other entity that might be involved. If the insured is a corporation, determine the state of incorporation. If a trade name, trust or other entity, obtain full details.
   2. *If an individual,* check his or her qualifications and background:
      a. Obtain the name of the professional schools, colleges or universities attended and indicate their ratings. Determine the year of graduation and whether the insured graduated with honors or with difficulty.
      b. Find out when and where the insured served his or her internship, residency and other apprenticeship.
      c. Find out if the insured has a license to practice, and, if so, in what states. Determine when and where the licenses were obtained.
      d. Determine what medical or honorary societies the insured belongs to and what his or her hospital connections are. If the profession involved is other than medical, make appropriate similar investigation.
      e. Determine what field of medicine, dentistry or law the insured specializes in, his or her qualifications, and how rated by peers. Determine how long the insured has practiced in his or her specialty, and where. Determine the extent of the practice and the type of clientele.
      f. By general inquiry among laymen and pro-

fessionals, determine the reputation of the insured both as a person and as a professional. Find out if the insured has written any professional papers, articles or books that have been accepted as authoritative.

    g. Find out if the insured was involved in any previous incident of possible malpractice, license suspension or termination of hospital affiliation. Find out if he or she was ever brought before a grievance committee or threatened with disciplinary action. Get details.

    h. Find out if the insured has had any experience as an expert testifying at trial. Get details.

    i. Find out if the insured is a teacher or professor at a recognized professional school and for how long.

3. Find out if any previous claims or suits have been filed against the insured and, if so, what disposition was made of them. Get details.
4. If necessary, obtain written permission to settle the claim or suit.
5. *Develop the factual details* from the insured:

    a. Obtain the date, time and place of the incident or incidents. Determine that coverage is in order and that the statute of limitations has not run out.

    b. Determine when the insured first learned that a claim was being made.

    c. Find out if drugs or alcohol were involved in in any way.

    d. Determine the exact nature of the act or omission complained of.

    e. Find out if anyone else was involved, such as associates, assistants, nurses, attendants, etc. If so:

(1) Obtain names and addresses and interview all such parties for complete details.
(2) Determine if they are covered under the insured's policy.
(3) Find out if they carry insurance of their own and, if so, see that they are put on notice.
(4) Obtain their qualifications and background.

  f. Determine if medication was involved and, if so:
(1) Get copies of any orders, notes, prescriptions, pharmacy records or any other records concerning the medication.
(2) Find out if the doctor's directions were specifically followed.
(3) Determine if there was anything wrong with the medication or if the wrong medication was prescribed. Have analysis made if warranted. Check with pharmacist.

  g. Find out if equipment failure of any kind was involved. If so, review the checklists suggested for the investigation of "General Liability" claims. The same applies if any defect in the floor, or the furniture, including the bed, was involved.

  h. Determine if the insured made any promise of a cure or other definite results either directly or indirectly. Get complete details.

6. Determine if the insured had other insurance that might provide coverage, as indicated under the section "Coverage," and see that such insurer is notified immediately.

7. *Obtain the insured's complete medical* or other records concerning the incident, including:
    a. Name, address, age, employment, marital and other pertinent information concerning the claimant.
    b. History of the accident.
    c. Previous medical history, if pertinent.
    d. Diagnosis and prognosis before and after the incident.
    e. Treatment rendered before and after the incident.
    f. Exact list of all visits to home or office.
    g. Report on all consultations with names of consulting physicians.
    h. Check insured's records carefully to see if any alterations were made and to see if pertinent records may be missing. If so, get detailed explanation.
8. Determine the amount of the insured's bill and find out if there was any controversy concerning it or any other matter. Find out if there was any ill-feeling between the doctor and the patient and, if so, get the details.
9. Check Index Bureau records carefully.

C. **Claimant's Investigation**

1. *Background and introductory matter:*
    a. Name and all previous names or aliases under which the claimant was ever known, including the maiden name of married females.
    b. Present address and, if warranted, any previous addresses.
    c. Age, general appearance and impression made by the claimant. Include any available information concerning the claimant's honesty, reputation, intelligence, education and other

factors that might bear on his or her impression as a witness.
    d. Possible criminal record, if it might be an indication, where possible fraud is involved.
2. *Marital status and dependency if pertinent:*
    a. Name, age and dependency status of wife, children and any other dependents.
    b. Marital status including details of previous marriages or widowhood. If necessary, obtain copies of records of all previous marriages, separations, divorces, children by former marriages and other pertinent births and deaths.
3. *Employment history:*
    a. Names and addresses of all present employers.
    b. Names and addresses of previous employers, where pertinent. This could be a source of information concerning the claimant's background.
    c. Time employed by each employer.
    d. Exact nature and duties of employment.
    e. Salaries received, including regular salary, commissions, overtime, tips, board and lodging, and any other remuneration of any kind.
    f. Time and exact earnings lost as a result of the incident.
4. *Educational background* where pertinent:
    a. Name and address of present school being attended.
    b. Names and addresses of previous schools, if applicable, to obtain background information.
    c. Obtain years in attendance and grades.
    d. Exact time lost from school as a result of the incident.

e. Review checklists on the investigation of claims involving minors.
5. Obtain details concerning claimant's economic status including pensions, insurance or welfare help where pertinent. Review checklists included in "Automobile Investigations" on this subject if necessary.
6. *Develop the factual details* from the claimant:
    a. Determine who referred the claimant to the insured, or how the insured came to the attention of the claimant.
    b. Obtain the exact date, time and place of the incident.
    c. If surgery was performed, determine if proper consent was obtained and from whom. If not, find out why. If consent was obtained, get a copy if in writing. If it is alleged that consent was oral, check for any witnesses.
    d. Find out if the claimant followed the doctor's instructions and, if not, why.
    e. Find out when the claimant first complained, and obtain a complete list of the complaints.
    f. Determine what subsequent treatment was received, if any. Get reports from all doctors and hospitals if possible.
7. Determine if the claimant made any settlement or received any compensation as a result of an injury which necessitated the medical treatment complained of. Obtain full details including copies of releases, drafts and court orders.
8. Try to determine if the claimant ever made a previous malpractice or other injury claim and check with the Index Bureau.

D. **Medical Investigation**
1. If possible, obtain medical reports from all attending doctors:

a. Personal and descriptive data concerning the claimant, as previously outlined.
b. History of the original accident or disability.
c. All details concerning the alleged malpractice.
d. Previous medical history, if applicable.
e. Details of the initial examination, including X-ray, laboratory or other tests and all consultant's reports.
f. Treatment rendered, including type and dates.
g. Original and subsequent diagnosis and prognosis.
h. Conclusions and recommendations.
i. Doctor's bills including estimate for future treatment.
j. Subsequent doctors and surgeons, their detailed reports and their relationship with the insured and with the patient.

2. *Hospital records:*

   It is especially important in malpractice claims to obtain a complete transcript of the hospital records. These usually contain:

   a. Admission information.
   b. Examinations by interns and doctors.
   c. X-ray, laboratory, pathologist's and other reports of a similar nature.
   d. Nurses' notes.
   e. Diagnosis and prognosis.
   f. Exit information (circumstances surrounding the patient's discharge from, or leaving, the hospital).
   g. Check carefully to make sure that no records have been removed, erased, or otherwise tampered with.

3. Arrange for physical examination where necessary, as outlined in the investigation of "Automobile Liability" claims.

4. Obtain the opinion of local practitioners to determine if the treatment rendered or the services performed were in accordance with ordinary good practice in that locality.
5. Enlist the aid of any medical societies or associations to which the insured belongs.

E. **Witnesses' Investigation**

Witnesses in malpractice claims will, for the most part, be confined to those who may have assisted in an operation, such as doctors, nurses and other attendants or observers. All such witnesses should be interviewed, where warranted, along the lines previously suggested, including:

1. Identification and background material.
2. Reason for witness' presence.
3. Qualifications of the witness, if pertinent.
4. Factual details.
5. Medical details if available.

F. **Special Damages**

1. *Lost time and earnings.* Remember that the claimant is entitled to take-home pay only:

   a. *Where the employee is salaried:*

   (1) Check the employer's payroll records.
   (2) Determine the amount of regular salary, overtime, commissions at that time of the year, gratuities and any other benefits.
   (3) Determine if the injury has necessitated a change of job or employment and, if so, determine the salary differential.
   (4) Determine if the injury has necessitated the claimant's going on part-time work and, if so, the salary differential.

   b. *Where the claimant is self-employed:*

   (1) If possible, check income tax returns,

including federal, state and local, and other tax returns.
      (2) If possible, check social security records.
      (3) Check licensing requirements.
      (4) If possible, check private books and accounts.
2. *Medical expenses.* Where possible, check all bills for authenticity and reasonableness:
    a. Obtain attending doctor's, specialist's and dentist's bills before and after the incident.
    b. Obtain registered and practical nurse's fees before and after the incident.
    c. Determine the amount of hospital or clinic bills.
    d. Obtain the cost of any ambulance charges.
    e. Determine the amount of any laboratory, X-ray or similar charges not listed on the hospital bill.
    f. Obtain the amount of any bills for prosthetic appliances or surgical therapy apparatus.
    g. Determine the amount of bills for medicines, drugs, etc.
    h. Determine if there were any travel expenses for medical reasons.
3. *Fatal claims:*
    a. Obtain funeral costs.
    b. Obtain cost of burial plot, crypt, or tombstone.
4. *Determine the expected future monetary losses:*
    a. Lost salary and earning capacity.
    b. Medical expenses.
    c. Household or other help needed as a direct result of the malpractice.
5. *Determine the extent of pain and suffering* as far as possible.

6. *Investigate any claim for loss of services or support.*
7. *Determine if there was any cosmetic or other disfigurement, or loss of a limb* or other vital part of the body.

CHAPTER VIII

Some Specific Professional Liability Investigations

Once again, it must be pointed out that no list can be complete in outlining all specific investigations that might be encountered by the claimsperson or attorney handling malpractice cases.

Acordingly, the following lists are representative only and include those that the investigator will most often encounter.

It is, therefore, necessary for the investigator to review the previous section concerning the general investigation of professional liability claims before referring to the specific category involved.

A. **Accountant's Liability**

1. Determine if the claimant is a regular client of the insured.
2. Find out how long the insured has been reviewing the claimant's books and records and how often.
3. Learn if the insured had any reason to suspect that anything was wrong.
4. Find out if the insured should have suspected that something was wrong if he or she had used reasonable diligence.
5. Determine the nature of the contract between the insured and his or her client and obtain a copy.
6. Determine the exact nature of any certification which the insured may have made.
7. Find out if the claimant was a party to any contract and obtain details.
8. Determine if the claimant had any proper reason to rely on the insured's certification.
9. Learn if the insured knew that the claimant was

relying on his certification and what action, if any, he took.
10. Find out if the claimant's negligence contributed to the defalcation.
11. If embezzlement was involved, find out if the insured's client had insurance covering the loss:
    a. Determine if there is a bond or other policy.
    b. Learn the name of all carriers that may be involved.
    c. Find out if subrogation rights are involved and get details.
12. Make sure that investigation is made to determine whether the loss arose as a result of any malicious or dishonest act or as a result of libel or slander.
13. Determine whether the insured has had any previous claims or losses as a result of alleged professional error and obtain complete details.

B. **Agent's (Insurance) Errors and Omissions**
   1. *Determine if the insured is an agent of the company.*
   2. *Find out if any representations outside the policy provisions were made by the agent or his or her employee:*
       a. Find out if any reliance was placed on such representation.
       b. Determine if the agent had the authority (written or oral) to make such representation and check with the company.
       c. Determine if the agent had ostensible authority and what actions or failure to act constituted such ostensible authority.
       d. Determine if the agent's representation contradicted any policy provision.
   3. *If failure to write a policy is involved:*
       a. Find out if there is definite proof that the policy was ordered.

SPECIFIC PROFESSIONAL LIABILITY

    b. Determine if a binder was issued.
    c. Find out if there is any record of the request for coverage in the agent's office.
    d. Determine, if possible, whether the failure could have been caused by an employee now unwilling or afraid to admit the error.
    e. Determine if there would be any valid reason for failing to write the policy allegedly requested.
    f. Determine if the insurance company would have accepted that type of risk.
    g. Determine if there was any undue delay in trying to obtain coverage.
    h. If the agent tried to obtain coverage and failed, find out if he notified his client in proper time.

4. *Where cancellation is involved:*

    a. Find out if the agent notified the client in proper time, how, and in what manner.
    b. Find out if proper return premium was made, how, and in what manner.
    c. Find out if notification and return premium conformed with legal requirements.
    d. Determine if the client requested reconsideration.
    e. Find out if there was a delay in replying to any request for reconsideration.
    f. Determine if the agent requested reconsideration from the company.
    g. Determine if the company had reconsidered previously on a similar risk and whether that was common practice.

5. *Determine if the policy or binder was issued effective as of the date requested:*

    a. Find out if there is a possibility that the client is trying to get coverage for an accident which occurred before requesting the policy.

        b. Determine if any request was made to pre-date the policy.
        c. Find out if the agent has a date stamped record of the request for coverage.
        d. Find out if the order was placed at the beginning of a week or over a weekend.
6. Determine if the coverage was written for the exact limits requested. Try to obtain proof.
7. Find out if the agent wrote the policy with the company specifically designated by the client, and, if not, why.
8. Determine whether the policy was written with a company not authorized to do business in that state.
9. Determine if the coverage requested was proper and legal.
10. Make sure that the loss did not result from the dishonesty, or criminal or malicious act, of the agent or his client.
11. Make sure that the action against the insured is not the result of libel, slander, assault or battery unless specific coverage for those items is alleged. Get details.
12. Determine whether the action involved tangible property damage or injury to the claimant.
13. Make sure that consideration is given to the deductible feature of the policy before settlement is made.

C. **Architects and Engineers**

Architects and engineers are held to the same degree of accountability as are medical practitioners. They ordinarily do not warrant that their plans are foolproof nor do they warrant the durability of the edifice or structure involved.

Some suggested avenues of investigation concerning this field are as follows:

SPECIFIC PROFESSIONAL LIABILITY

1. Determine who drew the plans. Get his or her background, including education, experience, professional associations and service with the present firm.
2. Obtain complete details concerning the contract, with names and correct legal entities of all parties. Where necessary, obtain copies of contracts.
3. Determine the correct legal name or entity for any contractors or subcontractors, including the names of their insurance carriers. If applicable, put them on notice.
4. Find out the exact nature of the supervision that was exercised by the architect or engineer and obtain complete details. Determine if there was any failure to supervise or whether there was any negligence in supervision.
5. Check the alleged negligence thoroughly and make a determination as to whether the alleged defect was hidden or open. Find out if it involved allegedly defective materials, improper materials, or allegedly improper construction or plans.
6. Determine whether the construction involved any deviation from the plans or blueprints and, if so, obtain all details. Obtain signed statements from the workmen involved.
7. Obtain copies of all progress reports and check these against the original plans and specifications.
8. Determine whether proper permits were obtained and if the work was in compliance with all local and state building codes and ordinances.
9. Find out whether there were any Hold Harmless Agreements between any of the parties and, if so, obtain copies. Determine whether there was any contractual insurance and get the names of all insurance carriers, and put on notice where pertinent.
10. Determine whether the structure was formally accepted by the owner and obtain proof of such acceptance including the exact date of acceptance.

D. **Druggist's Liability**
   1. Watch for possible overlapping coverages:
      a. Determine if the insured has another policy that may be involved.
      b. Find out if the insured's policy covers general liability features as well as professional liability.
   2. Determine if the product was asked for by name.
   3. Find out if the product was a patent medicine. If warranted, notify the manufacturer and ask him to take over. Proceed with the investigation as outlined under the "Products Liability" section.
   4. If the product was not requested by name, determine the exact language of the purchase.
   5. Learn if the seller recommended the product.
   6. Determine if the seller prescribed the medication or the treatment.
   7. Find out if the seller actually treated the claimant.
   8. Determine if the sale required a prescription.
   9. Find out if a prescription was presented.
   10. Determine if proper records of the prescription were kept, and, if warranted, get a copy.
   11. Determine if it was a new prescription or a refill. Find out if a refill was permitted under state law. Obtain the dates of the original prescription and all refills.
   12. Determine if the medicine was compounded exactly as called for in the prescription.
   13. *Learn if there was an error in the prescription:*
      a. Find out how and when the error was discovered.
      b. Find out if the druggist should have caught the error.
      c. If the prescription was not intelligible or if it was questionable for any other reason, determine if the druggist checked with the doctor

SPECIFIC PROFESSIONAL LIABILITY

    concerning the contents, quantities or directions.

    d. Find out if the doctor has been notified of the error and, if so, whether he notified his insurance carrier.

14. *Determine if the prescription was compounded or dispensed by a properly qualified person:*
    a. Determine what school he or she graduated from.
    b. Find out when the pharmacist graduated and for how long he or she has been practicing.
    c. Determine when he or she passed the state board examinations.
    d. Find out if the prescription was filled by or with the knowledge and consent of the insured.
    e. Determine if the person who dispensed the prescription ever had any previous trouble of a similar nature.

15. Determine if all local, state and federal laws were properly observed in filling and dispensing the prescription.

16. If a narcotic or poison was involved, determine if it was properly labeled, registered and dispensed. Make sure that a proper prescription was given and obtain a copy.

17. *Determine the exact ingredients that the prescription called for* and check with an outside specialist to see if it was proper. Have analysis made if warranted.
    a. Determine if it could have been harmful in any way, such as side effects. If pertinent, check to determine if proper tests or inquiries were made concerning allergies and side effects by the doctor.
    b. Determine if the prescription could have harmed the claimant if used properly. Find out if improper use was involved.

E. **Hospital Malpractice**
1. Determine if the insured is an individual doctor-owner, group, municipal or other entity. If the insured is a private hospital, owned by one or more doctors, check the coverage carefully to see if coverage is provided for the personal liability of the doctors in addition to any hospital involvement.
2. Check to see if the hospital or nursing home is properly licensed and get a copy of the last municipal or state and/or federal inspection report, if any.
3. Find out if the claimant was a patient.
4. Determine whether the act of commission or omission was committed by an employee of the hospital, such as an orderly, student nurse, practical nurse, attendant, porter, etc.
5. Determine if reasonable care was used in the employing of personnel. Check the previous record of the employee within and outside of the hospital, and on previous jobs. Any insurance?
6. *If the alleged illness might have involved medication:*
    a. Find out who ordered the medication or made the prescription.
    b. Determine the exact nature of the medication, drug or prescription and get copies of all written orders and instructions, including a copy of the prescription, if any.
    c. Learn who filled the prescription or dispensed the medication and determine if all was proper and in order.
    d. Check to determine if there might have been something wrong with the ingredients in the medication or prescription, by analysis if warranted.
    e. Find out the purpose of the medication or prescription and check with competent experts to see if it was proper.

SPECIFIC PROFESSIONAL LIABILITY

7. Determine whether a patient caused the injury and get details.
8. Determine whether the injury arose out of the operation of the hospital.
9. Determine if the act complained of was committed by an independent contractor such as an intern, doctor, nurse, etc., If so, and not covered by the hospital policy, put such individual and his or her carrier on notice. If covered, see if the individual has insurance which may be co-insurance or excess, if warranted.
10. Determine if the claimant was a paying or a charity patient.
11. Determine if a criminal act was involved and get police records and make interviews as called for.
12. If the claimant was an employee, find out whether he or she was in the course of employment at the time of the incident.
13. Determine whether liability arose out of contract.
14. Determine whether liability arose out of ownership, maintenance, use, loading or unloading of a motor vehicle or other conveyance.
15. *Determine if sedatives were administered:*
    a. Determine their exact nature.
    b. Find out when and by whom administered, and in what quantities.
    c. Learn if anyone else was in attendance.
    d. Determine what precautions were taken and if they were considered reasonably adequate.
16. *Determine if restraints were needed and properly provided* on bed or wheelchair:
    a. If not provided, find out why.
    b. Find out if it is customary to put up restraints in similar circumstances.
    c. Find out if the doctor instructed restraints to be put up, and, if so, whether the doctor's

instructions were verbal or in writing. If in writing, get copies.
17. Determine what general instructions were given by the doctor. Find out if they were followed and, if not, why.
18. Determine if there was bad feeling by the claimant against the hospital, which might have been provoked by the amount of the bill, or for other cause and get details.

F. **Lawyer's Professional Liability**

As with other professionals, an attorney is not an insurer of results. The fact that an attorney may lose a case will not ordinarily involve him or her in an action for malpractice.

An attorney can be held liable only for negligent acts or for failure to act in the handling of a case, aside from deliberate acts of misconduct which would not be covered under the policy.

1. *Check the lawyer's background:*
    a. Learn what school the insured attended, when and for how long. Find out what grades and honors he or she received.
    b. Find out what degrees the insured received.
    c. Determine when the insured was admitted to the bar and in what states and jurisdictions.
    d. Find out how long the insured has been practicing, and determine the nature of his or her practice.
    e. Learn the reputation of the insured for competency and honesty in the community.
    f. Determine whether the insured has ever been involved in a previous malpractice case and, if so, get details.
    g. Find out if the insured was ever suspended from practice and, if so, check this out thoroughly.

SPECIFIC PROFESSIONAL LIABILITY 221

  h. Find out if the insured was ever brought up on charges and whether reprimanded. Get all particulars.
2. *Determine the terms of the contract of hire:*
  a. Find out if the insured obtained a written retainer and, if so, obtain a copy.
  b. Find out if the case was accepted on a contingent fee basis and get the details.
3. Determine how the insured got the case and how the client was referred to him or her.
4. *Determine if the insured had the authority to act as he did:*
  a. Find out if specific instructions were issued to the insured by the client.
  b. If such instructions were issued, find out if they were practical, feasible and legal.
  c. Determine if such instructions were carried out and, if not, why.
5. Determine if the employment of the insured was terminated before the issue was brought to a conclusion. Obtain full details and copies of all letters and other pertinent papers.
6. Find out if the insured represented any interests adverse to those of his client.
7. Determine if there was any co-mingling of funds.
8. Determine if the insured acted maliciously or illegally.
9. Determine whether any acts of the insured were fraudulent or misleading.
10. If libel or slander is involved, find out if it was intentional.
11. *Learn if the insured was negligent in any way:*
  a. Determine if the insured defaulted in pleadings, appeal, or in notice to the client.
  b. Determine whether the insured abandoned

any suit or committed any other act of omission that could be considered as abandonment.
   c. Determine if the insured committed error in pleading, practice or advice given to the client.
   d. Determine if the insured committed an error in judgment.
   e. Determine if the insured failed to plead or file notice on time or whether he or she permitted the statute of limitations to run on an otherwise good cause of action. If so, determine if the action was deliberate or simply careless.

12. *If an associate was involved:*
    a. Find out if he or she was a partner.
    b. Learn if the associate was a member of the insured's firm and properly covered under the policy.
    c. Determine who assigned the case to the associate.
    d. Learn if this was done against the insured's express wishes or instructions. Find out if the insured should have been consulted even if no express instructions were given.

13. Determine if the insured was involved in any previous claims or suits based on malpractice and, if so, get the complete details including their disposition.

14. If it is possible that the malpractice action was encouraged or instigated by the insured to enable recovery on an otherwise worthless action, an intensive investigation should be made of the original action in all aspects.

G. **Nurse's Professional Liability**

1. *Determine the qualifications of the insured:*
   a. Determine the school or college attended and for how long. Learn what grades or honors were attained.

b. Determine the year of graduation.
   c. Find out if the insured passed the state board examination in the state where the incident occurred. Determine when such board examinations were passed.
   d. Find out how long the insured had been practicing and where.
2. Determine if the insured was a private nurse or on the hospital staff.
3. Find out who engaged the insured's services and under what conditions.
4. *Find out if the insured was under specific instructions from a doctor:*
   a. Find out if the insured followed such instructions properly.
   b. Find out if the instructions were in writing and, if so, obtain a copy. If not, try to get the exact wording of the instructions.
   c. Obtain a copy of all pertinent hospital notes and records.
   d. Determine the name of the doctor's insurance carrier and put both on notice if applicable.
   e. Determine if any instructions given by a doctor were obviously erroneous. If so, find out if the insured protested or called the error to the attention of the doctor. Determine how this was done and get all details.
   f. Determine whether the consequences of erroneous instructions were reasonably foreseeable.
5. Determine if the act complained of could have been malicious or criminal.
6. Determine if the insured acted illegally and, if so, get details.
7. Check the insured's previous record concerning

complaints or malpractice claims or suits and get details.

H. **Surgeons**

In addition to the investigation outlined under the general heading of "Professional Liability," the following are some special checklists that apply particularly to surgeons:

1. Determine how the surgeon came to the attention of the claimant.
2. *Check the qualifications of the surgeon:*
    a. Find out what undergraduate and graduate schools were attended and get a record of any honors bestowed. Determine where he or she served residency, under whom the surgeon studied and for how long.
    b. Determine when the surgeon became qualified and by whom.
    c. Find out how long the surgeon has been practicing his or her specialty and where.
    d. Determine the reputation of the surgeon from peers and find out if he or she was involved in any previous complaint, claim or suit involving alleged malpractice. If so, get complete details.
    e. Find out what medical associations and societies the surgeon belongs to and if he or she ever held office in such societies.
    f. Find out if the surgeon was ever brought up on disciplinary charges or was ever censured.
    g. Find out what teaching affiliations the surgeon had, with what colleges, universities or medical schools, and for how long.
    h. Find out what hospital affiliations he or she had, where, and for how long.
3. Determine whether the insured obtained proper written consent for the surgery and, if not, why.

Find out if verbal consent was obtained and if there were witnesses to such consent. Determine from whom such consent was obtained.
4. Determine what preliminary examinations were made and by whom. Find out if there was any consultation and, if so, interview the consultant.
5. Determine if proper tests were made to determine allergic or other possible reactions to drugs or anaesthesia.
6. Determine if proper preparation was made and by whom. If pertinent, check this out.
7. *Obtain all of the details concerning the operation:*
   a. Determine where and when the operation was performed.
   b. Determine if the surgeon who was engaged to perform the operation actually did so. If not, find out who did and why. If not performed by him, determine if the insured assisted or was even present at the operation.
   c. Get the names and positions of all who were present at the operation, includng assisting doctors, the anaesthesiologist, nurses, attendants and students. Interview them if warranted.
   d. Determine the purpose of the operation and whether it was or should have been routine. Find out if any new or untested techniques were used or if there was any experimentation. If so, find out if the circumstances required unusual action or treatment. Check this out thoroughly.
   e. Determine whether the surgeon encountered any unusual problems concerning instruments or procedures. Find out if all orders by the surgeon were followed and if the surgeon gave proper orders.
   f. Obtain all available medical records from the

doctors and the hospital and determine whether any are missing or were tampered with.

8. Check out on the post-operative examinations and care. Find out what visits were made at the hospital and when and where the insured saw his patient after he or she left the hospital. Determine if there were any complaints at any time and get their exact nature Find out what if any action was taken concerning any complaints.
9. Find out if the claimant went to another doctor, when, and under what conditions. Get the name of any subsequent doctors and interview for complete details.
10. Determine the final results, including prognosis and all special damages as previously outlined.

I. **Teachers**

The role of the teacher has changed considerably in recent years. Parental guidance has been considerably relaxed and is sometimes completely lacking because both parents are working and away from home. At the same time, corporal punishment in the schools has gone out of style. Violence has, in some large city schools, become almost a commonplace in recent years.

The problems of the teacher are complex and the investigator in this kind of malpractice action or claim is required to use a great deal of diplomacy. Here are a few suggestions for the investigation of such cases:

1. *If corporal punishment was involved:*
    a. Determine if it was sanctioned by state and local law.
    b. Determine if it was sanctioned by the Board of Education and the school where the incident occurred.

SPECIFIC PROFESSIONAL LIABILITY 227

- c. Determine the incidents leading up to the action and get corroboration or denial from students or others who witnessed the incident.
- d. Determine the exact nature of the punishment and whether or not it was excessive.
- e. Determine if any injury resulted and make the usual investigation to determine the nature and extent of the alleged injury. Check this out as previously outlined.
- f. Check the school records and the records of any other schools attended by the student and learn what previous problems have been encountered with this student.
- g. Obtain the grades and any other pertinent information from all school records.
- h. Check the past records concerning the teacher at all schools where he or she taught. Find out if the insured was involved in previous incidents of a similar nature.
- i. Find out if the teacher was ever cautioned or disciplined.

2. *If sports were involved:*
   - a. Where the incident arose out of spectator involvement, review the checklists under that heading in the investigation of "General Liability" claims.
   - b. Where the incident arose out of participation in sports:
     - (1) Describe the incident in detail.
     - (2) Determine if the participation was voluntary or required.
     - (3) Find out if parental permission was required and obtained for participation.
     - (4) Find out if the incident resulted from lack of, improper or insufficient supervision.

(5) Determine if supervision was required by law, custom or plain common sense and get details.
(6) If pertinent, find out if the equipment was adequate and in good condition.
(7) Find out if special equipment was required and available, such as gym mats, nets, knee or head guards, etc.
(8) If the injury resulted from defective equipment, make sure that the seller and manufacturer and their insurers are put on notice.

3. *If violence was involved:*
   a. Determine if the actions or attitude of the teacher might have provoked the incident.
   b. Get all of the facts leading up to and including the incident and interview witnesses where necessary.
   c. Learn if the teacher or principal acted in self-defense.
   d. Determine whether the defense was excessive.
   e. Find out whether any weapons were involved and describe in detail.
   f. Find out if drugs or alcohol were involved and check this out.
   g. Obtain the student's records giving past history of undisciplined behavior, past incidents involving violence, grades and other important information.
   h. Check juvenile delinquency records if available, or criminal records with the police if applicable.
   i. Check the past history of the teacher concerning problems of a similar nature.

CHAPTER IX

Workmen's Compensation Investigation

Ordinarily, the run-of-the-mill compensation claim does not require detailed investigation, nor does the expense involved warrant it. The average claim, involving little or no lost time, can and should be handled by mail or telephone. If, however, there is any question about compensability, or if fraud is suspected, the investigation should be complete, detailed and thorough. This is particularly true if there is any possibility of subrogation.

An accident involving vehicles, products, machinery or subcontractors may have such subrogation possibilities. Every compensation investigation must be conducted with an eye to these possibilities.

If a claimant is determined to accept compensation, no coercion should ever be used to persuade the injured to seek remedy against a third party. It is, however, the duty of an adjustor to explain to the claimant the full extent of his rights and remedies so that he or she may make an intelligent decision.

The third party must be placed on notice wherever subrogation rights are possible and the third-party insurer must also be brought into the picture as promptly as possible.

It is most important to inform the injured concerning the rights of the compensation insurer concerning any settlement made by him or her with the third-party insurer.

The following checklists will suggest avenues of investigation.

A. **Coverage Investigation**

    1. *Jurisdiction or Extraterritoriality:*

a. Determine the insured's principal place of business or home office.
b. Determine where the claimant is principally engaged in doing most of his or her work.
c. Find out where the claimant was hired and by whom.
d. Find out how the claimant was hired and whether there was an oral agreement or a written contract of hire. If written, obtain a copy.
e. Find out in what state the accident occurred.
f. Find out in what state the claimant maintains his or her principal residence.
g. Determine the nature of the claimant's regular duties.
h. Determine the exact nature of the claimant's work at the time of the accident.
i. Find out if coverage is provided for all of the states that might be involved in the incident.

2. *Occupational disease.* Our concern at this point is merely with coverage under the policy:

   a. Determine if an Occupational Disease Law has been enacted.
   b. If so, find out if it is part of the Workmen's Compensation Law.
   c. Determine if the employer is subject to the law.
   d. Find out if the employee is a beneficiary under the law.
   e. Determine if the particular disease involved is covered under the law.
   f. Learn whether an Occupational Disease endorsement was attached to the policy, if such endorsement was required.
   g. File a confidential risk report, if necessary.

3. *Dual or multiple employment:*

   a. Learn the names and addresses of all employers.

WORKMEN'S COMPENSATION

    b. Find out the occupations or businesses in which the employers were engaged.
    c. Find out if the employee of the insured was working for anyone else at the time of injury. If so, put such employer and his insurer on notice.
    d. Find out if the multiple employment was known to all interested parties and determine the salary arrangements.
    e. Determine whether there was a definite separation of duties.
    f. Check with the customer to determine exactly on whose business the claimant was engaged at the time of injury.

4. *Voluntary compensation:*
    a. Determine the nature of the insured's duties.
    b. Determine if the claimant's occupation falls within the coverage of the Act.
    c. If it does not, find out if the insured and the claimant complied with the elective requirements of the Act, if such election was required.
    d. Find out if the claimant indicated a desire to come within the scope of the Act.
    e. Learn if the policy contains a proper endorsement.

5. *General:*
    a. Determine the nature and location of all operations in which the insured was engaged. Find out if they are all properly covered under the policy.
    b. If the insurance was terminated, find out if proper notice was given to the Commission, where such notice is required.
    c. Find out if proper notice of termination of insurance was given by the previous carrier, if such notice was required.

d. Check with the insurer's auditing department to determine whether a premium was paid on the claimant's salary where warranted.

B. **Factual Information**

Details of the manner in which the incident took place, and of the surrounding circumstances must, of course, be obtained from all available sources, including the insured, claimant and witnesses. Corroboration or refutation must be made by comparison, not only with various versions, but also with the physical facts. If warranted, therefore, the same ground must be repeatedly covered with each separate inteview. For this reason, the following checklist is given under this caption only, rather than repeated under information to be obtained from the insured, claimant, or other witnesses.

The facts may, of course, be as varied as the circumstances of any particular accident can be. As the need arises, the investigator should accordingly review the specific checklists previously outlined, depending upon the type of accident under investigation.

The following lists will be confined to avenues of investigation that concentrate on the compensation feature in addition to the ground already covered.

1. *Determine the exact date and time of the occurrence:*
    a. Find out if it was a regular working day.
    b. Find out if it occurred before opening time or after closing time.
    c. Find out if it occurred during overtime period.
    d. Find out if it happened during lunch or coffee break.
    e. Determine the exact working days and hours of the claimant.
2. *Determine the place of the incident:*

- a. Find out if it occurred on the premises or the area adjacent thereto.
- b. Find out if the insured was conducting an operation at that point.
- c. Find out if the claimant was where he or she was supposed to be at the time of the incident.

3. *Obtain complete details as to how the incident occurred:* (Review liability checklists that fit the specific circumstances.)
    - a. Find out if the claimant was engaged in his or her regular duties, or whether there was any deviation therefrom.
    - b. If there was deviation, find out if such deviation was authorized, by whom, and when.
    - c. Find out if the claimant violated any rules or regulations:
        - (1) Find out if the rules were oral or written.
        - (2) Find out if they were posted, and, if so, where and for how long.
        - (3) Try to determine if the claimant was aware of them.
        - (4) Find out if the rules were enforced by the employer.

4. *Determine the likelihood of self-inflicted injury:*
    - a. Determine if there was any willful misconduct.
    - b. Try to find out if there was any possible motive, such as suicide, or fear of losing job.

5. *Determine if assault was involved:*
    - a. Determine if the act was obviously intentional.
    - b. Determine what provoked the original assault.
    - c. Find out if the altercation had anything to do with the business of the employer.
    - d. Determine who was the aggressor.
    - e. Find out if there was any ill-feeling between

the claimant and the one who allegedly committed the assault.

6. *Determine if horseplay was involved:*
    a. Find out who started the horseplay.
    b. Try to find out if the claimant was the instigator or the victim of the horseplay.
    c. Find out if the employer knew of the horseplay, and whether or not he objected to it.
    d. Find out if the employer had condoned such practice in the past.
    e. Find out if the employer had expressly forbidden such practice.
    f. Find out if the employer had previously punished or penalized or discharged an employee for similar acts.

7. *Determine if intoxication or alcohol was involved:*
    a. Find out if the insured permitted drinking on the job.
    b. Determine exactly how much the claimant had to drink.
    c. Find out if the claimant knew of any prohibition against drinking.
    d. Determine if anyone was with the claimant at the time and interview.
    e. Find out if the claimant appeared to be intoxicated.
    f. Find out if any tests were made to determine intoxication.

8. *Determine whether drugs of any kind were involved:*
    a. Find out if the claimant was under any kind of medication that might have affected his or her alertness.
    b. Try to find out if the claimant was addicted to drugs or pills and was under the influence at the time.

WORKMEN'S COMPENSATION 235

  c. Find out if the claimant had taken a heavy dose of pain reliever, such as aspirin, or similar medication.

 9. *Determine if illegal operations on the part of the insured were involved:*

  a. Determine if minors were employed without proper certificate.
  b. Find out if illegal immigrants were involved.
  c. Determine if other department of labor, health, or building regulations were disregarded or violated.
  d. Determine if required safety devices were present and in good operating condition. If present, find out if they were used properly. If disregarded, try to find out if this was done with the active or passive knowledge and agreement of the insured.
  e. Find out if the insured was engaged in gambling or other illegal activities (where gambling is illegal).
  f. Submit confidential report to the underwriters if pertinent.

 10. *Determine if the incidents resulted from Acts of God:*

  a. Find out if the incident was a result of lightning, tornado, windstorm, hailstorm, etc.
  b. Determine if the injury was a direct result of a force of nature.
  c. Determine if there was an intervening cause.

C. **Insured's Investigation**

 1. *Background information:*

  a. Find out if the insured is an individual, corporation, partnership, trustee or other legal entity.
  b. Determine if the insured is an owner, general contractor, or subcontractor.

c. If the insured is an owner or general contractor, find out if the subcontractor carries compensation insurance.
d. Determine the exact nature of the insured's business or operations.
e. Find out if the claimant works inside the plant, outside, or at home. If home and if necessary, find out if a license to do so has been obtained.
f. Check the days and hours of employment carefully.
g. Determine if the incident occurred within the regular hours of employment or overtime.
h. Find out if other accidents of a similar nature occurred previously and get details. Make up confidential risk report to the underwriters if pertinent.
i. Find out if the claimant is related to any member of the employer's firm, and, if so, whether collusion or conspiracy might be involved.
j. If warranted, check the background information and previous employment record of the claimant.
k. Find out how long the claimant has been employed by the insured and how long in the position occupied at the time of the incident.
l. Find out the accident record of the insured with the present, and, if warranted, past employers.
m. Make a thorough Index Bureau check.
n. Find out if the insured intends to pay the claimant's salary, or any part of it, during disability. If so, determine whether the employer expects reimbursement from the insurer. Check payroll records.

2. *Check the details of the incident* and obtain signed statements where necessary:

WORKMEN'S COMPENSATION

   a. Find out if the insured, another member of the firm, or an executive personally witnessed the accident.
   b. Find out if the insured or someone in an executive capacity came on the scene shortly after it happened.
   c. Find out when the insured first learned of the incident or disability, and how.
   d. Determine if the insured initiated any investigation of his own and if so, with what results.
3. *Determine the type of employment* (complete checklist for a determination of "independent contractor" relationship is given separately):
   a. *Find out if the claimant was on part-time work:*
      (1) Find out if he or she had definite hours of employment.
      (2) Find out if the claimant had a definite place of employment.
   b. *Determine if the claimant was a casual employee:*
      (1) Find out if he or she was regularly employed at definite intervals.
      (2) Find out if the claimant was periodically employed at indefinite periods.
      (3) Obtain verification from the records of the claimant's employment during the past year or more if necessary.
   c. *Determine if the claimant was a special employee:*
      (1) Find out if the claimant was hired for this particular job only.
      (2) Find out if the job required special skills.
      (3) Review the requirements concerning salary, tax deductions, control, etc.

d. *Determine if the claimant was a volunteer:*
   (1) Find out if the claimant offered his or her services without request.
   (2) Find out if the claimant asked for and or received any compensation.
   (3) Find out if there was any understanding concerning salary or payment of any kind.
   (4) Determine whether the claimant's services were needed at the time.

e. *Determine whether the claimant was a loaned employee:*
   (1) Determine what the understanding was between the regular and the temporary employer.
   (2) Find out who maintained control over the employee (right to hire, fire, or direct the work).
   (3) Find out who paid the claimant's salary.
   (4) Find out whether there was any transfer of employment made on the books of either employer.
   (5) Determine the duration of such employment and find out how long it was supposed to last.

f. *Determine if the claimant was a partner or corporate officer:*
   (1) Determine whether the claimant received a separate salary in addition to a share in the profits.
   (2) Find out if the claimant had any regular duties as an employee and check this out carefully on books and records.

g. *Determine if the claimant was an employee of a subcontractor:*

WORKMEN'S COMPENSATION 239

- (1) Obtain the name and address of the subcontractor.
- (2) Find out if he was insured and, if so, in what company. See that the insurer is properly notified and requested to take over.
- (3) If there was no insurance, place the subcontractor on notice that he will be held responsible for any amount paid and request him to take over personally.

h. Determine whether the claimant was an independent contractor. (Review complete checklist given separately.)

4. *Obtain complete salary details* (directly from the insured's records):

   a. Find out if the claimant was paid by the hour, day, week, month, year or fraction thereof.
   b. Find out if the claimant was on straight salary or on piecework.
   c. If piecework, obtain the rate.
   d. Find out if the claimant worked on a commission basis:
   - (1) Find out whether it was commission only and get rates.
   - (2) Determine whether the claimant had a drawing account.
   - (3) If it was salary plus commission, get the details.

   e. Find out if the claimant received any tips or other gratuities:
   - (1) Determine if they were considered as part of the claimant's salary.
   - (2) Find out if an accounting was kept and if social security or other tax was paid or collected.

        f. Determine whether the claimant received other benefits and obtain copy of available records on such matters as bonuses, board and lodging, and transportation.
        g. Find out if the claimant received an allowance for expenses:

           (1) Automobile, either company or personally owned.
           (2) Hotel, meals, transportation and other incidentals.
           (3) Find out if the claimant received a definite sum allowance for expenses.

        h. Find out if the claimant will return to work at the same salary. If not, obtain details, including the salary expected and the reason therefore.

    5. *Forms:*

        a. Determine whether the proper forms were completed and filed on time.
        b. Explain the need for prompt, complete and proper filing to the insured.

D. **Claimant's Investigation**

    1. *Background information:*

        a. Obtain the claimant's name, address, social security number, and any previous names or addresses if pertinent.
        b. Obtain claimant's age. If the claimant is a minor, determine whether or not certificate of employment was obtained.
        c. Obtain birth records or proof of citizenship.
        d. Determine the claimant's union affiliations.
        e. Obtain history of previous accidents with this or previous employers and check with the Index Bureau.

WORKMEN'S COMPENSATION

    f. Obtain complete employment history, if necessary.

2. *Dependency.*

Those who may properly claim dependency under the various Acts are not always obvious. Occasionally, all of the dependents will not be revealed unless careful investigation is made. A former marriage may not have been properly dissolved, or children by a former marriage may be in existence but unknown to the investigator until he or she digs it out. It is therefore essential that all avenues of investigation be checked thoroughly before payments are made on a fatal claim.

In some instances, dependency for certain cases of persons is presumed under the Act. In other jurisdictions, dependency must be proven for the same individuals. In the latter case, it will be necessary to determine the exact extent of the dependency. If records of marriage, birth, death, separation, divorce and annulment are available, copies should be obtained. This kind of investigation is especially important where the claimant had a job requiring absence from home base for long periods of time, such as salesmen, oil well workers, etc. It is not unknown for some such deceased employees to have left several families, unknown to each other, but each with legitimate claims.

    a. Determine the present marital status of the claimant.
    b. Learn the name, address and age of the last wife.
    c. Obtain the names, addresses and details concerning all previous wives and women alleged to have been married to the claimant, or with whom the claimant lived as man and wife.

d. Obtain the names, addresses and ages of all children by all marriages.
e. Obtain the names and addresses of any children born out of wedlock if possible.
f. Obtain the names and addresses of any incompetent or disabled dependents and get details.
g. *If the insured lived with a woman for any protracted time out of wedlock:*
   (1) Determine if common-law marriages are recognized in the jurisdiction involved.
   (2) Find out how long they lived together and where.
   (3) Find out if they held themselves to be man and wife.
   (4) Find out if they were recognized as husband and wife in the locality where they lived.
   (5) Try to determine if they underwent any ceremony or by personal vows gave evidence of intent to be considered as husband and wife.
   (6) Try to find out if they intended to get married officially in the future.
   (7) Determine why no marriage ceremony was ever performed.
h. Obtain as much detail as possible concerning any divorce, separation or annulment.
i. Determine whether there are other dependents such as a mother, father, other close relatives, ward, adopted children, etc.:
   (1) Obtain the names, addresses and ages of all such alleged dependents.
   (2) Determine their relationship to the claimant.
   (3) Determine the exact degree of dependency.

(a) Find out if the claimant was their sole source of support.
(b) If not, find out exactly how much he did contribute, including board and lodging.
(c) Determine who else contributed to the support of the dependents and how much.

3. *General information:*
   a. Corroborate the salary and employment information obtained from the insured.
   b. Determine when the claimant first made a claim, to whom and how.
   c. Obtain the names of any witnesses from the claimant and interview them, obtaining signed statements if necessary.
   d. Determine if the claimant is related to the insured.
   e. Determine whether the claimant is a partner or officer of the insured's corporation. If so, corroborate information concerning his or her status as an employee.
   f. Determine whether the claimant expects to return to the same employer and the same job.
   g. Corroborate all factual information as previously outlined, if warranted.

4. *Medical information to be obtained from the claimant.* Much of this will be obtained from various state forms required to be filled out by the doctors:
   a. Detailed description of all objective (noticeable) evidence of injury.
   b. Detailed account of any unconsciousness and the exact duration, as closely as possible.
   c. Complete list of subjective complaints (those not accompanied by noticeable evidence of

injury), when they first developed, and their duration.
- d. Determine what medical assistance was given at the scene of the accident.
- e. Determine the name of the doctor or hospital to whom the claimant was taken after the accident.
- f. Learn the name and address of the family doctor who subsequently treated the claimant.
- g. Obtain the names of all doctors and specialists who were consulted.
- h. Obtain the dates of all visits by and to doctors, clinics, hospitals, etc.
- i. Obtain the dates of admission to and discharge from any hospitals, rest homes, etc.
- j. Obtain information concerning X-rays, scans, laboratory tests, etc.
- k. Obtain details of any operations or casts.
- l. Obtain the details of the treatment given.
- m. Determine the exact extent of the confinement to bed.
- n. Determine the length of disability from work.
- o. Obtain details of previous medical history as previously outlined, if applicable.

E. **Medical Investigation**

In the investigation of compensation claims, it is now, more than ever, important to check the background and capabilities of the attending physicians. The investigator should have a direct interest in the treatment given in order to effect the quickest recovery or rehabilitation.

1. Detailed information to be obtained from the claimant as outlined in the previous section.
2. Determine whether any pre-employment physical examinations were made and, if so, obtain copies, if pertinent.

3. Determine who engaged the doctors and who authorized the medical treatment and hospitalization.
4. Make a check on the qualifications of the attending doctors.
5. *Obtain attending doctor's reports.* In compensation cases, doctors are required to complete medical forms, which should include:
    a. Personal and descriptive data concerning the claimant:
        (1) Date, time and place of the initial examination.
        (2) Name and address of the claimant.
        (3) Claimant's age, weight, height, occupation and marital status.
    b. History of the accident. This should include as much information as can be obtained concerning the time, location and manner in which the accident occurred, as reported to the doctor by the claimant. Admittedly, in this day and age, the investigator will have to be content with as much information as he or she can get.
    c. Previous medical history, where applicable, with special emphasis on any condition which would have any bearing on the disability, or any possible effect on the manner in which the accident happened, as follows:
        (1) Family history, including inherited tendencies or weaknesses, and the history of family deaths which might have had a connection with the present or future disability of the claimant.
        (2) Names and addresses of all doctors and hospitals that were involved in previous serious ailments which might have some connection with the present disability.

(3) List of previous operations, with details including X-rays, scans, etc.
(4) Details concerning any previous protracted treatments.
(5) History of previous diseases such as asthma or heart disease, which may have been aggravated as a result of the accident.
(6) History of previous ailments or diseases which might have left after-effects such as scarlet fever, rheumatic fever, measles, mumps, etc.
(7) History of any previous diseases which might affect healing in any manner such as tuberculosis, syphilis, gonorrhea, diabetes, etc.
(8) Previous dental history, if applicable.
(9) History of all extensive previous physical examinations such as those made by life insurance companies, armed forces or induction examinations, private company employment examinations, etc.

d. Details concerning initial examination, including any X-rays, scans or laboratory tests, and consultant's or other reports.
e. Treatment given, including the type and dates of office and home visits.
f. Diagnosis. This should include a detailed account of the doctor's findings concerning injury, ailments and disability, with special emphasis on trauma.
g. Prognosis. This concerns the estimated disability and the possibility of ultimate partial or complete recovery, with emphasis on any possible partial or permanent disability.

h. Conclusions and recommendations. Here, the doctor should comment on recommendations concerning future treatment, operations, or further hospitalization that may be necessary, as well as any other details that might affect the medical picture.
i. Diagrams. Diagrams of various parts of the body are often imprinted on the opposite side of medical forms in order to enable the doctor to show scars or indicate the location of fractures, burns or other injuries.
j. Doctor's bills. The doctor should indicate the amount of his bill up to the time the report is made.

6. *Obtain hospital records.* These records usually contain:

    a. Admission information. This may include information concerning the claimant's economic status as well as personal background, police reports, an itemized list of the clothes and possessions of the claimant at the time of admission, etc. It will ordinarily include the extremely valuable history of the accident.
    b. The examination reports by attending doctors and interns, X-ray and similar reports, notes and instructions by interns and doctors, details concerning treatments, pathologist's and laboratory reports and nurses' notes.
    c. Diagnosis and prognosis of the various attending doctors and specialists, including the date and circumstances under which the patient left the hospital.

7. *Obtain physical examination,* if warranted.

Physical examination should not be ordered indiscriminately without giving the following factors serious consideration:

a. Determine the purpose of the examination. If the purpose is merely to corroborate information, the hospital records and the reputation of the claimant's doctor, together with the information obtained from him or her, may be all that is needed.
b. Determine the type of examination that is needed. Don't use a general practitioner if a specialist is called for.
c. Determine the time when the examination is to be made. If the object is to prove that the claimant is fully recovered, don't press for an examination while he still has evidence of substantial injury or disability.
d. Furnish the doctor with all of the medical information possible before he or she makes the examination. This should include attending doctor's reports, hospital records, X-ray reports, and anything else that may be pertinent to the examination depending on the severity of the injury or condition. Wherever possible and necessary, the examining physician should be permitted to personally examine X-rays previously taken.

8. Make periodic check-ups on claimant's recovery.
9. Check all medical bills against available fee schedule rates.
10. Determine at regular intervals what further medical attention may be required.
11. Make an effort to determine, as soon as possible, whether there will be any degree of permanent disability.
12. Determine, as closely as possible, when the claimant is expected to return to work. Try to observe whether the claimant wants to return as soon as possible.
13. Try to determine if the claimant will be able to carry out his or her regular duties or whether the claimant

will have to be assigned to lighter work for some period of time, or permanently.
14. In fatal cases, determine the advisability of an autopsy and obtain permission for one if possible. If an autopsy has been made, obtain a copy of the report.

F. **Physical Facts**

The physical facts will, of course, be as diverse as the type of claim under investigation, as has already been seen. Review the checklists previously outlined for the investigation of various types of liability claims.

Particular emphasis should be placed on local ordinances and state laws concerning safety measures. An effort should be made to find whether there were any definite rules or regulations governing the manner of work or affecting safety measures, and, if so, whether they were posted properly. Determine whether the employees were aware of the rules and regulations, and whether disobedience of them was tolerated by the employer.

Such details as complete description of the scene of the accident, including a comprehensive description of the machine or device involved, are, of course, elementary.

In general, investigation of the physical facts on a compensation case should parallel that on a liability claim. There is little point in repeating checklists already contained in this volume on this subject.

G. **Occupational Disease**

Investigation of Occupational Disease claims may fall within either the Workmen's Compensation or the Employers' Liability sections of the policy. If the investigation is being conducted under the Employers' Liability provisions, the investigator will have to determine whether there was any negligence on the part of the employer. If there was, the investigation must be just as comprehensive as that of any other public or general liability claim.

It is always difficult to determine the degree of exposure necessary to contract a disease. Ordinarily, disability must begin within a specified time from the date of last exposure in order to bring such claim within the Workmen's Compensation Law. It is essential to determine the length of exposure and to determine the names of any previous carriers that may have possible overlapping or concurrent coverage for the claimant's disability.

In addition to the ordinary investigation as previously outlined, it is suggested that the following details be checked when investigating Occupational Disease claims:

1. Determine the exact nature of the materials with which the claimant worked.
2. Determine the amount of material used and the duration of use.
3. If the claimant did not work directly with or on the questionable material, determine what contact he or she did have with it.
4. Determine the size and location of the room or area in which the claimant worked.
5. Find out how many people worked in the same room or area.
6. Learn the duration of the exposure. Obtain the hours per day, days per week, and so on.
7. Determine the date of last exposure.
8. Describe all safety devices:
    a. Find out if gloves or a mask was required. If they were not used, find out why.
    b. Describe all ventilation facilities such as fans, blowers, windows, exhausts, air conditioning, etc.
    c. Describe all other safety measures.
9. Determine if any safety measures were required by the Building, Health or other local or state or federal departments or authorities.
10. Determine if a chemical or dust analysis is necessary.

If such an analysis was made previously, obtain a copy of the report.
11. Obtain complete record of the claimant's previous employment.
12. Obtain detailed information concerning the employee's previous medical condition, as outlined.
13. Obtain records of previous illnesses of any employees in similar working conditions in the same plant.
14. The investigator should discuss the situation with his or her company Safety Engineering Department for additional ideas.
15. Check local or state Building and Factory Inspection Departments.
16. Determine whether a pre-employment or other physical examination was given by the employer and get copies of any available reports.
17. Find out if the claimant first indicated any manifestations of illness or disease to the employer and exactly when and to whom.
18. Obtain physical examination after your doctor has made a complete review of the medical and X-ray reports.

H. **Determination of Employee Status**

The following checklist should help in making a determination concerning the status of the injured:

1. Find out if the claimant was a loaned employee.
2. Determine the circumstances involved in the lending.
3. Learn if there was a transfer of payroll and tax deductions.
4. Find out how the injured understood the situation.
5. Learn who directed the work.
6. Determine if there was a transfer of the right to fire the employee.
7. Determine if there was any specific time limit or job limit specified.
8. Learn what type of work was involved.

9. Determine if the injured was a general or a special employee.
10. Find out if the claimant was working for more than one employer.
11. Determine if the claimant was either a subcontractor or the employee of a subcontractor. Get a copy of the contract.
12. Determine if the claimant was a volunteer.
13. Learn if the claimant was a casual employee not engaged in the regular course of his employer's trade.
14. Find out if work was performed at home. If so, find out if a certificate of permission was necessary and obtained.

I. **Employee v. Independent Contractor**

The following checklist should help to determine the status:

1. Learn if the claimant was engaged in work that required specialized skill.
2. Find out who hired the claimant.
3. Find out who paid him.
4. Find out on whose payroll records he is listed.
5. Determine who controlled the activities of the injured.
6. Determine who had the right to fire the employee.
7. Find out if he or she was paid by the hour, day, week or month.
8. Learn if the injured received a regular salary or was on piecework or commission, or a combination of both.
9. Find out if the injured was on an expense account, and if he or she had to account for expenses.
10. Determine if there was any other consideration in lieu of salary, such as board, lodging, use of a car, etc.
11. Learn if there was any contract in existence between the parties, either oral or written. If written, obtain a copy.

WORKMEN'S COMPENSATION

12. Find out if a contract was made in advance for a definite consideration.
13. Find out if there was any regulation concerning the hours worked, and, if so, get details.
14. Determine who directed the method of operation.
15. Learn who had the right of inspection.
16. Find out if a lump sum was agreed upon in advance for the entire job.
17. Learn who furnished the materials, supplies, tools and work clothes and who paid for them.
18. Learn who furnished transportation.
19. Find out if the injured was permitted to hire extra help and, if so, find out who did the hiring and who paid the help.
20. Determine if the injured maintained a separate business establishment either at an office or at home.
21. Determine if the injured pays the maintenance costs such as rent, electricity, water, telephone, etc.
22. Find out if the injured has a business card or a sign at his or her place of business that advertises the services to the general public.
23. Learn if the injured holds himself or herself out for hire by the public.
24. Find out if the injured performs similar work for others on a contract basis and check with former clients.
25. Determine if it was necessary to obtain an official license or special permit to perform the work and, if so, obtain a copy.
26. Learn if the injured has a social security number.
27. Determine if social security was deducted from pay or any other withholdings made for tax purposes such as unemployment tax, disability benefits, etc.
28. Find out if the injured was on any pension plan and if such a plan was of his or her own creation.

CHAPTER X

Crime Insurance Investigation

BURGLARY AND ROBBERY

Generally speaking, crime insurance includes burglary, robbery and fidelity policies. Since fidelity insurance has special qualities of its own, it will be treated as a separate category.

The following checklists, accordingly, apply principally to the investigation of policies covering the various types of burglary and robbery insurance.

A. **Residence Investigation**

1. *Insured's information:*

    a. Name and address of the insured and other personal information.
    b. Previous loss records of the insured:

    (1) Find out if the insured ever sustained a previous loss or damage as a result of burglary, robbery, theft or larceny. If so, obtain details including the exact time and place of all losses.
    (2) Find out if theft was involved and, if so, learn if the thief was ever discovered.
    (3) Obtain the names of all those who were involved in previous losses and get the details.
    (4) Determine what action, if any, was taken against them.
    (5) Find out if any of the previous losses were insured. If so, obtain the name of

the carrier and the amount of payments made in addition to other details.
(6) Find out if any previous policy covering crime insurance was ever canceled. If so, obtain details, including the names of the companies and the approximate date of the cancellations.
(7) If warranted, make a check on previous losses through the police and previous carriers.
(8) Find out if there is any other insurance coverage for the loss being investigated. If so, obtain the name of the company, the type of policy, its limits and other specifics.
(9) Check previous record with the Index Bureau.

B. **Loss From Premises**

1. Determine if the loss was sustained at a private residence.
2. Find out if it was a permanent dwelling or a summer or other temporary residence.
3. Find out if it was a one-family or multiple-family house, an apartment dwelling, a hotel or a motel.
4. Find out if it was a rooming or boarding house.
5. Find out if any business is conducted on the premises from which the loss was sustained and, if so, get details.
6. Determine if the insured owns or leases the premises. Determine the insured's exact interest in the premises. If he or she leases it, find out if the insured is responsible for damage to the premises.
7. Obtain a list of all residents, their ages and relationships to the insured. Find out if they are regular members of the insured's household.
8. Find out who occupied the premises at the time of the loss. If unoccupied, determine the exact time

during which it was left unoccupied. If partially occupied, obtain all details as to who occupied what portions.
9. Determine what precautions were taken against unlawful entry:
    a. Find out if the doors and windows were locked.
    b. Describe the type of locks, bars or other excluding devices.
    c. Find out if a watchman was employed and if he was on duty. Get details.
    d. Find out if there was a burglar alarm and, if so, whether it was set and went off. If not, get an explanation.
    e. Find out if there is a dog on the premises. If so, find out where it was located, what kind it was, and whether or not it gave warning. If it did not, find out why.
10. Describe the exact point of entry and draw diagram if necessary for a full understanding.
11. Describe all marks at the point of entry, such as jimmy marks, broken window or lock, etc. Give a detailed description.

C. **Loss From a Depository**
1. Determine if the loss was sustained at or from a bank, trust company, building and loan association, credit union or similar institution.
2. Determine if an outside receptacle was involved and, if so, get complete details concerning its operation and use.
3. Determine if the loss was from a public warehouse.
4. Determine if the loss was sustained from a private dwelling other than the insured's home:
    a. If so, find out if it was occupied at the time of the loss.

b. If occupied, find out by whom, and give relationship to the insured.
   c. Find out who owns the premises or leases it. Check the deed and lease if warranted.
   5. Find out who placed the property in the depository.
   6. Find out when it was placed there and obtain copies of records if available.
   7. Determine exactly where the personal property (money, securities, etc.) was ordinarily kept and where it was before being placed in the depository.
   8. Find out exactly how it was placed in the depository and by whom.
   9. Find out who had access to the property.
   10. Find out if the property was taken from an automobile, motorcycle, trailer, truck, etc. If so, find out if it was unattended.
   11. Find out if the property was taken from a public conveyance.
   12. Find out if the depository owner has any insurance coverage and, if so, obtain the name of the carrier and the policy limits.

D. **Nature of the Loss**
   1. Describe the articles or personal property in detail. If it includes fur, obtain an exact description of the amount, kind, quality and age.
   2. Find out who owns the missing or damaged property, whether a residence employee, a member of the household, a relative or a roomer.
   3. Find out if the property was obsolete or out of style.
   4. If the insured did not own the property, find out if he or she was responsible for its loss.
   5. Find out who used the property.
   6. Determine where and when it was bought, and what it cost originally. Obtain bills or receipts if available, and check the original value, if warranted.
   7. Determine if the property was a gift, and, if so, who

was the donor, when given, and what the occasion. Find out if the purchase and the price can be traced through the donor, if warranted.
8. Find out if the property was one of the specified articles listed in the policy.
9. If checks were stolen, obtain details concerning the payees and arrange for "stop payment."
10. Find out who last saw the object that is missing and when last seen.
11. Determine if the loss was reported to the police, when and to whom. Obtain a copy of the police report.
12. Check pawn shop police details for possible recovery of the missing property.
13. Find out who had access to the premises or property. Check all servants, employees, gas, electric or water meter readers, tradesmen and others if warranted.
14. Find out who discovered the loss, when and how.
15. Interview all witnesses who have any knowledge of the loss and take signed statements where warranted.
16. Have a thorough search made of the premises, including waste baskets, particularly if the loss involves certificates or documents.

E. **Damage to Property or Premises**
1. Obtain a complete list of all damaged property including a description of the nature of the damage.
2. Determine the exact location of the damaged property.
3. Determine whether the damage can be repaired or whether it must be replaced. Obtain estimates or bills and arrange for appraisal if warranted.
4. Determine who owns the property. If the insured is not the owner, find out if he or she is legally responsible for it. If the insured is not legally responsible for the property, find out who is and whether or not he or she was a resident in the place where the loss occurred when damaged.

5. Find out if the property was held as a sample. Determine if it was being held for sale and, if so, whether it was sold.
6. Determine if the loss or damage was caused by fire or as a result of attempting to put out a fire.

F. **Suspects**
1. In order to obtain the names of any possible suspects, interview all people who had any connection with the loss, directly or indirectly, including tenants or other occupants of the household, neighbors, employees, etc.
2. When interviewing possible suspects, try to obtain their name, address, age, marital status, dependents, salary, financial condition, debts or any other cause for financial temptation.
3. Where advisable and warranted, obtain history of previous employment of any suspects, including previous bonding history.
4. Check for possible criminal records of any suspects.
5. Check associates, where they are of questionable character.
6. Check the suspect's habits, where questionable.
7. Make a detailed investigation to determine if any suspect is a drug addict.

G. **Settlement Negotiations**
1. Whenever a substantial savings can be affected, consider replacement of the article if this can be done to the satisfaction of the insured and if warranted.
2. In any settlement based on cash value, depreciation should always be considered, where warranted.
3. Whenever a damaged article still has any monetary value, and where a cash settlement is being made, salvage must be taken into consideration either by deduction from the settlement figure, or by taking over the property itself. Review the chapter on this subject.

4. If the article is taken over as salvage, an attempt should be made to sell it as economically as possible and as soon as possible, particularly if the article or object is large and involves storage charges.

MERCANTILE INVESTIGATION

A. **Commercial Losses—General**
   1. *Insured's information:*
      a. Name, address and other personal information concerning the insured.
      b. Determine the exact location of the loss.
      c. Determine if the insured is an individual, partnership, corporation, trade name, trustee or other entity.
      d. Determine what kind of business the insured was conducting and get details.
      e. Determine the previous loss and insurance record.
      f. If a broken lock was involved, obtain a description of the type of lock, the nature of the break and describe all marks of damage. Describe all other bars and protective measures of a similar nature that might be pertinent to the loss.
      g. Obtain the exact time then the premises were closed and locked and find out by whom this was done and how.
      h. If a watchman was involved:
         (1) Get his name, address, age and other personal details.
         (2) Find out how long he was employed by the insured and obtain his previous employment record.
         (3) Find out if he was ever involved in a previous loss and get the details including anything of a suspicious nature.

(4) Determine if the watchman was on duty at the time and, if not, find out why.
(5) If a watchman was on duty, find out if he was supposed to make regular rounds and did so. If he did not, make a detailed investigation to find out why. Determine if there is any clock record of the timing.

i. Find out if a burglar alarm system was involved:

(1) Determine whether it was in operation and, if not, why.
(2) Obtain a description of the type of alarm and whether it was tied into the police station.
(3) If it was in operation, find out if it was heeded, what action was taken and by whom.
(4) Determine whether it was adequate for the purpose and make a report to the underwriters if warranted.

j. Find out if all policy warranties, including watchmen, alarms and others, were complied with and, if not, find out why. Report to the underwriters if warranted.

2. *Nature of the loss:*

a. Obtain the exact date and time of the loss.
b. Determine if the premises were occupied, unoccupied, or partially occupied and get details.
c. Determine if the premises were open for business at the time. If so, find out if it was during the regular business hours.
d. List all empoyees who had access to the premises or to the particular property involved. Obtain the length of their employment and

previous records, including bonding, criminal or other pertinent data.

e. Obtain the names of all people who were lawfully in the vicinity and who might be able to give useful information. Obtain the names of adjacent tenants and observe the general character of the neighborhood.

f. Determine how the loss was discovered and by whom. Take a signed statement.

g. Check to see whether the police have been notified, by whom, when and to whom. Obtain a copy of the report.

h. Describe the nature of the property that was lost or damaged.

i. If checks were involved, obtain itemization of all payees where possible and place a "stop payment" on them.

j. If the loss occurred from a cash box, determine who had the keys or other access. Find out where the keys were kept. Determine when the money was last checked and by whom.

k. *Where money loss is concerned:*

  (1) Determine the amount as closely as possible, with denominations and serial numbers if available.

  (2) Find out who knew about, and had access to it.

  (3) Find out who discovered the loss and how.

  (4) Check the amount usually on hand for that day and hour from previous records. Check all amounts paid that day and get the details concerning the payments.

  (5) Check the books if necessary, and consider the advisability of an auditor's review.

l. *Where the loss involves securities:*

    (1) Obtain complete description, including serial numbers where available.
    (2) Where possible, have "stop payment" placed with the registrar or transfer agent.
    (3) Check all deliveries of securities carefully.

3. *Suspects.* Check all possible suspects and proceed as previously outlined.

B. **Safe Burglary Claims:**

   1. Describe the safe or depository:

      a. Obtain the make, model, serial number, year of manufacture and similar details. Determine if it was fireproof and anchored.
      b. Determine the cost, date of purchase and whether it was bought new or second-hand, where and from whom it was purchased.
      c. Describe the locking devices.
      d. Determine if there was any damage to the safe or whether there were any marks of entry. Obtain photographs, if warranted.
      e. Determine if the safe can be repaired effectively and, if so, obtain estimates for repair.

   2. Determine where the safe was located and describe in detail.
   3. Find out who had the combination and where it was kept. Find out who had access to the combination.

C. **Messenger Losses**

   1. Obtain the name, address, age and other personal details and background information of all messengers that might have been involved.
   2. Obtain the bonding record and previous criminal record, if any.

3. Obtain the same information concerning anyone who accompanied the messenger.
4. Obtain the exact time when the messenger left the insured's premises.
5. Determine the exact route taken, including all stops and persons with whom any contact was made.
6. Try to find out as much as possible about the messenger involved concerning his education, previous employment, recreational activities, associates and general reputation.
7. If any securities were involved, find out if any deliveries were actually made. If so, find out where and to whom.

D. **Robbery Claims**

1. Determine if violence or the threat of violence was involved.
2. Obtain full information concerning any involved custodians, as previously outlined.
3. Obtain detailed description of any guards including their ages, physical appearance and other pertinent details. Check their backgrounds as previously outlined, and their past employment record with the insured and previous employers. Check their bonding and criminal record.
4. Obtain complete description of any vehicle involved in the loss.
5. Obtain full information concerning any alarm system, if the loss was from the inside, as previously outlined.

E. **Subrogation, Salvage or Contribution**

1. Make sure to obtain pro-rata contribution from any other insurers that may have covered the loss, or request that they take over, if warranted.
2. Make recovery from the wrongdoer, relatives, etc. wherever possible.

3. Arrange for the sale of any recovered property at the best possible price.

F. **Confidential Report to Underwriters**

If ever there is a need for close cooperation and communication between the claim representative and the underwriters, it is in the area of crime insurance. An observant investigator can save the company from continuing on a bad risk, or give information that will lead to needed corrections in order to make a risk acceptable.

Some of the factors that the investigator should be aware of, and report on, are:

1. The character and reputation of the insured. Report on personal habits that could invite a loss such as unnecessary ostentation, public notoriety, etc.
2. The type of business and whether it is borderline legal.
3. Neighborhood conditions and whether they are hazardous.
4. Condition of the premises and accessibility to break-in.
5. Moral hazard. Report on large sums of money that may be kept on the premises or transported without proper protection.
6. Any question about under-insurance or over-insurance.
7. Unguarded or vacant premises.
8. Construction of walls, floor, ceiling, locks, bolts, etc.
9. Type of alarm or the need for it.
10. Type of watchmen, or the need for them.
11. Hours during which business is being conducted.
12. Previous burglary or robbery record.

FIDELITY CLAIMS

The handling of fidelity claims involves settlement negotiations with insureds and brokers, since they are first-party claims, and, for that reason, require the highest degree of tact and diplomacy. In addition, such claims present complications and legal pitfalls with which the adjuster must be able to cope, with the aid of supervisors and counsel. The following guidelines are recommended:

A. **General Guidelines**

1. Upon receipt of the first notice of claim from the insured, agent or broker, "Notice of Claim" and "Proof of Loss" forms should be sent to the insured or his representative. The covering letter should be carefully worded to avoid any statement which could later be interpreted as an admission of acceptance on the part of the company. The letter can be written along the following lines:

    "This will acknowledge your letter of _____. Attached are bond "Notice of Claim" and "Proof of Loss" forms in duplicate, to be executed by the insured and returned together with any other documentation in support of this matter.

    Upon receipt of the above requested information and forms, this claim will be given our further consideration in accordance with the provisions of the captioned bond."

2. There may be instances when the amount of information furnished in the initial report will permit the company to waive the requirement of having a "Notice of Claim" form prepared. In such instances, the "Proof of Loss" form should be submitted to the insured with a request for completion and submission of any additional documentation necessary to properly determine whether there is a valid fidelity claim.

3. While it is the responsibility of the insured to prove that he or she has sustained a fidelity loss covered under the bond, this does not mean that the adjuster

should adopt a negative attitude toward the insured, In most instances, the case will warrant immediate investigation.
4. Awareness of all subrogation or restitution rights and provisions is essential as previously indicated. Only by immediate investigation and proper handling can the company protect these rights to the fullest extent.
5. Discrete, tactful and careful handling is an absolute necessity because the law of defamation, libel, slander, false arrest and other criminal as well as civil consequences can be disastrous. In many jurisdictions, extreme care is necessary to prevent the wrongdoer from getting the impression that there was a promise of immunity from criminal prosecution upon receipt of restitution.
6. Special care should be taken initially in order to legally tie up monies or properties that may rightfully belong to the company under subrogation and salvage rights.

B. **Investigation**

There are many forms of fidelity bonds and each requires some specialized handling. It would be impractical to outline claim handling instructions concerning the finer points in each of these separate situations. The following outline is, therefore, to be considered as general instructions which will cover the immediate investigation that should be made on all fidelity claims.

Generally speaking, the investigation should proceed along the following lines:

1. *Determine the nature of the loss,* as for instance:
    a. Employee dishonesty, whether by theft or embezzlement.
    b. Mysterious disappearance.
    c. Misplacement.

CRIME INSURANCE INVESTIGATION

  d. Outside theft.
  e. Holdup.
2. *Check coverage* and review the bond form and all endorsements. In view of the fact that some employees are sometimes excluded from coverage, it is particularly pertinent to review all exclusions and endorsements which might affect coverage.
3. *Make preliminary investigation* and determine when, how and by whom the loss was first discovered.
   a. If the loss was in currency, obtain the exact amount of money involved.
   b. If property, determine the value by bills, bookkeeping entries, warehouse receipts or bills of lading, etc.
   c. If the property is merchandise, obtain details or inventory and check the bookkeeping records. It may be necessary to order an audit by qualified public accountants, but this should be done only with the approval of the home or office or counsel.
4. *If the defaulter is known:*
   a. Obtain the name, position, home address and addresses of close relatives.
   b. Obtain as much of his personal history as is pertinent, including his age, family, education, previous employment, previous criminal record if any, and full details concerning any previous losses. This is particularly important since coverage is usually excluded where the insured retains an employee who is known to be a defaulter. In this respect, it is important to review the defaulter's personnel file.
   c. Determine whether there was any collusion involving others. If so, get details concerning the other party or parties, since this may be an important source of salvage.

d. Obtain a signed confession. However, it is important that the investigator become familiar with the laws of his or her jurisdiction before such confession is obtained. Such a confession must be voluntary, without duress, promise of a reward or promise not to prosecute. If necessary, obtain the services of an attorney who is familiar with this type of loss to assist in obtaining such a confession.
e. Make sure that the matter was reported to the police and keep in close contact in order to obtain any information that may be available.
f. Try to determine what happened to the money and whether it can be recovered.
g. Determine the financial status not only of the defaulter, but of his or her family and friends who might be willing to lend the money for restitution. Check the defaulter's bank accounts, insurance policies, real estate holdings, stocks, bonds, credit or other notes or mortgages due him or her, and other property such as automobiles, jewelry, boats and household or other personal property. If possible, and advisable, obtain confession of judgment, with the help of proper legal guidance.

5. If bonds, stocks or checks are involved, get the insured to place stops and make sure that he or she goes through all necessary legal steps to stop payment as soon as possible. Determine if claim can be made against the bank in the event of forged checks.
6. Determine whether there might possibly be other insurance involved in the loss and, if so, whether it is co-insurance or excess.
7. As soon as the first report is obtained, try to obtain enough information to make a realistic appraisal of the loss and to make a recommendation for a realistic reserve.

8. Keep the insured advised as to the progress of the investigation unless collusion is suspected, or for other reasons making this inadvisable.
9. Check every possible avenue to determine the relationship of the insured and the defaulter, whether by blood or otherwise.
10. Obtain proof of loss as soon as possible and submit it promptly, together with recommendations resulting from the investigation. Make sure the proof of loss does not result in an admission of liability on the part of the company.
11. Finally, whenever the investigation of a fidelity loss indicates, for any reason whatsoever, that continued exposure to coverage would be dangerous to the company, a confidential report should be made to the Underwriting Department. Care must be exercised so that defamatory material may not rightfully be used against the individual making the report or the company he or she represents.

CHAPTER XI

Accident & Health, Personal Injury and Plate Glass Investigations

There is no logical reason for combining these categories in one chapter except for convenience in gathering together areas of investigation not as yet treated.

ACCIDENT AND HEALTH CLAIMS

For the most part, investigations of claims under Accident and Health policies do not require the detailed information that is usually essential in liability, fidelity or workers' compensation claims. While signed statements, police reports and witnesses' statements are not ordinarily necessary in the average accident and health claim, it is essential that reports which warrant investigation should receive them promptly and that they should be made thoroughly, particularly since they are first-party claims. Danger signals that highlight the need for detailed investigation fall chiefly into the following categories:

A. **Coverage Problems**
1. *Verification of personal details* concerning the ininsured. His or her age, economic status and physical condition should be determined. The insured's occupation may warrant looking into, particularly if there is any question of extra hazard.
2. *Delayed notice.* The policy provisions always require notice within a specified or reasonable period of time. A slight delay in reporting will ordinarily be overlooked, especially if there is some legitimate reason therefor. Considerable delay should give warning to the investigator that there may be some

questionable elements to the claim. In cases of protracted delay, the investigator should obtain a signed statement from the insured giving reasons for the delay.

3. *Other policy provisions.* The investigator must review the policy to make sure that the claim falls within all of the provisions. Exclusions should be particularly scrutinized.

B. **Misrepresentations in the Application**

Material misrepresentations may affect the acceptance of a risk or they may involve a higher premium charge, and are, accordingly, most important to investigate.

Once a material misrepresentation has been discovered, notice should immediately be given to the underwriting department so that there may be no waiver of company rights by the acceptance of additional premium payments.

C. **Reasonable Bills**

Accident and Health policies are rated on the assumption that bills presented by the insured will be fair and reasonable for the locality where the services were given. Excessive treatment can also cause unreasonable billing. Investigation of these items may call for the assistance of a qualified physician, and such help should be requested where the amount involved warrants it.

D. **Over-Insurance**

It is important, particularly when dealing with large limits, to determine what other insurance might have been purchased by the insured. Over-insurance should act as a red flag to indicate the possibility of fraud. The investigation should, of course, be conducted with tact, since over-insurance might be completely innocent.

E. **Dismemberment, Loss of Sight or Total Disability**

Cases in these categories always deserve complete investigation, not only because of the amounts involved, but

ACCIDENT, HEALTH, PERSONAL INJURY & PLATE GLASS

because of the possible questionable nature of total disability allegations. Check the medical with especial care as previously outlined. Also check carefully the past employment records of the insured. Make sure that all names and aliases that the insured has ever used are checked with the Index Bureau.

F. **Physical Examinations**

The company has the right to make physical examinations of its own at its discretion and the investigator must keep this in mind whenever the situation warrants it. As previously indicated, such examinations should not be made indiscriminately. Review the previous checklists on this subject.

G. **Death Claims**

All death claims warrant complete investigation. In addition to doctors' and hospital reports, where available, copies of death certificates, coroner's reports, autopsy reports and any other applicable reports or records should be obtained. A thorough investigation of the possibility of suicide and possible misrepresentation concerning previous health should be made. The financial condition of the deceased should also be checked carefully.

H. **Suicide or Voluntary Injury**

Obviously, if suicide or voluntary injury is suspected, investigation of a most intensive nature must be made. It should include the insured's personal and family history, physical, mental, financial and occupational background, among other items as indicated in the following checklist:

1. *Determine the physical facts.* A complete description of the scene of the death should be obtained including the area where the death occurred, the position of the body, the nature of the objective evidence of injury, and general information which might lead to a determination as to whether or not suicide was likely or possible.

The physical facts should include determination of whether a suicide note was left in the vicinity of the body or in the possession of someone to whom it may have been addressed. Examination of the suicide note should determine whether it was in the handwriting of the deceased and whether the tenor of the note was rational. It is important to determine whether the note was dated, since a previously written note could be used to obscure murder.

2. *All reports of any nature* that might bear on a determination of suicide should be obtained, such as:
    a. Death certificate.
    b. Coroner's report.
    c. Autopsy report.
    d. Police report.
    e. Ballistics expert's report.
    f. Newspaper reports. Whenever possible, the reporter should be interviewed to see if he or she can throw any extra light on the subject.

3. *Possible motive for suicide.*
    a. Determine if bad health or recent notice of serious illness was involved.
    b. Find out if the insured was in financial difficulties. Check the insured's bank accounts, stocks, bonds, mortgages or other outstanding loans or debts.
    c. Try to determine if the insured had made a recent bad financial or business investment. Check his or her credit rating.
    d. Try to determine if the insured had a large outstanding gambling debt and if he or she was involved with loan sharks. Try to find out if the insured had a reputation for gambling.
    e. Determine if the insured was facing bankruptcy or an outside audit.
    f. Find out if the insured had recently suffered

a large fire or other casualty loss either without insurance coverage or with insufficient coverage.
- g. Find out if the insured recently lost his or her job.
- h. Find out if the insured's home life was troubled and whether infidelity might have been a cause. Find out if the insured was divorced, separated, or on the verge of either. Try to find out if there were any unusual problems with children.
- i. Determine whether alcoholism or drug addiction could have been involved.
- j. Find out if the insured was involved in any illegal or criminal activity and, if so, whether exposure might have affected him or her seriously. Find out what kind of friends and associates the insured had.

4. Determine if the insured was religious and to what degree. Deeply religious people seldom commit suicide unless they have suddenly become disillusioned with their religion. Find out if the insured or one or more of his or her children was a member or a potential member of one of the religious sects or cults that is in questionable esteem.
5. Finally, it is of the utmost importance to find out if the insured had ever previously tried to commit suicide or had threatened to do so. Try to find out if the insured had ever, and particularly recently, gone to a psychiatrist, psychologist or quack regularly.

I. Forms

The average Accident and Health Claim requires little more investigation than that which is provided by the completion of necessary forms. It is therefore important that such forms be filled out completely and accurately, and returned promptly. The claimsperson should review them carefully, since, even in what appears to be a minor case, he or she may find something that needs further explanation. Occasionally, the investigator may get a "sleeper." This is a claim that appears small and innocuous on the surface, purposely and in order to lull the company into a false sense of security, in the hope that it will allow the claim to rest unattended long enough to make detection of disability difficult or impossible. Once a company has been put on notice concerning a possible claim, it cannot afford to let the matter rest, awaiting further word from the claimant, particularly if proofs of loss have not been completed and forwarded.

J. **Independent of Other Causes**

No discussion of the investigation of accident claims would be complete without mentioning the importance of investigating possible related cases to disability or death not due to accident. A pre-existing condition might make a person accident prone. Disease or sickness may have contributed to the disability or death. Review the section dealing with this subject and keep it in mind when investigating any Accident and Health claim.

K. **Medical Substantiation**

The company is entitled to all of the medical information that is at the disposal of the insured or his physicians to corroborate a claim under an Accident and Health policy. It is, therefore, essential that the investigator review very carefully the checklists and information provided in the various sections dealing with the investigation of injury and illness previously outlined. In a claim under this type of policy, the investigator has the advantage of policy requirements not present in a liability claim.

PERSONAL INJURY CLAIMS

Personal Injury Liability, in insurance terminology, must be distinguished from "personal injury" as often used snynonymously with "bodily injury" as applied to automobile or public liability claims.

Personal Injury Liability coverage refers to protection for the insured against claims and suits arising out of actual or alleged libel, slander, defamation, false arrest or detention, malicious prosecution and invasion of privacy.

A. **Defamation, Libel and Slander**

In addition to the basic investigation to be made in any casualty claim, the claims person should determine:

1. If the statement or publication was defamatory. If possible, determine the exact nature of the statements or publishings, pictures, radio, television or whatever.
2. Whether the alleged statements or publications were true.
3. The exact nature, circumstances and manner of publication, to whom and how. Obtain and interview all witnesses.
4. If malice was involved. Determine the reasons for the publication.
5. If the statement was so reckless as to amount to malice.
6. If the claimant suffered any damage financially or to his or her reputation of a substantial nature.
7. If the statement or publication was privileged.

B. **False Arrest or Imprisonment**

The false arrest or imprisonment coverage of Personal Injury insurance is ordinarily involved in cases of suspected theft or pilferage from a store. In recent years, a more devious and much more potentially lucrative con game has become prevalent. This involves fraudulent actions of men or women who make it appear as though they have stolen some merchandise in order to invite arrest and a false accusation of theft and subsequent arrest. The danger to the perpetrator is almost non-existent since the worse that can happen is the "embarrassment" of the incident itself, unless he or she is a repeater and detected as such. The rewards, on the other hand, depend on the gullibility of the average jury.

There are, of course, cases of honest mistake but it is the job of the investigator not only to try to distinguish between the honest and the fraudulent claimant, but to determine whether the actions of an insured were justified, even when the mistake was honest. It is most important for the investigator to determine if there was probable cause, and, if so, whether the action taken was reasonable under the circumstances.

I would suggest that the investigator:

1. Examine the coverage carefully to determine exactly who is insured.
2. Obtain the complete facts of the incident from all available parties to it.
3. Obtain statements from all known witnesses and try to discover witnesses not reported by the insured.
4. Determine, as closely as possible, the exact words used by the parties involved in the incident.
5. Learn the exact nature of any physical acts or force used by all parties concerned.
6. If the polcie were involved, make a check and interview the police officer.
7. Make an exhaustive check of the claimant:
    a. Background and reputation in the neighborhood or previous neighborhoods, schools, etc.
    b. Police record of arrests and convictions. Check with juvenile authorities where warranted.
    c. Employment record and past employment records.
    d. Church affiliation. Interview the minister,

ACCIDENT, HEALTH, PERSONAL INJURY & PLATE GLASS

   priest or rabbi to check out the claimant's reputation.
   e. Credit record.
   f. Activities of any other kind that would help to determine whether the claim under investigation is an honest one and what approximate embarrassment such a claimant would have suffered.
   g. Check past claim record through the Index Bureau.
8. Try to determine damages, both actual and consequential. The investigator must familiarize himself or herself with the law of damage pertaining to this subject in the jurisdiction involved.

PLATE GLASS LOSSES

In the processing of plate glass losses, the following routine steps are suggested:

1. Check coverage:
   a. Determine if the broken or damaged glass is listed or otherwise properly covered.
   b. Determine if lettering or ornamentation is separately covered.
   c. Determine if the loss was caused by fire, and, if so, get the fire insurer to take over.
2. Determine whether any other insurance covered the loss. Insistence on cash settlement may sometimes indicate this possibility.
3. While the amount involved usually requires that investigation be kept at a minimum, a brief description of the occurrence should be obtained, including the following information:
   a. Date and time of the loss. Watch for losses that allegedly occurred close to the inception date of the policy.

      b. Obtain the facts of the incident.
      c. Obtain a description of the glass, including the exact size, thickness, composition, location, number of panes, type (plate, mirror, beveled, shatter-proof, etc.), setting, lettering and ornamentation.
4. Arrange for the immediate boarding up where necessary and advisable.
5. Arrange for replacement after checking the cost against price book or competitive estimates.
6. Determine subrogation and salvage possibilities and follow up for recovery.
7. Make a report to the underwriters if warranted.
8. Arrange for discounts to be given for prompt payment of all bills.
9. Where the loss involves a substantial amount of money, a more thorough investigation may be warranted if subrogation appears possible.

CHAPTER XII

Some Special Aspects of Liability Investigations

A. **Investigation of Accidents Involving Children**
   1. Statements obtained from children should be written in the language of the child and, wherever possible and practical, by the child.
   2. *School records* should be obtained, including the following information:
       a. Attendance record before the accident, as a basis for comparison after the accident.
       b. Time lost as a result of the accident and attendance record for some time subsequent to it.
       c. Grades before and after the accident.
       d. Physical, dental and psychiatric examinations.
       e. Aptitude, intelligence or psychological tests.
       f. Curriculum before and after the accident.
       g. Recorded complaints to teachers, athletic directors or principal.
       h. Athletic activities before and after the accident.
   3. Interview teachers for personal reactions to the difference in the child's behavior, if any.
   4. Where warranted, interview all school doctors or psychologists who examined the child.
   5. Where warranted, interview gym teachers, athletic directors or others connected with the child's athletic activities.
   6. If discreetly possible, interview other children with whom the claimant associated, in order to get their reaction to any change in the child's behavior.

B. **Investigation of Fatal Accidents**
   1. Learn how long the decedent lived after the accident. in order to determine the amount of possible pain and suffering.
   2. Learn the age and sex of the decedent.
   3. Learn the general health of the decedent, determined by:
       a. Neighborhood canvass.
       b. Life insurance examinations.
       c. Army or school examinations.
       d. Other evidence produced by dependents.
   4. Make a medical history investigation, if warranted.
   5. Learn the general habits of the deceased including any evidence of alcoholism or drug use.
   6. Determine the life expectancy of the deceased.
   7. Determine the previous earnings of the deceased, as previously outlined under "Special Damages."
   8. Determine potential earning capacity of the deceased and any increases which could logically have been expected.
   9. Obtain the names and addresses of all close relatives and check their relationship.
   10. Obtain the ages, sex and number of dependents together with their relationship to the deceased.
   11. Determine the general economic condition and social status of the deceased and his or her family.
   12. Determine the marital status of the deceased and obtain certificates and other documentary proof, or written corroboration where warranted.
   13. Obtain all medical bills.
   14. Obtain all funeral expenses, including incidentals such as burial plot, tombstone, etc.
   15. *Determine the causal relationship between death and the accident, derived from:*
       a. Coroner's report and transcript of hearing, if any.

SPECIAL ASPECTS OF LIABILITY 285

    b. Death certificate.
    c. Autopsy report, if any.
    d. Available medical reports.
    e. Medical history.

C. **Investigation of Claims Involving Fraud**

The investigation of claims involving possible fraud should be as thorough as possible. Important information may be obtained from almost any aspect of the investigation. If the claims have gone into suit, leads may be obtained from depositions, interrogatories, and bills of particulars.

Where possible fraud is involved, emphasis should be placed on the following points, all of which have been previously covered in the checklists for the investigation of specific cases.

  1. *Obtain details of the claimant's background:*
      a. General reputation and character through neighborhood canvass and other sources.
      b. Financial condition, including inspection of books and other records where possible. Determine the general living conditions of the claimant, including possessions such as automobiles, jewelry, residences, etc.
      c. Business or employment. Find out if there is anything shady, suspicious, mysterious or illegal about the claimant's business or employment. Check the reputation of the business with the Better Business Bureau, Manufacturing Associations and similar organizations.
      d. Hobbies and sports, such as gardening, golf, etc. Find out, if possible, with whom the claimant associates in these or other activities.
      e. Social activities. Find out if the claimant is active in any borderline social activities.
      f. Religious affiliations. Find out if the claimant

is active in religious activities and whether such activities appear sincere or are being used as a cover-up.
  g. Previous history, including all previous residences and employers or businesses. Make all necessary neighborhood investigations to check these out.
  h. Insurance, including particularly life and accident and health policies and check with the insurers to determine the past claim record of the claimant.
  i. Police records.
  j. Index Bureau. Check back with the companies reporting and check out not only the claimant, but any suspicious indications concerning doctors, lawyers and even witnesses.
2. *Obtain complete medical information:*
  a. Check the reputation and qualifications of all attending doctors.
  b. Arrange for a thorough medical examination by an outstandingly qualified specialist.
  c. Hospital records. Consider the necessity of obtaining new X-ray reports, scans and laboratory tests.
  d. Check the claimant's physical activities by neighborhood canvass and personal observation by an expert, including photographs and motion pictures, where warranted.
3. *Make a complete investigation of all special damages:*
  a. Lost time and earnings and all details as previously indicated under checklists outlined previously in the investigation of "Special Damages."
  b. Thorough check of all special damages as previously outlined.

SPECIAL ASPECTS OF LIABILITY

D. **Suit Reviews**

   1. *Attorney's review.*

   The company, after assigning a case to an attorney for defense or settlement recommendations, has the right to expect an early written report, including his or her opinions and evaluation. Such a report should include:

   a. A review of the facts contained in the claim file, or a complete review of them (which should, of course, be sent to the attorney at the time of assignment or very shortly thereafter), upon which the attorney's opinion concerning liability and value are predicated.
   b. A review of the law.
   c. A review of the coverage, including recommendations concerning the ad damnum letter, reservation of rights or non-waiver, declaratory judgment action or disclaimer.
   d. Opinon as to whether the case will reach the jury and a recommendation concerning whether or not a jury would be advantageous.
   e. Medical review and an opinion as to its probable effect on the jury and comment concerning medical expert witnesses.
   f. Review of the special damages and an indication of their credibility.
   g. Opinion concerning the impression which the insured, claimant and all other witnesses may make on a judge or jury.
   h. Opinion about the ability, qualifications, peculiarities and prejudices of the plaintiff's attorney, the trial judge and local juries.
   i. Opinion concerning the trend of recent verdicts.
   j. Opinion concerning the likelihood of a verdict.
   k. Settlement evaluation.

l. Report on any settlement negotiations.
m. Last minute instructions for additional investigation and work to be completed by the investigator.
n. Present reserve recommendations.

2. *Claim manager's or supervisor's review.*

   Most companies require the opinion of the claim manager or supervisor, in addition to that of the trial lawyer, when a serious claim goes into suit. If necessary, such information should include:

   a. Opinion of defense counsel's ability and reputation in the community where the trial is being held.
   b. Opinion of the plaintiff's attorney.
   c. Trend of recent verdicts in that locality.
   d. Opinion concerning liability and additional investigation needed, as well as an opinion concerning settlement value.
   e. Report on any settlement negotiations.
   f. Any additional recommendations, including a report on the availability of all witnesses, the plaintiff (if known), and the defendant.
   g. Condition of all evidence and a review of the physical facts.
   h. Review of the reserves and recommendations for any changes.

3. *Checklist for trial preparation.*

   a. *Some guidelines for defense counsel:*

      (1) Review the case shortly after it has been received and outline the investigation needed. Pre-trial investigation begins on the day the attorney gets first notice of the suit.
      (2) When all basic investigation has been

SPECIAL ASPECTS OF LIABILITY

received, make settlement evaluation in the light of all pertinent information.

(3) Reserve recommendations should be made and altered in accordance with the information at hand.

(4) Check the coverage carefully so that ad damnum letter may be sent to the insured if this has not already been done. Make sure that proper consideration is given to the question concerning the necessity for a reservation of rights, non-waiver, declaratory judgment action or disclaimer.

(5) Make periodic reviews of the file to make sure that the requested investigation is being completed.

(6) Arrange the claim file chronologically so that all information is available with the least confusion. Keep the file in neat order.

(7) Outline and index the case where warranted.

(8) See that all pleadings have been reviewed and are in order, all motions properly filed, all interrogatories made and answered and all necessary depositions taken.

(9) Determine if proper consideration has been given to the venue where the case is to be tried.

(10) Make sure that the necessary investigation, reports, records and other evidence have been received and that all loose ends have been followed up.

(11) Determine if all avenues for possible settlement have been explored, where justified.

(12) Make sure that final check has been made to determine the availability of all witnesses including the defendant, any passengers, outside witnesses, doctors, appraisers and engineers, photographers or any other experts.
(13) See that arrangements have been made for the service of subpoenas or court orders where required, in order to produce witnesses, policemen, hospital attendants and records, salary records and any other needed witnesses and records.
(14) See that arrangements have been made to see the defendant and other key witnesses in order to properly evaluate them and to determine that there has been no lapse of memory or change of opinion concerning important details.
(15) Make a last minute review of the scene of the accident where warranted.

b. *Final review of the file by the claim representative and defense counsel.*

(1) *Coverage information.* Review the policy and the facts to make sure that all questions concerning coverage have been resolved. If a question still exists, make sure that proper reservation of rights has been made. Consider the advisability of declaratory judgment action. Make sure that a proper excess ad damnum letter has been sent where necessary. *Make sure that all proper precautions have been taken to avoid the possibility of an excess verdict in the future.*

(2) *Review the facts.* Determine if the

following statements and reports have been obtained:

- (a) Insured's statement. If a signed statement was taken from the defendant, make sure that it is available.
- (b) Plaintiff's version, obtained from him or her, or from the plaintiff's attorney.
- (c) Statements taken from all witnesses, including passengers in vehicles, outside witnesses as well as negative witnesses.
- (d) Expert's reports. Make sure that all experts are properly qualified to testify.
- (e) Police, motor vehicle, hospital, coroner's, autopsy, P.U.C. and I.C.C. and other reports and records that may be pertinent.

(3) *Review of the physical evidence.* Check to make sure that all evidence and exhibits are available, identifiable and in proper condition.

- (a) Equipment of any kind, including products, parts, broken bottles, descriptive, advertising or instructional matter, labels, etc.
- (b) Certified copies of all public records.
- (c) Make sure that all necessary photographs are on file. Rescrutinize the pictures in order to make sure that there is no danger of disqualification because of distortion, or for other reason.

(d) Review any movies that may have been taken and make sure that they were taken by an expert who can testify concerning the rate of speed at which the film was taken and that the result is a true representation of what was photographed. Make sure that the movies can be qualified by being able to prove that they were not tampered with or cut.
(e) Find out if all other visual aids have been obtained and are ready for trial, such as plats, mats, cutouts, scale models, etc., including medical charts and models.
(f) Determine whether all survey and appraisal reports are available, including chemical and other laboratory analysis and tests.
(g) Determine if all necessary reports have been obtained and ready for trial such as Index Bureau reports, police, motor vehicle, school records, etc. Make sure that proper subpoenas have been served where necessary.

(4) *Medical information.* Review and evaluate again all medical reports such as:

(a) Plaintiff's version of the injuries and disability.
(b) Autopsy reports.
(c) Reports of attending doctors, dentists and surgeons. Evaluate their potential as witnesses.

(d) Hospital records.
(e) Veteran's records.
(f) X-ray records.
(g) Determine if a physical examination is needed and make sure of the availability of the examining doctor. If possible, have a pre-trial interview with him or her to avoid surprises.

(5) *Special damages.* Check to see if information needed concerning the special damages has been obtained and see if it has been corroborated to the extent possible:

(a) Wage and salary records including tax reports if available and employer's records.
(b) Information concerning the plaintiff's business if he or she was self-employed and make sure that a proper request was made to produce all necessary records and accounts.
(c) Medical bills, including doctors, dentists, nurses, ambulance, hospital, etc.
(d) Property damage of any kind, including automobiles, jewelry, clothes, etc.

(6) *Evaluation.* Make a final pre-trial evaluation to determine if there is any possibility of a reasonable settlement, *with some very serious consideration given to the possibility of an excess action and verdict.*
Make a last pre-trial reserve review.

E. **Locating the Missing Witness**

It is most important that the investigator keep track of all witnesses that may be needed in the trial of a case. Initially, this involves obtaining not only the addresses of transient witnesses, but the names and addresses of relatives who may have a permanent address and who can always locate the transient.

In the event that a witness apparently disappears, much can be done by way of long-distance telephone calls, especially in rural communities. Various "skip-trace" organizations specialize in this field, and good results are often obtained if the need warrants the fee.

If none of these is successful, and the magnitude of the case warrants it, here are some suggestions that might help to locate the missing witness:

1. Registered letter, return receipt with address requested, sent to the last known address of the witness.
2. Long-distance telephone calls on a person-to-person basis.
3. Telephone directories.
4. City directories.
5. Interview the janitor or landlord at the last known address for possible leads, including:
    a. Names and addresses of relatives and friends.
    b. Names of company or collector on industrial life insurance.
    c. Name of a credit or collection agency that had previously checked on the individual.
    d. Name of fraternal, veterans or other organizations that the witness may have belonged to.
6. Canvass of the neighborhood or building for any possible leads from friends, relatives or acquain-

SPECIAL ASPECTS OF LIABILITY 295

tances. Such investigation should be repeated several times if warranted, because the investigator will never find everyone at home on the first canvass.
7. Business establishments, stores and banks in the immediate vicinity of his last known address.
8. Churches and church organizations in the vicinity.
9. Local doctors and dentists that may have treated the witness.
10. Local parochial or public schools.
11. Name of a moving firm whose vehicle may have been observed by the janitor or neighbors.
12. Any former employer of the witness or any member of his family. From this source you may obtain, if not the present address, leads such as:
    a. Union affiliations.
    b. Names of references on employment records.
    c. Type of work or employment.
    d. Information from fellow workmen.
13. Automobile or motor vehicle bureaus may have information concerning the witness' address if an automobile has been registered in his or her name, or if a driver's or chauffeur's license has been issued.
14. Local election records.
15. Utility and telephone companies.
16. Military service or Veteran's Administration records.
17. Credit accounts in department or other retail stores.
18. Welfare and unemployment agencies.
19. Police and parole records.
20. Tax records.
21. Marriage, birth or death records of the witness and family.
22. Judgment records.
23. Golf, tennis, bowling or other athletic clubs and leads through any known hobby organizations or merchants.

CHAPTER XIII

Factors Involved in Taking Signed Statements

It is not the purpose of these lists to discuss the nature of or the reasons for the taking of signed statements. This has been adequately covered in my book *Successful Handling of Casualty Claims*.

The following lists are meant merely to highlight the important aspects of the subjects covered for quick and easy reference under conditions that may not lend themselves to more protracted study.

A. **Rules for the Taking of Statements**

1. *Coverage problems.* Whenever a coverage problem is involved, two separate statements should be obtained from the insured: one reviewing the facts of the accident, and the other reviewing the information to be obtained concerning the coverage problem. The latter will usually contain references to the agent or broker as well as to the insured's carrier, which are matters that might disqualify the statement concerning the accident facts from being used at trial if both subjects are included in the same statement.
2. *First person.* The statements should be written in the first person in order to show that the witness or other person being interviewed is doing the talking.
3. *Separate statements.* No two people will ever see an accident exactly alike. It is, therefore, better practice to obtain a separate signed statement from each witness. The investigator should refrain from having one witness add either his or her signature to the statement of another, or even to add a paragraph to the effect that his or her version of the accident

corresponds with the version as stated by the other witness. While there are unusual circumstances that could make such a practice acceptable, such as where the alternative would be no statement at all from the second witness, this should be the exception rather than the rule.

4. *Legible writing.* The handwriting on the statement must be legible. If the investigator's handwriting is difficult to read, he or she should get a portable typewriter or have the witness write out the statement. This, however, has its dangers. If the witness writes the statement without any direction, it will usually be inadequate. If the investigator directs the statement, it may be discredited at trial. In any event, the investigator should never urge a witness who is self-conscious about his or her education or spelling to write the statement.

5. *Narrative form.* Unless a court reporter's statement is being taken, the straight narrative form is ordinarily best. The question and answer type of statement looks too legalistic and may cause the average layman some concern.

The statement should be specific, brief and to the point, without overlooking important material.

6. *Although every effort should be made to arrange a statement chronologically for easy reading,* the writer should not be afraid to add paragraphs at the end, either upon request by the witness or in order to cover information that was overlooked.

Paragraphing makes for easier reading. In my opinion, that is more important than the suspicion that might be aroused by leaving part of a line unfilled.

7. *Solitary interview.* If the investigator can possibly avoid it, he or she should not try to take a signed statement from a witness when that witness is surrounded by family or friends. In such event, it is best

to suggest tactfully that the noise and disturbance will be too great for concentration. There are, of course, exceptions, such as if the witness is a minor, is in an institution, or is illiterate or unfamiliar with the English language, but, even in such conditions, the bystanders should be kept at a minimum.

It must be recognized that there may be times when taking a statement under adverse conditions is better than getting no statement at all.

8. *Style.* Whenever it is appropriate, simple language and short sentences should be used. The statement should record, as closely as possible, the witnesses' manner of speech, but purposely bad grammar or very objectionable verbiage should be avoided unless a definite point is being made. When quoting, the exact language must, of course, be used. The writer should also try to avoid the use of unfamiliar legal, medical or technical language where the education of the witness does not warrant it.

9. *Pre-printed forms.* The use of forms that are partially pre-printed should be avoided when taking signed statements. They serve no useful purpose and may create suspicion and be less effective as evidence.

10. *Factual material.* Whenever possible, the investigator should try to give factual information and avoid opinions and conclusions in a signed statement taken from a witness. While this is not always possible, or, perhaps, in some circumstances, even advisable, an effort should be made to keep opinions and conclusions at a minimum. Statements overheard by a witness should be quoted as close to verbatim as possible, Also, where possible, recognized designations of speed, distance and direction should be used in as exact a figure as the witness can designate. Care must be used to avoid a dogmatic attitude on the statement unless that is the attitude of the witness.

11. *Insurance.* All mention concerning the name of the company for whom the investigator is working, or the phrase "insurance company" should be avoided where the company is not a party defendant.
12. *Conditions affecting the statement.* A signed statement should not be taken from anyone who is under the influence of alcohol or narcotics, or who is in a state of shock, following an accident. If a witness is obviously thick of tongue, drowsy, or unusually slow in his or her reactions, the investigator should be doubly cautious and make thorough inquiries concerning the witness' condition before taking a statement from such witness.

    In order to obtain an effective signed statement, and to keep the ethics of the investigator above reproach, he or she must observe local laws, ordinances, codes and statutes that regulate the time or place for the taking of such statements. If, for instance, a statement is being taken in a hospital under circumstances that permit it, the investigator should try to have a nurse, attendant or possibly a doctor present as a witness. Such an attendant should be able to attest to the fact that the patient was free from apparent unusual pain and from the influence of narcotics, and seemed to be in a rational state of mind.
13. *Objectionable phraseology.* The use of objectionable words or phrases should be avoided unless the investigator is quoting directly. Otherwise, any reference to race, religion, foreign background or other evidence of bigotry or obscenity should be avoided unless a specific point concerning the witness is being made for a legitimate reason. Otherwise, a completely innocent remark concerning race, religion, etc., intended merely as descriptive, could easily be misinterpreted.
14. *Preserving the statement.* The investigator should refrain from physically mutilating a statement in

any way. It is a valuable piece of evidence and should not be soiled, torn or shopworn. It should also not be date-stamped by an office clerk or otherwise marked so as to make it unacceptable as evidence.

B. **Construction of a Signed Statement**

There will be times when, because of pressure, peculiarities of an individual, the facts of an accident, or for other adequate reasons, the statement will not follow an orderly pattern.

By and large, however, the general construction of a signed statement obtained from a witness, be it from an insured, claimant, or disinterested outside witness, should follow an orderly, chronological form.

An outline of a good construction pattern for a signed statement should include the following subjects, generally in the order given:

1. *Date, time and address* where the statement is being obtained, preferably in the upper righthand corner.
2. *Identification of the subject.* The first paragraph of a signed statement should be concerned with the identification of the subject who is giving the statement. It should include his or her name, address, age and other details necessary to prove the authenticity of the statement.
3. *Location and reason for the witness' presence.* This paragraph should be devoted to a description of the location of the accident and should include the reasons for the witness' being there at that time. The direction in which the witness may have been walking or riding should be given, as well as the exact spot from which he or she viewed the accident.

   This paragraph should also include the introduction to the factual matter by indicating what attracted the attention of the witness to the accident.
4. *Factual details.* This paragraph should include the

factual information concerning the details of the accident. It should, as far as possible, be confined to the facts. Hearsay information should be avoided unless it involves spontaneous remarks made directly before or after the accident, or unless the remarks contain information which will attack the credibility of a witness.
5. *Physical description.* The physical description of the scene of the accident should be as complete as possible. It should include weather and lighting conditions, road surfaces, road contours, all measurements and other pertinent details.

   Wherever possible and advisable, some effort should be made to get the witness to draw some form of diagram illustrating the manner in which the accident occurred, and it too should be signed and dated.
6. *Injuries and damages.* The next section of the statement can include details concerning the nature of the property damage and the injuries received. This should include not only as complete a description of the damage as possible, but an estimate of the cost of repairs if one has been obtained. Description of the injuries should be as complete and detailed as possible. It ought to be in the language used by the claimant. The names of all attending doctors and their addresses should also be included, as well as other pertinent medical information as previously outlined.
7. *Special damages.* In statements obtained from claimants, a complete list of all special damages should be obtained and itemized. The items that make up the special damages have been outlined previously.
8. *Police action.* An indication of any possible arrests or other police action should be included toward the end of the statement.
9. *Corrections.* Having finished the body of the statement, it is now the duty and responsibility of the

investigator to make sure that the statement contains the information given by the witness and that it does not deviate from that information. This is the time to give the statement to the witness and ask him or her to read it and to point out any inadvertent errors or any parts of the statement that may not be clear, or any parts which the witness, for any reason whatsoever, wishes to have changed. Wherever possible, all changes or corrections should be in the witness' handwriting, or at least initialed by the witness. Erasures should not be made.

10. *Acknowledgment.* After the witness has completed the corrections, request him or her to acknowledge the fact that he or she has read the statement and affirms the truth of the statement by adding, in his or her own handwriting, the words "I have read the above and preceding — pages and state that the information contained therein is true and correct," or words of a similar nature. This sentence should be written on the line following the end of the statement, allowing for no empty space between them.

11. *Signature.* If the investigator has obtained the acknowledgment, he or she should usually have little difficulty in obtaining the signature of the person giving the statement on each and every page of it. The signature should be located immediately under the last written line, with no empty space between the last line and the signature.

12. *Witnesses to the statement.* Whenever practical, signed statements should be witnessed by one or two disinterested parties who should place their full names and addresses on the statement. The investigator taking the statement should not ordinarily witness it.

CHAPTER XIV

Casualty Reserves and Evaluation
and
Reports to Underwriters

RESERVES

The factors that go into the setting up of an individual case reserve are the same ones that must enter into the settlement evaluation of a claim or suit.

There are many methods used for setting reserves and evaluating claims. For a thorough discussion of these subjects, see *Successful Handling of Casualty Claims* by this author.

The following are factors to be considered:

A. **Serious Injury Liability Claims**
   1. *Coverage.* Any problems concerning coverage should be weighed in favor of the claimant in setting up a reserve. Where possible, such coverage problems should be resolved as soon as possible since proper settlement evaluation cannot otherwise be made.
   2. *Liability or negligence.* Liability is, of course, the most important factor to be considered in setting up a reserve or in evaluating a claim. It is wise to remember that whenever a question of fact requires the determination of a jury, the odds are against the defendant.
   3. *Contributory or comparative negligence.* Again, although this is an item to be given serious consideration in the overall evaluation, any doubt should be resolved in favor of the claimant.

4. *Other legal defenses.* Additional legal defenses such as assumption of risk, agency, fellow servant rule, etc., might have a bearing on the ultimate outcome of a claim or suit. Such defenses, unless very strong, however, should not be given too much consideration in setting up reserves. They are more important in settlement evaluation.
5. *Injury.* It is most important that the adjuster learn the true nature and extent of the injury received by the claimant. This will often necessitate a medical examination by an outside physician if there is some reasonable doubt about the hospital or the claimant's medical report.
6. *Pain and suffering.* Long and painful disability always greatly increases the value of a claim. This is the factor which in recent years has been the principal reason for some exceedingly high verdicts.
7. *Possible punitive damages.* Occasionally, damages will be permitted in some jurisdictions where there has been wanton disregard for the safety of others. In evaluating a liability claim, the possibility of punitive damages, or for liability in excess of the policy limits, must be given consideration.
8. *Age of the claimant.* It is obvious that an older person will suffer a greater disability from an injury than a younger person. It has been estimated, for instance, that every ten years over the age of forty increases disability by about ten percent. Age is also very important in evaluating a death claim. The deceased's life expectancy is an important factor in establishing monetary loss to dependents.
9. *Sex of the claimant.* In many instances, disability to women will be twenty to twenty-five percent greater than the average for men. On the other hand, life expectancy for women is longer than that for men.
10. *Dependency.* This is an item to be considered partic-

ularly in death cases. The claimant may leave a dependent wife or husband, minor children or other dependents.

11. *Loss of salary.* This item speaks for itself. It is essential that the amount of time allegedly lost be checked, preferably from payroll records. In cases of long disability or death, it is also important to give consideration to the salary potential of the injured or deceased.
12. *Medical expenses.* This is one of the items of special damages, along with loss of salary and other items listed in previous outlines.
13. *Property damage.* This item, as previously outlined, might include a claimant's automobile, jewelry, clothing or other personal effects. Loss of use is a factor that must be given consideration, if pertinent.
14. *Economic status.* This item is not one that can usually be pinned down to a definite amount like some of the others previously listed. However, a claim involving a person in the higher income brackets is usually going to cost more than a similar claim by someone whose out-of-pocket expenses are not as great.
15. *Past experience of tendencies of local juries and courts.* It is a known fact that juries in certain areas are more liberal than they are in others. By the same token, certain judges, being only mortal, have their prejudices and predilections. These, where known, should also be given consideration in setting up reserves or in evaluating a claim.
16. *Realistic appraisal of the ability of defense counsel.* This item speaks for itself.
17. *Knowledge of the ability of opposing counsel.* Here again, the item speaks for itself.

B. **Fatal Liability Cases**

Although many of the factors involved in a consideration of the reserve or settlement value figures for fatal cases have already been outlined, there are others that apply only to this type of claim.

1. Age and life expectancy of the decedent.
2. Marital status.
3. Number, age, sex and relationship of all dependents.
4. Economic status, to approximate funeral and other expenses.
5. Health and habits.
6. Earnings.
7. Earning capacity and future earning prospects.

C. **Workmen's Compensation Cases**

As in all other casualty claims, the reserves on Workmen's Compensation cases should be based upon the best appraisal of what the claim will ultimately cost. Unlike other casualty claims, however, the Workmen's Compensation Acts of the various states do give some specific information that enables a more exact figure or appraisal for both reserving and evaluating purposes. Each state for instance, lists the weekly benefits to which a particular employee may be entitled. Most states have a time limit for the running of such benefits and list lump-sum benefits that may be payable. A thorough knowledge of the Workmen's Compensation Law of the jurisdiction involved is essential for a proper reserve appraisal.

Compensation reserves are divided into two sections:

1. *Indemnity reserves:*

    a. *Disability:*

    (1) *Extent of the injury.* Whether it is an initial injury or an aggravation of a pre-existing condition, it is important to determine, as quickly as possible, the full extent of the injury so that some appraisal of the length of disability can

be made.
- (2) *Age of the claimant.* As has already been indicated, the age of the claimant is an important consideration in estimating his or her recovery time.
- (3) *Sex of the claimant.* Again, as previously indicated, it is important to remember that the disability of women is usually greater than that of men.

b. *Allowance under the Compensation Act:*
- (1) Temporary total disability.
- (2) Temporary partial disability. It is important to know if the Act involved permits recovery for partial disability over and above any temporary disability allowed.
- (3) Total partial disability.
- (4) Total permanent disability.
- (5) Dependency and death benefits.

2. *Medical reserves:*
   a. Doctors', surgeons' and dentists' bills, including associated expenses and cost of therapeutic or other treatments. If the jurisdiction involved has a fee schedule, consult the fee schedule for the extent of the probable medical expense.
   b. Hospital, sanitorium or nursing home bills.
   c. Nurses' bills.
   d. X-rays, laboratory and similar expenses.
   e. Cost of practical nurses. In many instances, it is advantageous to pay for the cost of a practical nurse where hospitalization or registered nurses' care would otherwise be required.
   f. Fee for surgical and prosthetic appliances.

CONFIDENTIAL REPORT TO THE UNDERWRITERS

One of the important functions and duties of an investigator for an insurance company is to observe and report on any information that may affect the desirability of a risk or the adequacy of the premium rate, to the Underwriting Department of the company.

Ordinarily, it is not the province of the Claim Department to recommend the cancellation of a risk. There may be other reasons why the underwriters may decide to retain a risk, despite some undesirable features. It is, however, the duty of the Claim Department to bring to the attention of the Underwriting Department any information that may aid them in arriving at a proper decision concerning cancellation, or which may necessitate corrective action. In the course of the investigation of an accident, much information will come to the attention of the investigator that might affect the desirability of a risk.

Most companies have some form for this purpose which is variously termed "Questionable Risk Report," "Confidential Risk Report" or some similar designation used for the same purpose.

The types and kinds of deficiencies that should be noted and brought to the attention of the underwriters can be grouped into five categories. These, and some examples of each, are:

1. *Physical defects:*
    a. Poor condition of an automobile, building or area.
    b. Defective equipment, such as brakes, headlights, horn or steering mechanism on an automobile; defective machinery or working conditions on compensation risks, etc.
    c. Improper equipment.
    d. Machinery safeguards not being used, or no safeguards provided.
    e. Dangerous machinery.

f. Unoccupied premises.

2. *Moral hazards:*
    a. Bad reputation of the insured or driver with reference to speeding, reckless driving or bad traffic violation record.
    c. Intoxication or drug abuse.
    d. Apparent collusion.
    e. Fraudulent acts or deliberately false statements.
    f. Illegal operation of vehicle, elevator, machinery or equipment.
    g. Previous questionable Index Bureau record with reference to previous claims.

3. *Physical infirmities:*
    a. Poor vision; glasses required but not used; or blind in one eye.
    b. Loss or impaired use of arm, leg, fingers.
    c. Insured or regular driver afflicted with epilepsy, heart condition or other infirmity that could momentarily disable the driver.
    d. Insured or driver aged or infirm.
    e. Alcoholism or drug abuse.

4. *Matters affecting premium:*
    a. Age of the driver.
    b. Usual traveling distance on truck under a local truckman's endorsement.
    c. Principal garaging of automobiles.
    d. Operations or employment not covered under compensation policy.
    e. Improper classification of automobile or job.
    f. Failure to cover all jobs on compensation policy.

5. *Other hazards:*
    a. Accident frequency or excessive traffic violations.

b. Poor class of drivers or employees.
c. Truck used to transport employees.
d. Gross negligence or wanton disregard involved in accident under investigation.
e. Improper registration or no driver's license.
f. Catastrophe hazard such as transportation of butane gas, asphalt or other highly flammable or otherwise inherently dangerous substance; fire-trap type of building, etc.
g. Non-cooperation in defense of case.
h. Illegal employment of minors.
i. Unusual occupational disease exposure.
j. Unsafe practices.

INDEX

References are to pages

A

Accident and health claims, 273-278
  Coverage problems, 273-274
  Death claims, 275
  Dismemberment, loss of sight or total disability, 274-275
  Forms, 277-278
  Independent of other causes, 278
  Medical substantiation, 278
  Misrepresentations in the application, 274
  Over-insurance, 274
  Physical limitations, 275
  Reasonable bills, 274
  Suicide or voluntary injury, 275-277
Accountant's liability, 211-212
Agent's (insurance) errors and omissions, 212-214
Alcoholic consumption, 11-12
Amusement parks and fairs, 105-107
Animals, 107-113
  If claim involves a dog, 109-110
  If claim involves a saddle horse, 110-113
Architects, 214-215
Areaways, liability for, *see* **Public liability investigations**
Attractive nuisance, 113-114
Attorneys, *see* **Lawyers**
Auditoriums and theaters, 162
Automobile liability and property investigations, 1-72
  Automobile medical payments investigations in, 55-57
  Automobile physical damage investigations in, 59-63
  Claimant's investigations in, 21-34
  Claimant passengers, 25-26
  Claimant pedestrians, 26-27
  Claimant's background information and introductory matter, 21-23
  Claimant's marital status and dependency, 23
  Determine if claimant made any report, 27
  Determine insurance carriers for any claimants, 27
  Develop the factual details, 27-30
  Driver's experience, 24-25
  Driving distractions, 25
  Educational background, 23-24
  Employment history, 23
  Medical information to be obtained from claimant, 30-32
  Pensions, insurance or welfare help, 24
  Property damage, 32-33
  Report on claimant's economic status, 27

INDEX

References are to pages

Automobile liability and property investigations *(cont.)*
  Witnesses obtained through claimant, 33-34
  Coverage information, 1-3
  Identification of insured's vehicle, 3-6
  Insured's investigation in, 6-21
    Alcoholic or drug consumption, 11-12
    Determine if any report was made, 14
    Develop the factual details, 14-18
    Driver fatigue, 11
    Driver's background and introductory matter, 6-7
    Injuries, 18-19
    Injury to passengers in insured's vehicle (guest statutes), 12-14
    Permissive use of vehicle, 8-10
    Property damage, 19-20
    Witnesses obtained from insured, 20-21
  Investigation of claims involving I.C.C. or P.S.C. certificates, 63-65
  Investigation of coverage problems in automobile claims, 65-71
    Review application or daily with care, 66
    Where alleged date of accident is close to inception date of policy, 66-67
  Investigation of coverage

Automobile liability and property investigations *(cont.)*
    problems where there is a question concerning:
    Commercial radius endorsement, 71
    Delayed notice, 67-69
    Ownership of vehicle involved in accident, 69
    Possibility of uninsured vehicles in named insured's household, 70
    Purposes for which vehicle is used, 70
    Who regularly drives vehicle named in policy, 69-70
  Investigation of uninsured motorists' claims, 71-72
  Medical investigation, 34-38
    Additional interviews, 38
    Attending doctor's report, 34-36
    Detailed information from claimant, 34
    Determine if malpractice evident or probable, 38
    Hospital records, 36
    Physical examination, 36-38
  Physical facts in, 38-44
  Special damages in, 49-53
    Automobile property damage, 50-52
    Cosmetic disfigurement, 53
    Expected future monetary loss, 53
    Fatal claims, 53
    Loss of services or support, 53

INDEX

References are to pages

Automobile liability and property investigations *(cont.)*
  Lost time and earnings, 49-50
  Medical expenses, 52-53
  Other property damage, 52
  Pain and suffering, 53
  Witnesses' investigation in, 44-49
Automobile non-ownership coverage investigations, 57-59
Automobiles
  Product liability claims, 177-178

B

Blasting, 114-115
Blind accidents (no known witnesses), 89-90
  In public liability investigations, 115-117
Boiler explosions, 117-119
Bottling claims, 179-180
Buildings, liability for, *see* **Public liability investigations**
Bus or trolley passengers, 29-30

C

Carbon monoxide, 119-122
Casualty reserves, 305-309
  Fatal liability cases, 307-308
  Serious injury liability claims, 305-307
  Workers' Compensation cases, 308-309
Ceiling cases (falling plaster), 122-124

Children
  Accidents involving, 283
Claimant's investigations
  In automobile liability investigations, *see* **Automobile liability and property investigations**
  In product liability investigations, *see* **Product liability investigations**
  In professional liability claims, 204-206
  In public liability investigations, *see* **Public liability investigations**
  In Workers' Compensation investigations, 240-244
Commercial losses, 261-264
Confidential reports to underwriters
  In casualty reserves, 310-312
  In crime insurance investigations, 266
Construction, road, 149-151
Construction cases, 124-127
Contribution, 265-266
Cosmetic disfigurement
  In automobile liability investigations, 53
  In public liability investigations, 104
Cosmetics and drugs, 182-185
Coverage
  In accident and health claims, 273-274
  In automobile liability investigations, 1-3

References are to pages

Coverage *(cont.)*
  Investigation of problems of, in automobile liability investigations, *see* **Automobile liability and property investigations**
  Non-ownership of automobile, 57-59
  In product liability claims investigations, 165
  In professional liability investigations, 200-201
  In public liability investigations, 75-77
  In Workers' Compensation investigations, 229-232

Crime insurance investigations, 255-272
  Damage to property or premises, 259-260
  Fidelity claims, 266-271
    General guidelines, 267-268
    Investigation, 268-271
  Loss from depository, 257-258
  Loss from premises, 256-257
  Mercantile investigation in, 261-266
    Commercial losses, 261-264
    Confidential report to underwriters, 266
    Messenger losses, 264-265
    Robbery claims, 265
    Safe burglary claims, 264
    Subrogation, salvage or contribution, 265-266
  Nature of loss, 258-259
  Residence investigation in, 255-256

Crime insurance investigations *(cont.)*
  Settlement negotiations in, 260-261
  Suspects in, 260

Crop dusting
  In public liability investigations, 127-130
  Or spraying, in product liability claims, 180-182

D

Death claims, 275
  See also **Fatal cases; Fatal claims**
Defamation, 279
Depository, loss from, 257-258
Disability, total, 274-275
Dismemberment, 274-275
Doors, 130-131
Driver fatigue, 11
Drug consumption, 11-12
Druggist's liability, 216-217
Drugs and cosmetics, 182-185

E

Earnings
  Lost time and, in automobile liability investigations, 49-50
  Lost time and, in public liability investigations, 101-102
Electrical appliances, 185-186
Elevators, 131-136

INDEX

References are to pages

Employees, *see* **Workers' Compensation investigations**
Engineers, 214-215
Entrances and lobbies, 136
Escalators, 137-138

F

Fairs and amusement parks, 105-107
Falling objects, 138-140
Falling plaster, 122-124
False arrests, 279-281
Fatal accidents, 284-285
Fatal cases, casualty reserves, 307-308
Fatal claims, 275
   In automobile liability investigations, 53
   In public liability investigations, 103
Fidelity claims, 266-271
   General guidelines, 267-268
   Investigation, 268-271
Fire losses, 62-63
Floor accidents, 140-142
Food contamination or foreign substances, 186-188
Forms for accident and health claims, 277-278
Fraud, 285-286

G

General liability investigations, *see* **Public liability investigations**

H

Health claims, *see* **Accident and health claims**
Hospital malpractice, 218-220

I

I.C.C. or P.S.C. certificates, 63-65
Imprisonment, 279-281
Inflammables, 189-190
Insured's investigations
   In automobile liability investigations, *see* **Automobile and property liability investigations**
   In product liability investigations, 166-169
   In professional liability investigations, 201-204
   In public liability investigations, 77-83
Insured's vehicle, identification of, 3-6

L

Lawyers
   Professional liability, 220-222
   Suit reviews, 287-293
Leased trucks, 64
Libel, 279
Liquor law liability, 142-143
Lobbies and entrances, 136

M

Machinery claims, 143-144

References are to pages

Medical expenses
  In automobile liability investigations, 52-53
  In public liability investigations, 103
Medical investigations
  In automobile liability investigations, 34-38
    Additional interviews, 38
    Attending doctor's report, 34-36
    Detailed information from claimant, 34
    Determine if malpractice evident or probable, 38
    Hospital records, 36
    Physical examination, 36-38
    Physical facts, 38-44
  In product liability investigations, 174
  In professional liability claims, 206-208
  In public liability investigations, 93-97
Medical payments investigation
  In automobile liability investigations, 55-57
Medical substantiation
  Of accident and health claims, 278
Mercantile investigations, 261-266
  Commercial losses, 261-264
  Confidential report to underwriters, 266
  Messenger losses, 264-265
  Robbery claims, 265

Mercantile investigations *(cont.)*
  Safe burglary claims, 264
  Subrogation, salvage or contribution, 265-266
Messenger losses, 264-265
Misrepresentations in the application
  In accident and health claims, 274
Monetary loss
  Expected future, in automobile liability investigations, 53
  Expected future, in public liability investigations, 103-104
  See also **Earnings**
Mopeds, 190-191
Motorcycles, 190-191

N

Nurse's professional liability, 222-223

O

Ownership and control, 74-75

P

Pain and suffering
  In automobile liability investigations, 53
  In public liability investigations, 104
Percussion caps, 191-192

INDEX

References are to pages

Personal injury claims, 278-281
  Defamation, libel and slander, 279
  False arrest or imprisonment, 279-281
Physical damage investigations, 59-63
Physical facts
  In automobile liability investigations, 40-44
  In public liability investigations, 97-98
  In Workers' Compensation investigations, 249
Plate glass losses, 281-282
Playgrounds, 144-146
Pollution claims, 146-147
Porcelain handles, 148-149
Power mowers, 192-195
Premises
  Damage to property or, in crime insurance investigations, 259-260
  Loss from, crime insurance investigations, 256-257
Pressure spray containers, 195
Products liability claims investigations, 163-198
  Claimant's investigations in, 169-174
    Claimant's background information, 169-170
    Employment history, 170-171
    Factual details, 171-172
    Marital status and dependency, 170

Products liability claims investigations *(cont.)*
    Medical information, 172-174
    Witnesses obtained through claimant, 174
  Coverage, 165
  Description and identification of the product in, 165-166
  Insured's investigations in, 166-169
  Medical investigation in, 174
  Special damages in, 174-176
  Specific, 177-198
    Automobiles, 177-178
    Bottling claims, 179-180
    Crop dusting or spraying, 180-182
    Drugs and cosmetics, 182-185
    Electrical appliances, 185-186
    Food contamination or foreign substances, 186-188
    Inflammables, 189-190
    Motorcycles, mopeds and snowmobiles, 190-191
    Percussion caps, 191-192
    Power mowers, 192-195
    Pressure spray containers, 195
    Trichinosis, 196-198
Professional liability policies investigations, 199-228
  Claimant's investigation in, 204-206

INDEX

References are to pages

Professional liability policies investigations *(cont.)*
  Coverage information in, 200-201
  Insured's investigation in, 201-204
  Medical investigation in, 206-208
  Special damages in, 208-210
  Specific, 211-228
    Accountant's liability, 211-212
    Agent's (insurance) errors and omissions, 212-214
    Architects and engineers, 214-215
    Druggist's liability, 216-217
    Hospital malpractice, 218-220
    Lawyer's professional liability, 220-222
    Nurse's professional liability, 222-223
    Surgeon's liability, 224-226
    Teacher's liability, 226-228
  Witnesses' investigation in, 208
Property investigations, *see* **Automobile liability and property investigations**
P.S.C. or I.C.C. certificates, 63-65
Public liability investigations, 73-162
  Claimant's investigations in, 83-93
    Blind accidents (no known witnesses), 89-90

Public liability investigations *(cont.)*
    Claimant's background information and introductory matter, 83-84
    Determine if claimant's clothes were material to accident, 87
    Education background, 84-85
    Employment history, 84
    Factual details, 88-89
    Marital status and dependency, 84
    Medical information to be obtained from claimant, 90-92
    Nature and purpose of the trip, 87-88
    Obtain previous and subsequent accident records, 87
    Pensions, insurance or welfare help, 85
    Physical condition or possible deformities, 85-86
    Possible distractions to claimant, 86-87
    Previous knowledge of condition, 88
    Witnesses obtained through claimant, 92-93
  Coverage in, 75-77
  Description and identification of premises, 73-74
  Insured's investigation in, 77-83
  Medical investigation in, 93-97

References are to pages

Public liability investigations *(cont.)*
  Ownership and control in, 74-75
  Physical facts in, 97-98
  Special damages in, 101-104
    Cosmetic disfigurement, 104
    Expected future monetary loss, 103-104
    Fatal claims, 103
    Location of, and reason for, witness' presence, 100
    Loss of services or support, 104
    Lost time and earnings, 101-102
    Medical expenses, 103
    Pain and suffering, 104
    Property damage, 102-103
  Specific, 105-162
    Amusement parks and fairs, 105-107
    Animals, *see* **Animals**
    Attractive nuisance, 113-114
    Blasting, 114-115
    Blind accidents (possible fraud), 115-117
    Boiler explosions, 117-119
    Carbon monoxide, 119-122
    Ceiling cases (falling plaster), 122-124
    Construction cases 124-127
    Crop dusting, 127-130
    Doors, 130-131
    Elevators, 131-136
    Entrances and lobbies, 136-137

Public liability investigations *(cont.)*
    Escalators, 137-138
    Falling objects, 138-141
    Floor accidents, 140-142
    Liquor law liability, 142-143
    Machinery claims, 143-144
    Playgrounds, 144-146
    Pollution claims, 146-147
    Porcelain handles, 148-149
    Road construction, 149-151
    Sidewalks, 151-154
    Sporting events, 154-156
    Stairways, 156-158
    Swimming pools, 158-160
    Tenancy claims, 160-162
    Theaters and auditoriums, 162
  Witnesses' investigations, 99-101

R

Residence investigations, 255-256
Road construction, 149-151
Robbery claims, 265

S

Safe burglary claims, 264
Salvage, 265-266
Serious injury liability claims, 305-307
Services or support, loss of
  In automobile liability investigations, 53

References are to pages

Services or support, loss of *(cont.)*
   In public liability investigations, 104
Settlement negotiations, 260-261
Sidewalk claims, 151-154
Sight, loss of, 274-275
Signed statements
   Factors involved in taking, 297-304
      Construction of signed statement, 301-303
      Rules for taking, 297-301
Snow and ice cases, 153-154
Snowmobiles, 190-191
Special aspects of liability investigations, 283-296
   Investigation of accidents involving children, 283
   Investigation of claims involving fraud, 285-286
   Investigation of fatal accidents, 284-285
   Locating the missing witness, 294-295
   Suit reviews, 287-293
Special damages
   In automobile liability investigations, *see* **Automobile liability and property investigations**
   In product liability claims, 174-176
   In professional liability claims, 208-210
   In public liability investigations, *see* **Public liability investigations**

Sporting events, 154-156
Spray
   Crop dusting or, in product liability claims, 180-182
   Pressure, containers, 195
Stairways, 156-158
Statements, *see* **Signed statements**
Streets, liability for, *see* **Public liability investigations**
Subrogation, 265-266
Surgeons, 224-226
Suicide or voluntary injury, 275-277
Suit reviews, 287-293
Suspects
   In crime insurance investigations, 260
Swimming pools, 158-160

T

Teachers, 226-228
Tenancy claims, 160-162
Theaters and auditoriums, 162
Theft losses, 61-62
Time, *see* **Earnings**
Total disability, 274-275
Total losses, automobile, 61
Trichinosis, 196-198

U

Uninsured motorists' claims, 71-72

V

Voluntary injury, 275-277

References are to pages

W

Witnesses' investigations
In automobile liability investigations, 44-49
In professional liability claims, 208
In public liability investigations, 99-101

Workmen's Compensation cases
Casualty reserves in, 308-309

Workmen's Compensation investigations, 229-254
Claimant's investigation in, 240-244

Workmen's Compensation investigations *(cont.)*
Coverage investigation in, 229-232
Determination of employee status, 251
Employee v. independent contractor, 252-253
Factual information, 232-235
Insured's investigation, 235-240
Medical investigation, 244-249
Occupational disease, 249-251
Physical facts, 249